‣ ‣ ‣ RALPH
LAUREN

RALPH LAUREN

The Man Behind the Mystique

BY JEFFREY A.
TRACHTENBERG

Little, Brown and Company
BOSTON · TORONTO

FIRST EDITION

The author is grateful for permission to include the following previ-
ously copyrighted materials:
Excerpts from "Men's styles recall Douglas Fairbanks," by Anne-Marie
Schiro (April 17, 1973), "New York goes western, too," by Bill Cun-
ningham (June 20, 1978), "Divergent moods for fall," by Bernadine
Morris (April 24, 1982), "Lauren look permeating city," by Lisa Belkin
(December 8, 1986), and "Lauren's quiet way with sport clothes," by
Bernadine Morris (August 13, 1987). Copyright © 1973, 1978, 1982,
1986, 1987 by the New York Times Company. Reprinted by permis-
sion.

Excerpt from the "Polo Fall 1977 Catalog." Reprinted with permission
of Polo/Ralph Lauren Corporation.

Excerpt from *The Ultraconsumers — A Grey Study.* Reprinted by permission of Grey Advertising.

Excerpt from *Confessions of an Advertising Man,* by David Ogilvy. Copyright © 1963 David Ogilvy Trustee. Reprinted with the permission of
Atheneum Publishers, an imprint of Macmillan Publishing Company.

Library of Congress Cataloging-in-Publication Data

Trachtenberg, Jeffrey A.
  Ralph Lauren : the man behind the mystique / by Jeffrey
A. Trachtenberg.
    p.   cm.
  Bibliography: p.
  Includes index.
  1. Lauren, Ralph. 2. Costume designers—United States—Biography.
I. Title.
TT505.L38T73 1988
746.9'2'0924—dc19
[B]   88-12823
                                 CIP

10 9 8 7 6 5 4 3 2 1

Published simultaneously in Canada
by Little, Brown & Company (Canada) Limited
PRINTED IN THE UNITED STATES OF AMERICA

For my loving wife, Elizabeth

‣ ‣ ‣ RALPH
LAUREN

▸▸▸ INTRODUCTION

Ralph Lauren has built the most successful apparel company in the United States. He often wears blue jeans to work, and he has been married to the same woman for more than twenty years. His favorite declaration about himself is, "What you see is what you get." When he describes his work he insists that it does not constitute "trendy fashion" and that his customers care more about well-made clothes than the latest party dresses from Europe. He takes such distinctions seriously. Once, when I lumped him together with a handful of other designers during casual conversation, he snapped: "Don't put me with those designers. My business is not compared to anybody else's."

Ralph Lauren is important because he has influenced not only the way we dress but the advertisements we see in our magazines and newspapers, the sheets and pillowcases on which we sleep, and the way in which we decorate our houses. Inadvertently he has also affected the publishing world (the recent spate of books on English home decorating and English country homes), the way retailers decorate their windows and accessorize their boutique displays, and our own expectations — cashmere not wool, crocodile not leather, pima cotton

sheets, not cotton/polyester blends. Moreover, no other designer's image is so closely identified with baby boomers, the
postwar generation that now dominates politics and the national economy.

From the day Ralph sold his first wide tie, he has kept
asking his customers to dig deeper into their pockets. He has
never been satisfied, never said, "Enough!" After the ties came
ever-more-expensive shirts, sport jackets, slacks, suits, and
dresses. For this he has been strongly criticized; many critics
believe that his customers represent the worst in over-
materialistic self-servers. To some Ralph is symptomatic of a
generation that values Häagen-Dazs ice cream, designer jeans,
and foreign sports cars more than marriage, kids, and good
credit ratings. Ralph Lauren customers have always been pic-
tured as insecure usurpers willing to pay almost any price to
be accepted. Some see in these strivers an almost appalling
lack of sensitivity to others, and consequently resent both the
large salaries such consumers earn and their self-indulgence.
In turn, they resent Ralph Lauren.

This is an unauthorized biography. I knew before starting
this project that Ralph Lauren was guarded about his personal
life. I also knew he rarely appeared at black-tie society dinners. This reserve is due to shyness, not modesty. In practice
Ralph Lauren is a tough, intensely ambitious businessman who
thinks his work has never received the recognition it deserves.
Ralph has always possessed immense self-confidence; it is central to his character, an asset as valuable as his sense of color,
fabric, style. That explains why Ralph has always been willing
to break the rules to do things his way. He sells establishment-
looking clothes, but Ralph Lauren is not part of the fashion
establishment. Indeed, at different times in his career he has
refused orders from such top retailers as Macy's California,
Wallachs, Abraham & Straus, and Rich's. For years he griped
that the retailers he did do business with didn't display his
clothes with enough elegance. Finally, he decided he would do
it himself. In April 1986 he opened his Rhinelander Mansion
store on East 72nd Street, filling four floors of that New York
City landmark building with thousands of his products and
boldly putting his thumb in the eyes of his biggest retail accounts.

Ralph Lauren's attitude and convictions amounted to business heresy. A designer/manufacturer is not supposed to compete with his customers for their customers. When some retailers nervously complained that their sales of Ralph Lauren merchandise would be crippled, Ralph predicted their business would increase. He was right. During the summer of 1987 Bloomingdale's even redid its Ralph Lauren's women's department on the fourth floor, expanding it from a bit over 2,000 square feet to more than 3,500 square feet. With its mahogany-paneled walls, its leather books, and its silver frames, the area soon resembled a scaled-down version of the Rhinelander Mansion. Ralph inspected it for himself. After moving some of the suits about from this place to that, he said Bloomingdale's had done a good job. Then, in the same breath, he suggested that Bloomingdale's redo his men's department on the first floor. Ralph said this with a smile, but he was serious.

Today Ralph Lauren lives in a Fifth Avenue duplex, owns a 12,300-acre ranch in Colorado, a home on five-and-a-half acres in Montauk, Long Island, a villa in Jamaica, an island as well as a 200-acre estate in Westchester County, New York, and a fleet of antique cars; he sometimes jets from home to home in his own Gulfstream II. His possessions symbolize great wealth, and on paper Ralph Lauren, with a fortune valued in the proximity of $400 million, is one of the richest self-made men in the United States. His friends say he is warm, generous, sensitive. His former friends say he has a short memory and loses interest in people without apparent reason. Money doesn't improve character; it exaggerates it. Once a man's estimated holdings reach the $400 million mark, even the way he washes his face is studied with intent. At this level of wealth a man with common good values becomes a hero; a man who ignores old acquaintances an ingrate.

Ralph Lauren acquired his fortune by emerging as a design leader, not only in men's, women's and children's clothes, but also in home furnishings. He is conceded to be an insightful marketer at a time when marketing drives even the most technology-minded companies. He is also a fine merchandiser — which means he knows how to put together collections of hundreds of items that are attractive when worn apart or together. This ability has made him especially popular with the department stores, many of which won't pay the salaries necessary to attract attentive sales people.

Certainly Ralph is prolific. The fall 1987 product list of the Ralph Lauren Home Collection alone numbered 2,200 pieces. They included towels, sheets, polyester-filled comforters, down-filled comforters and pillows, comforter covers, throw pillows, shams, bedskirts, placemats, napkins, tablecloths, blankets, challis throws, rugs, robes, rattan furniture, upholstered furniture ranging from wing chairs to sofas, rugs, and various potpourri products. There was also a separate spring collection of about the same size.

A complete listing of all the different products bearing Ralph's name or logo may well number over 110,000. The Polo men's division alone produces 40,000 different styles a year. Bidermann Industries, which manufactures Ralph Lauren's women's wear, makes over 50,000 styles. Then there are the shoes, the scarves, the socks, the ties, the entire cornucopia of Ralph Lauren designs. One market survey commissioned by a competitor estimated that each year more than 7 million Ralph Lauren products, excluding fragrances, are sold in this country. However, since Polo/Ralph Lauren sells 4 million men's polo shirts alone, a more accurate estimate is about 10 million units, or one for every seventeen adults over the age of eighteen. The numbers boggle the imagination.

Ralph Lauren insists he sees and works on each product that bears his name. "What do you think, I leave the room and come back and it's all done?" he asks. "Why do you think I'm in design meetings all day? I do it. It's not done for me. I'm not an overseer."

Ralph Lauren has built an empire by maintaining a consistent product and by promoting an image of exclusivity. His advertising cannily blends images of family, wealth, and romance, drawing on universal archetypes, and he has used it successfully throughout the world. Most global advertising fails because images that appeal to one culture may be insulting or incomprehensible to another. For this reason Seibu Department Stores, Limited, in Japan creates its own advertising for its Giorgio Armani and Missoni lines. Seibu also holds a Ralph Lauren license, but by contract it must use only advertising supplied by Ralph. The images work because they fulfill Japanese fantasies about how Americans live. Today, with a business that does over $200 million at retail, Ralph Lauren is the most successful of all American designers in Japan.

The Polo/Ralph Lauren label is so strong in this country that Ralph has built a strong following among students at private elementary schools, public high schools, and colleges. As these customers grow older and earn more money, they advance from the less expensive Ralph Lauren collections, such as Chaps and Polo University, to the more expensive Polo line. Ralph uses much the same marketing strategy that General Motors uses to move its customers from Chevrolets to Cadillacs.

What makes Ralph Lauren's company almost unique is that it is vertically integrated. Ralph not only designs and manufactures, he also sells his clothes to a network of more than sixty independently owned Ralph Lauren stores in such places as Aspen, Palm Beach, Salt Lake City, Tulsa, Denver, San Jose, and Houston. Those shops do in excess of $150 million a year in sales. His own stores, including twenty-four factory outlets in such places as Appleton, Wisconsin, and Freeport, Maine, plus a fully owned store in London and the Rhinelander Mansion, generate over $80 million at retail. Both his own stores and the independently owned freestanding shops carry only Ralph Lauren products, which means that even if every department store and specialty retailer in the country dropped his lines, Ralph would still have a thriving business.

"You go into the Ralph Lauren/Polo shops and you see the world of Ralph Lauren. You can't overestimate their value to us," says Peter Strom, president of Polo/Ralph Lauren. (Ralph launched his business as Polo Fashions in 1967. In 1987 the corporate name was changed to the Polo/Ralph Lauren Corporation in recognition of the fact that Ralph's name is on every label.) When Strom joined the company at the end of 1974, it generated $5 million in men's wear sales at wholesale and $2 million in women's wear at wholesale. For fiscal 1988, which ended March 31, 1988, worldwide revenues of Ralph

Lauren products amounted to $925 million at wholesale. Some in the industry think hiring Peter Strom was the best decision Ralph Lauren ever made. They may be right. Most fashion designers fail because they never find somebody able to manage their business, not because they lack talent.

Often it is said that Ralph Lauren is less a designer than he is an editor, an adapter, a copyist. This statement is misleading, because all art is derivative. "You are always a thief — a selector, not a director," filmmaker Adrian Lyne told the *New York Times* after his film *Fatal Attraction* was released in 1987. That may be, but because Ralph Lauren never attended design school and can't draw worth a lick, he is rarely given credit as a top creative force. He was, however, the first American designer to draw inspiration from uniquely American images, such as the Southwest. And in the early 1970s, he helped make the American sportswear industry the most exciting in the world.

There will always be those who dismiss Ralph Lauren's design skills. There may be less argument about his influence on other tastemakers. As did the leading industrial designers from the 1920s and 1930s, Ralph Lauren has made an impact on numerous industries. There are the retail imitators, who have built major businesses selling Ralph Lauren–like khaki pants and cotton shirts and rugged outdoor clothes; the major textile mills, which now make flannel and 200-thread, all-cotton sheets; the countless Ralph Lauren look-alike ads in magazines and newspapers, and the dozens of low-price manufacturers who cheerfully prosper making cheap Ralph Lauren knockoffs. Even the smallest details are copied. After Ralph Lauren put a crest on his shirts and sportcoats, manufacturers such as Clubroom, Thomson Company, and Reebok (the apparel licensee) ran ads featuring their own crests. Virtually every high-quality men's specialty store, from Brooks Brothers to Paul Stuart, now has a large women's wear department stocked with gray flannel skirts, blue blazers, and oxford button-down shirts. Ralph Lauren was the first to design those products specifically for women. In 1986, when Ralph reintroduced expensive accessories made from crocodile, the major retailers quickly followed suit. By the end of 1987 stores like Saks Fifth Avenue were running large ads selling crocodile pocket secretaries ($300), crocodile wallets ($185), and crocodile keycases ($55). Notice, too, how many other fashion designers have since opened, or announced intentions of opening, their own retail stores. The list includes Calvin Klein, Liz Claiborne, and Geoffrey Beene.

Economics also tells us something about Ralph Lauren's design skills. If retailers already carried the clothes Ralph Lauren made, they wouldn't pay the exorbitant prices for which he is best known. Retailing today is increasingly dominated by a handful of superchains whose computers monitor designer sell-through as carefully as bookies read the *Daily Racing Form*. If Ralph Lauren's clothes did not sell, the chains would stop buying almost instantly.

Moreover, if Ralph appealed solely to the nouveau riche, his would be a small business in terms of unit sales. According to a 1985 U.S. Census Bureau report, only 3.3 million households earned over $75,000 that year — the dividing line between the well-off and the affluent. Those 3.3 million amounted to 3.7 percent of all 86.8 million U.S. households. Such a small base would not be enough to support a business the size of Ralph Lauren's. Therefore investment bankers and lawyers are not Ralph's only customers.

In fact, anybody walking through the Rhinelander Mansion store in December 1987 would have seen that the customers included teenagers in jeans and jean jackets; leather-clad French, Italian, and German tourists in their thirties, and many older shoppers in corduroys, heavy sweaters, and stadium coats. One middle-aged man spent fifteen minutes running his fingers over a $2,500 shearling bed throw, smiling to himself, before turning to a stranger and saying, "The day is going to come when I'm going to get one of these." Then his wife dragged him away by the arm. A tuxedo-clad trio played classical music. People pointed, prodded, touched, and compared. One woman picked up a paisley shawl ($315), turned to her husband, and whispered, "Just like the ones we saw at Liberty in London."

Many shoppers were not clutching blue Polo/Ralph Lauren bags when they left. But they looked happier than many leaving nearby $7-a-ticket movie theaters. Here admission was free. If nothing else, the entertainment value was outstanding.

Nobody has to buy clothes made by Ralph Lauren; necessity isn't an issue to somebody spending more than $90 for a simple cotton sweater. The customers come back because they think the clothes wear well, and because they want to identify with the images of a world Ralph has so obsessively promoted. His label obviously fulfills a variety of psychological needs, including the need to conform. Otherwise fewer people would want to wear a polo player on their breast.

This, then, is the story of how Ralph Lauren built his business and why it succeeded. It is also the story of what that success has done to him.

It was a good dream, he had worked hard to achieve it, and now it was about to come true. So designer Ralph Lauren had every reason to welcome with pride the two hundred fashion editors, reporters, and longtime supporters expected that evening in April 1986. Ralph, better than anybody else, knew how much this store opening had cost in time, anxiety, and that most fragile of coins, prestige. For this was more than yet another East Side designer boutique. Rather, Ralph Lauren had renovated the Rhinelander Mansion, a five-story, gray limestone building at the southeast corner of Madison Avenue and 72nd Street. In 1894 wealthy Gertrude Rhinelander Waldo instructed her architects to recreate a French château, investing more than $500,000 in a home that included a ballroom with 1,100 light bulbs, a billiard parlor, and a bowling alley. Yet when all was finished five years later, Gertrude eccentrically decided to live across the street with her sister.

Ralph and interior designer Naomi Leff had restored the Rhinelander Mansion in spirit if not in exact detail, for only one corner remained of the original blueprints. More challenging yet, the building had sheltered numerous commercial tenants during the past fifty years, including E.A.T. Gourmet, a specialty foods shop, and the Phillips Auction Gallery. Walls had been knocked down, decorative motifs destroyed, moldings ruined. Those interior details which did survive had to be restored and the vaulted ceilings completely replastered. A sweeping new staircase was built, modeled after that of London's Connaught Hotel. As many as ninety electricians at a time were employed, plus squads of painters, plumbers, and carpenters. Then there were the specialists, such as the woodcarvers and the stone and plaster carvers. Workers added 82,000 feet of Honduran mahogany before they were through.

The plans, hardly modest at the start, became increasingly ambitious. Ralph decided he needed four selling floors, not three, which meant more delay and more overtime pay. Add the antiques, the construction costs, the cabinetry costs, the architectural fees, and all other related costs, and the final bill topped $30 million, or more than four times the original $7 million estimate. This sum was mind-boggling even in a city where minor fortunes are invested to launch trendy restaurants. It is one thing to commission a $500,000 mural and then sell pumpkin-stuffed ravioli. It is another matter to reconstruct a life-style out of favor even with the Rockefeller and Whitney clans.

What made this venture even more daring was that Ralph did not own the building. Rather, it belonged to a group of investors led by Saudi Arabian businessman Yousef Jameel. (Jameel owns Jaymont Holdings, Inc., a Delaware corporation with offices in New York, which in turn is the majority partner in a real estate company called the 867 Madison Partnership. The 867 Partnership bought the Rhinelander Mansion on April 28, 1983, for nearly $7 million.)

A bit complicated, that, but what matters is that in late December 1984, Ralph leased the mansion for twenty years, with an option for another twenty. He agreed to pay $1.4 million annually in rent, not outrageous considering the 20,000 square feet of selling space. There was a kicker, however. The lease specified that if the store's annual sales topped $17.5 million, he would pay a rent equivalent to 8 percent of sales. No wonder realtors later reported that after the Rhinelander Mansion opened, commercial rents in the neighborhood more than doubled.

Renovating the store was a major investment even for a company Wall Street then valued at $300 million, or ten times earnings. Peter Strom, Ralph's patient and deliberative partner, said that thinking about the project and the bank loans it required sometimes left him dizzy with anxiety in spite of the company's growth. Worldwide wholesale revenues, including licensing fees, had grown almost fourfold from $168 million in 1980 to $625 million for the fiscal year ended March 31, 1986.

Strom worried because he knew that more than dollars and cents were at risk. The name Ralph Lauren had meant selling power at store level since the late 1960s. So strong was the label, so loyal the public, that Bloomingdale's, Saks Fifth Avenue, and Macy's had all built million-dollar Ralph Lauren businesses within thirty blocks of each other. These retailers were not only among the most prestigious in the country, they were also among Ralph Lauren's strongest supporters. Now some store executives were disgruntled. They didn't want to compete with their suppliers for customers. Many remembered with relish how Bergdorf Goodman had dropped its Halston collection like soiled goods soon after Halston announced that he would design clothes for J. C. Penney.

Maybe somebody would take Ralph Lauren down a notch or two.

But nobody did.

Bloomingdale's, Saks Fifth Avenue, Bergdorf Goodman, and Macy's couldn't threaten Ralph. They needed him. The customers who bought Ralph Lauren came back season after season, and if they couldn't buy his clothes at those stores, they would shop somewhere else.

Years earlier, Bloomingdale's had turned its Lexington Avenue Store into a singles' scene, blurring the lines between retailing and entertainment. Ralph wanted to go one better. He intended to transform the store itself into an object of desire.

But would his customers shop at the mansion? Nobody knew, because nobody had seen a store like this before. Maybe the public would think it an overblown house of chintz and gewgaws, spectacular in concept, but like the remake of *King Kong*, dumb in execution. If that happened, Ralph's clothes would lose their cachet and his business would suffer.

Nobody wants to buy a $1,000 hand-tailored suit from a dummy.

There was reason for concern. Because even before the store opened, it was obvious that it was going to provide a shopping experience that could only be described as intense. Every square inch of wall space seemed to be covered with paintings or animal trophies or mirrors or old prints. An inadvertent elbow, an unwatched sleeve, and kaboom, over went an obsessively perfect display of leather books or mechanical toys. Indeed, the bric-a-brac and mementos that skilled antiques buyers had been dispatched to acquire seemed more appropriate to a rambling country estate than a store at one of the great retail intersections of New York. Into the mansion had gone the memorabilia of nineteenth-century England: straw picnic baskets, salmon fishing rods, mahogany highboys, steamer trunks, oriental carpets, leather-bound books, flowered hat boxes, monogrammed luggage, and silver-framed photographs.

Not all the antiques were acquired overseas, though. The three etched-glass panels of polo players that graced the first floor were designed by Paul Robinson in the late 1920s, and for more than fifty years they decorated the Polo Lounge at New York's Westbury Hotel. Ralph bought them at Sotheby's in November 1984. They were his first purchases for the mansion, and he paid $20,800 for them, or about four times the preauction estimate.

Thus a pattern of extravagance was established even before Ralph signed his lease. Do it right, he told Naomi Leff when she went to work. Doing it right meant sheetrocking the building; adding a sprinkler system; taking original slates from the rear of the roof and moving them to the front to replace slates damaged or lost; reglazing and weather-sealing each window, as well as removing and cleaning the original hardware; installing central air conditioning; handcarving the balustrades on the second-floor balcony; and matching the original decorative copper ridgecaps and replacing those that had rotted. Even the stone columns at the front door had to be special-ordered from Indiana; the capitals were handcast and handcarved.

This is how a $7 million estimate grows to $30 million plus.

Why risk damaging retailer relationships, the status of his label, and his financial security? Because Ralph saw the Rhinelander Mansion as the key to his independence. In the 1970s American designers had been transformed into celebrities by merchants anxious to add sparkle to a business of bean counters: so many goods bought, so many goods sold. Creating the designer mystique was brilliant marketing. It revived the men's wear industry, it boosted women's wear sales, and it meant higher retail prices and greater profits. The designers themselves shared in the riches, buying country estates, hiring private chefs, and emerging as eager bidders at the famous auction houses. They could afford it. They made even more money than baseball players.

Then greed set in. There were designer diaper covers, designer chocolates, designer key chains. Bill Blass was even asked to put his name on a line of funeral caskets. By the mid-1980s the country was so cluttered with malls, shopping centers, and rebuilt downtown shopping districts that customers could buy designer brands anywhere. The pretense of exclusivity ended, and many big stores began to develop and promote their own private labels. Ralph Lauren would meet this challenge directly: if the stores were becoming manufacturers, he would become a retailer.

His move was a bold one. It also violated the savvy investment strategy that had made Ralph rich. With the exception of his men's wear business and his store in London, Ralph had never put his own money in new ventures. Even the freestanding Polo/Ralph Lauren stores were owned by others. Few outsiders understood fully how lucrative the licensing business had become. Ralph would have been a successful designer in his own right. However, he would never have qualified as one of the world's richest men without licensees willing to pay him 5 to 7 percent of sales.

Deciding to open the Rhinelander Mansion, then, was a bold, even reckless move, and some of Ralph's friends, including Steve Ross, chairman of Warner Communications, and Arnold Cohen, Ralph's accountant and financial adviser, were against it.

"I fought him in three or four meetings, because I didn't think it was justified on a risk/reward basis," says Ross. "But it was his dream. He wanted to take his shot."

Ralph may have been running a business, but it was a personal business. And since it was his personal dream to open the store, he went ahead.

On opening night in April 1986, Ralph was dressed in what can only be described as his serious grown-up clothes: a dark, double-breasted, pin-striped suit, which was all the more striking because Ralph usually wore blue jeans and denim work shirts. The pressure showed, too. Before the first guests arrived, he fussed about the tuxedo-clad young men assembled in a line near the front door on Madison Avenue, as nervous as a Hollywood producer on opening night.

"Why are so many of them standing around," he groused, finally quieting after learning they would check raincoats and umbrellas. Minutes earlier, heavy spring rains had stopped. Overhead, the sky turned faintly pink as the day's storm clouds blew past the Manhattan skyline and out to sea. A good omen, Peter Strom joked. Strom had reason to sound relieved. Only a few hours earlier, workmen had still been painting, moving furniture, and unloading racks of clothes off trucks. The store had resembled a construction site.

Now everything was in place. Even the handwritten invitations, complete with the admonition "No cameras please," had been hand-delivered without a hitch. Everything was exactly how Ralph wanted it. His guests included the top editors from the *New York Times, Women's Wear Daily, Vogue,* and *Harper's Bazaar,* the very crowd he'd spent years wooing and agonizing over. They were the tastemakers whose decisions influenced retailers and the buying public. A favorable review, an expansive photo spread, could help launch or maintain a career.

This party, then, was an opportunity to play host to those whose coverage over the years had helped build his business. This made his fussing more understandable, although it had been years since the critics had panned his work. "Tailored wool dresses are impressive in herringbone patterns . . . nonchalant elegance . . . luxury in the black fitted coats with swirling skirts," wrote one New York fashion critic about his fall 1986 collection. "Lauren at his best," advised another.

Unlike fellow designers Calvin Klein, Bill Blass, and Oscar de la Renta, Ralph shied away from the charity events and late-night dinners that dominated New York's social circuit. He almost never ate lunch at La Grenouille or Le Cirque, the favored restaurants of the fashion industry, and he rarely entertained at his Fifth Avenue duplex. Ralph didn't like being in the public eye.

But bashful or not, he'd decided to make this evening as

lavish as possible. And that was very lavish indeed. New York caterer Gay Jordan served thinly sliced Scotch salmon and caviar canapés mimosa. For those with more exotic tastes, there was creole crab meat in snow pea pods, wild-rice crepes with wild duck and plum sauce, and a puff filled with sun-dried tomatoes, Camembert, and almonds. A crew of forty-two waiters carried heavy silver trays, offering Dom Perignon or Perrier in champagne flutes.

It was an exciting moment and those invited responded to it. Women made dramatic entrances; Ralph welcomed them with open arms, kissing them on the cheek. "I'm proud, very proud," he said as he greeted his guests. "This is something we've worked very hard to achieve. I hope you like it."

Soon the crowd was sipping its drinks and walking past the elegant hand-finished ties on the main floor to the green-carpeted stairs. Up they marched, admiring, as they went, the women's $500 crocodile shoes, the $700 black silk evening dresses. More extraordinary still, on the fourth floor, was Ralph's white Jamaican room, complete with a bed anchored by four seven-foot bamboo posts. Nearby, a country-room motif had been faithfully executed with Navaho-style cotton blankets, handcrafted baskets, and even old postcards of Vermont. As the guests mingled they marveled to each other at the sheer luxury on display. There were the carved ornaments covering the ceilings, the round arched windows, the leather tuxedo sofas. Many of the selling areas resembled private rooms, with inventories carefully concealed in drawers of English highboys and chests. Each room was perfect and precise in each of the hundreds of details that determined its character. Add the cashmere sweaters flung over a chair's arm, the walking canes, and the personal jewelry, and the total effect was overwhelming. Some complained that the memorabilia and richness of the store made them feel claustrophobic. Most found it as imaginative and impressive as an opulent movie set.

"You know, Ralph always felt that the stores never understood him, never displayed his clothes properly," remarked Peter Strom. "Now he has his chance."

As Strom talked he walked up the stairs, rechecking every display. The store had opened for business that morning, and he was interested in which departments had sold what, and for how much. He stopped momentarily at a small area leased to Baker-Benjes, Inc., the New York–based company that manufactures Ralph Lauren Footwear.

"We sold forty pairs of shoes today," said a tired saleswoman. "At least a third of the shoes were made from crocodile, which means they cost at least five hundred dollars each. If we could only get some more inventory space . . ."

Strom nodded and walked off. Now that he was a full-fledged New York retailer, there was nothing more satisfying than seeing cashiers counting the day's take. It had been an excellent day's business, too. When the receipts were totaled, sales amounted to about $100,000. By the end of the week, the store had already passed the $1 million mark. (The store would ultimately produce sales of $31 million its first year. This meant it paid about $2.5 million in rent. The losses topped $5 million.)

"Ralph always said that this store would sell his highest-priced goods," Strom continued. "It looks like he may well be right. He's a genius."

Not all agreed. Many fashion insiders viewed Ralph's ascent with bemused skepticism. He knocked off Brooks Brothers, they said. Or, he copied L. L. Bean. Ralph is a stylist, they said, or Ralph is a brilliant editor. But not a designer, not somebody who understands how to cut fabric or create something new. A top merchandiser? Certainly. But not a great designer. Ralph can't even sketch.

On that April evening, though, those in attendance put their doubts aside. Congratulations were exchanged, heads nodded in approval, compliments were on everybody's lips. As the night drew to a close, Ralph's smile deepened, his eyes sparkled even more intently. For watching with pride, and not a little astonishment, were family and friends who knew and loved him. All were impressed. There had never been a store like this before, not on Fifth Avenue, not in London, not in the fantasies of Hollywood. This evening, then, was the pinnacle of a career that had started so many years ago in the Bronx, where Ralph, the third son of Russian immigrants, had grown up wearing hand-me-downs.

▶ ▶ ▶ 2

This is what it meant to grow up in the Bronx: public schools stayed open late one night a week so there was a place to dance, ice cream parlors made chocolate malteds, and kids didn't have to lock their bikes. If a family was wealthy, they lived in a building with an elevator. If not, most likely the kids shared their bedrooms. Everybody knew everybody else in a ten-square-block area, and if somebody got out of line, a neighbor called their parents, not the police.

There was an intimacy about the 1950s, an intimacy based on shared purpose. Television became a national passion, and its programming reflected the sense that life was good and about to get better. Those were the years of grand aspirations, dreams neatly framed and gently mocked by comedians like Milton Berle and Sid Caesar. It was a young decade, too, a decade whose best rock-and-roll musicians, Elvis Presley, Buddy Holly, and Little Richard, were barely past adolescence. There were two-toned Studebakers with fins, amoeba-shaped cocktail tables, pole lamps, and movie stars like Marilyn Monroe, Audrey Hepburn, Grace Kelly. Everybody drank Coca-Cola, and flying saucers made headlines. Teenage girls wore ponytails and rhinestone earrings. Their boyfriends copied the leather motorcycle jackets, tee shirts, and boots worn by Marlon Brando and James Dean in pictures like *The Wild One* and *Rebel Without a Cause*. The famous women's wear designers were Christian Dior, Balenciaga, Chanel. *Cosmopolitan* magazine devoted its entire November issue in 1957 to teenagers, and a *Newsweek* article the following month framed the pressing dilemma: "The Male Animal: How to Get Him Dressed." In most cases, getting dressed meant boxy suits in blue, gray, or brown, dumb but comfortable.

There was a dark side, too. Senator Joe McCarthy destroyed the careers of New York City school teachers. The first hydrogen bomb was exploded. The Russians crushed the

Hungarian uprising. And there were dozens of ugly racial confrontations, south and north. Still, this was a decade dominated by plain-speaking Dwight Eisenhower, the low-key, firm midwesterner more given to compromise than confrontation. President Eisenhower reflected the outlook of most Americans. Somehow, they felt, even the most difficult problems would be fixed. This was a postwar generation, and collectively it was incandescently optimistic about its future.

Few believed more strongly than the families living in the Mosholu Parkway section of the Bronx. Theirs was a tree-lined neighborhood with grass so green and thick some called it "Little California." On the north it was bounded by Van Cortlandt Park, on the south by the Bronx Botanical Garden, on the west by Jerome Avenue, and on the east by Bainbridge Avenue. The neighborhood was named for the Mosholu Parkway, a wide boulevard that connects Van Cortlandt Park and the Bronx Park. John McNamara, author of a history of Bronx streets, has written that Mosholu is an old Indian word referring to a small stream now called Tibbett's Brook.

This neighborhood would never be confused with the much quieter, white-picket-fence houses to the north, but if it was boisterous, it was also mannerly. The morality here was dominated by old-fashioned first- and second-generation Jews, Italians, and Irish. Here were the homes of those who had climbed one step up the ladder, of parents who spoke English with a foreign accent and dreamed of seeing the day when their children would become doctors, lawyers, or accountants. There were few drugs in the schoolyards; there was even less teenage sex. It was a neighborhood in which homes were clean and well-kept. Typical was 3220 Steuben Avenue, a sturdy six-story red brick apartment building rented mostly to Jewish families. Ralph Lauren grew up here in a small two-bedroom apartment with a tiny bathroom and a kitchen as narrow as a lemon slice. Public School 80 with its six two-story white columns was next door; the Mosholu Parkway itself a few short steps away. Today there are still Italians on Villa Avenue, Irish on Bainbridge, but the Jews are mostly gone, replaced by Asians, Hispanics, West Indians, blacks, and even some Albanians.

Ralph Lauren was born Ralph Lifshitz on October 14, 1939, the youngest of four children. There was Thelma, born September 2, 1930; Leonard, born March 4, 1932, and Jerome, born November 4, 1934. The parents, both Russian immigrants, were opposites in character and habit. Frank Lifshitz was a house painter and muralist, who wore tweed jackets and always tipped his hat to women. He saw himself not as a craftsman but as an artist. Frieda Lifshitz was more pragmatic and deeply religious. Where Frank was whimsical, she was serious. Where Frank dreamed of becoming another Chagall, another Picasso, Frieda wanted her children to get a good Jewish education and then have careers as professionals.

Ralph's home life reflected that sense of push and pull, says Rabbi Zevulun Charlop, who at twenty-three joined the Young Israel of Mosholu Parkway Temple, the neighborhood synagogue the Lifshitz family attended. Rabbi Charlop is an enthusiastic, energetic talker, and when he becomes excited he bounds out of his chair. Rows of books line his office at the Rabbi Isaac Elchanan Theological Seminary, an affiliate of Yeshiva University, where he is dean. He prides himself on his ability to explain why people act the way they do, casually referring to an essay by Freud to make his points.

"The mother was a strong, forceful figure, very Jewish-minded," says Rabbi Charlop. "Her disappointments in life are that the children didn't necessarily follow in her footsteps in religion. Her profoundest disappointment with Ralph may have been in this area. Not that he went away, that he wasn't a good boy. He had tremendous success . . . how could it have happened otherwise? But she always said, 'I only want Jewish *nachas*.' Meaning, a kid becomes famous, that's fine, but I want him to be Jewish. If I can get Jewish celebrity, Jewish nachas, that's great. She doesn't care if he dresses the WASPs or not; she's concerned with his personal life. She's a real Jewish mother.

"The father, Frank, earned a living as a house painter. But he was really an artist. Everything he did, he did with an artistic touch. He wasn't the ordinary run of house painter. Frank looked like a French artiste; he still does. He had an impressive mane, kept his figure, was always nimble. He was a little quixotic, because his feet were on the ground and you knew he wanted to soar into the heavens. The realities of his life, the exigencies of raising a family. . . . He was an immigrant, the Depression, other things . . . he was glued to realities. But he wanted to soar. In that way he was altogether different. He had dreams.

"Frank was also the one who changed his name to Lauren. How do I know this? There is a tradition, a law, that on the Passover holiday you must get rid of all certain kinds of properties. Nonkosher dishes, for example, you put away. Not only are they not supposed to be there, but you're not supposed to keep possession of them. So you come to the rabbi and put your name on a list. The rabbi then sells that list of the neighborhood's belongings to a Gentile. After Passover, we repurchase it.

"Anyway, Frank used to sell his things, and one day he put down the name Lauren. This was about twenty-five years ago. You have to understand. He is one of the most dedicated Jews, but he thought if he were an artist called Frank Lauren it might help him. He wanted to shoot out of the coop. He wanted to reach the heavens. He really believed he had the goods. For every Picasso there may be ten others that never made it, not that they didn't have the art. You could write a Broadway musical about Ralph Lauren, but the star would have to be his father. He walks nimbly. He dances. He's got vitality. And always the hat cocked in the jaunty manner with a feather. Frank isn't the ordinary European immigrant who came to America and had a lucky son. His son made it in ways that came from home. In concepts of painting and art. In having dreams. If Ralph has these qualities now, that's where they come from."

Everybody in the Mosholu Parkway knew Frank Lifshitz. When a neighbor on nearby Kossulth Avenue wanted the window panes on a bedroom door frosted, Frank Lifshitz walked over, paints in hand, and frosted them. Then he wrapped a rag around his finger and drew an ornate design that was both simple and beautiful. Those windows stayed that way for the next fifteen years.

Frank Lifshitz took his work seriously. He would support

his family painting houses; his satisfaction came from the murals he created in the lobbies of New York office buildings. Some still survive. Inside 130 West 30th Street, a building occupied by fur manufacturers, is his mural of New York City. The most striking view is a broad scene of Fifth Avenue painted in grays, blacks, and whites and anchored by the Empire State Building on the left and the Public Library on the right. Here are dozens of buildings squeezed so tightly together they seem on the verge of knocking each other over. Here, too, are hundreds of New Yorkers filling the sidewalks and crossing the street. This is a grand and monumental Fifth Avenue, and it bespeaks a world far different than that of the Mosholu Parkway. A separate city scene covers each of four walls. All are neatly signed: "F. Lifshitz, 1949."

Few of the well-dressed women rushing in to buy their minks and sables at a discount notice, though, because the mural is well above eye level.

When Ralph Lauren grew up in the Mosholu Parkway, a long cast-iron fence called The Rail enclosed the grassy divide separating both directions of traffic. At night the guys would gather here opposite Public School 80 and talk about sports and boast about sexual encounters they now say few experienced. Some wore tight black leather jackets, which meant they were what the neighborhood called "rocks." Others were preppy, wearing crew neck sweaters, khaki pants, and penny loafers. There were also clubs like the Sharks and the Falcons, whose members wore satin jackets with their club names emblazoned on the back. The girls wore skinny, black, tight skirts with Capezio slippers and long earrings, pedal pushers, tight sweaters, crinoline petticoats under full skirts. They had their own clubs, too, with names like the Magnets, Earth Angels, or Evols, which is *Love* spelled backwards with an *s* thrown in.

Few had cars, because in a neighborhood of shopkeepers, furriers, and garment workers not many could afford them. Here, where so many of its members lived, the Amalgamated Clothing Workers built New York's first cooperative apartment buildings. There was little crime. Everybody knew the local toughs, and they were so few in number that those who grew up there can recite their names on one hand. Mainly, the memories are sweet.

"What you did was work the Rail," recalls Garry Marshall, the television producer who based much of his hit series "Happy Days" on his childhood in the Mosholu Parkway neighborhood. Marshall was a friend of Ralph Lauren's oldest brother, Lenny. "That was the social life, and it didn't cost any money. The girls would parade around; some even had their own groups. There was one, the Magnets, which I put in 'Happy Days.' Not that there was much sex. Pregnant was a big scary word. That meant you got married. Each boy had one prophylactic to carry in his wallet and he didn't use it up on just anybody. Prophylactics were hidden in the back room.

"In most neighborhoods, only two things counted: how well you played ball and how tough you were. Our neighborhood was unique in that a sense of humor was respected. So was looking cool and going out with the girls. The Rail itself was one of the most colorful places in town because of the gangs with their satin jackets and pants with pistol pockets; we were fashion plates. That's why Ralph and Calvin Klein went into the business; they had to save the poor souls on the fence. You could be funny, or you could dress up and nobody would call you a sissy. That was a little different from other neighborhoods where those things were put down."

A big date meant a trip to the Fordham Paradise, a handsome movie theater complete with balcony. The local hangouts had names like Gold's Candy Store, where malteds were the drink of choice. Schweller's, a local deli, had pickle barrels in front. The local movie house, the Tuxedo, was renamed the David Marcus theater after a hero in World War II. When there were fights, guys used their fists, not knives or guns. On Friday nights everybody met at the Night Center at nearby Public School 94, where they would play the latest Bill Haley or Elvis Presley records. It was a world that would nurture comedian Robert Klein; Broadway composer Stanley Silverman; actress Penny Marshall, sister of Garry; and dozens of others who went on to careers as scriptwriters, filmmakers, entertainers. Many of those who grew up there say they made their best friends during that period; others formed business partnerships that still exist.

Ralph Lauren had none of the artistic skills of his father. But he didn't like painting or drawing or going to the museums. What Ralph Lauren wanted to do was dominate the basketball courts like Bob Cousy or Sweetwater Clifton, a great City College basketball player who later played for the New York Knickerbockers. Ralph pursued this dream so intensely that as a freshman in high school he made the basketball team at the Boy's Talmudical Academy, an affiliate of Yeshiva University, although most of the other kids towered over him.

"My dream was to be an athlete," says Ralph. "I lived sports. That's what I did all day long. My life was playing basketball and stickball. My biggest influences were Joe DiMaggio, Bob Cousy, Sweetwater Clifton. And maybe Randolph Scott, because I loved cowboys. I didn't know what a fashion designer was in high school. It never dawned on me. It was the last thing on my mind."

He was, say those who grew up with him, pudgy, easygoing, self-involved. He lisped slightly. He made friends without problems, he fit in, he was not an outsider. "Ralph dressed his own way, lived his own style, was very low-key," says Dr. Oscar Cohen, who frequently played against Ralph on the courts. "He was a good basketball player, not great, above average. He was gentle, not aggressive in any way, shape, or form. He didn't have any airs. If you fouled him playing ball he didn't make a big deal out of it."

Ralph's parents raised four children on a salary of $50 to $75 a week. There wasn't much left over for clothes, for restaurants, for nights out with the kids. Neither was there money to move into the larger apartment that would have meant more privacy.

Almost everybody else in the neighborhood lived the same way.

"I was the baby brother," says Ralph. "The clothes went from Lenny to Jerry to me. I guess it was important to have new things, but some of those clothes I really wanted, some of them I couldn't wait to get. We weren't poor. There's a difference.

"I was very preppy when most kids didn't know what that
was. I wore a lot of oxford shirts and crew neck sweaters. I
also wore duffel coats, camel-colored English sailor coats with
wooden toggles. It was a taste level that I related to. I'm not
saying I discovered it; it was out there. I just at an early age
appreciated a look that was collegiate. It was unusual in the
Bronx at that time because kids were wearing motorcycle jackets and singing 'Earth Angel.'

"Then I got more imaginative. I wore white bucks. The
kids were loving rock-and-roll and I was loving Frank Sinatra.
Later, I got a chance to tell him that. When I was thirteen I
read that he was going to take on a TV series. I thought, 'Wrong
thing, Frank.' I knew what made him so popular: his rarity.
He was hard to get to. Seeing him every day was not what he
needed. What he needed to be was special, not to be Johnny
Carson.

"But I wasn't a fish out of water. I didn't know any different. Certainly I wasn't running away from anything. You see
these James Cagney movies, where he's running from the slums
on the Lower East Side, the 'I gotta get out of here, Mom,'
movies, but it was never like that for me. I had a nice childhood. We might have been poor by other people's standards,
but in my neighborhood we were comfortable. My parents
struggled, but I never sensed that struggle. The schoolyard
was right next to my house, and in the mornings I'd run out
and see who was there. It was a great neighborhood. There
was no such thing as not being out late at night. I used to
roller-skate in the schoolyard, roller-skate down the streets, play
stickball. Saturdays I'd hear my friends bouncing the basketball on the court."

Ralph had a team, the Comets, with whom he played at
nearby public schools. There he made friends who were to
stay close for many years, including Michael Bernstein, who
would later be Ralph's business partner, and Steve Bell, now a
New York stockbroker.

"You'd go over to his room, and it looked like a typhoon
had gone through it," says Bell. "It would take him two hours
to find a sock. What made him different was that as a kid he'd
show up dressed in outrageous stuff, like oversized army pon-

chos. Or he'd wear these preppy crew neck sweaters in bright colors, and on him they looked great. We were sort of straight kids, not rocks, which is what we called the tough kids. The crew neck sweaters he wore then he sells today. He had two sharp older brothers, and he saw what they were doing."

His upbringing was unusual in only one way. Through the end of his freshman year in high school, Ralph Lauren went almost exclusively to yeshivas, private Jewish schools where he was taught Hebrew and religious studies. His parents were both active in their temple, and a Jewish education was especially important to Ralph's mother. Such schooling was expensive, and Ralph often attended on partial scholarships. Jerry had gone to yeshivas, and Ralph's parents insisted he go also. Ralph was a good son; he attended without complaint.

Not that Ralph excelled at school.

"He wasn't a particularly good student," says Armand Lindenbaum, a New York realtor who attended Boy's Talmudical Academy with Ralph in 1953 and played on the basketball team there with him. "Like myself, he struggled under heavy pressure from one exam to the other. Kids were very bright, competitive intellectually. Most of them, like Ralph, had been in Jewish elementary schools from first through eighth grades. Later they became doctors, lawyers, researchers. These were poor kids from poor families, and they didn't think in terms of wealth, they thought in terms of jobs. The hours were very long, and what you did was eat, sleep, and study. It wasn't so bad — if you didn't know better. School started before nine A.M. and lasted till six. Then basketball practice would last another two hours. I don't know when we had time to study.

"Ralph was short but aggressive, a fast, good player. Making the team was tough; you had to be a better-than-average player. And the coach was very hard on the younger guys. You couldn't fool around. You had to be serious. If you didn't put out, you were gone."

By the end of freshman year, Ralph had had enough. He wanted to go to DeWitt Clinton, an all-boys high school across the parkway from his apartment. He didn't understand why he had to attend a yeshiva, and he was sick of the forty-five-minute subway ride. Finally he told his parents how he felt.

"That was it," says Ralph. "My dream was to be an athlete. The yeshiva had good teachers; some of them also taught at local colleges during the day. But I wanted a change. I lived sports. That's what I did all day long. I played basketball, stickball in the schoolyards, baseball, that was my whole life."

Ralph was also interested in girls. And they were interested in him. They liked his blue eyes, his petulant manner of cocking his head, his knack for offbeat clothing — white high-top sneakers, safari jackets, a brown leather bomber jacket — and his stylish swagger. (It would be Jerry Lauren, though, Ralph's older brother, who was remembered in the neighborhood as the best-looking Lauren. Ralph seemed to agree. Years later he would introduce Jerry to friends and then say, in all seriousness, "Isn't Jerry good-looking?")

June Ainsworth was Ralph's first girlfriend. She was thirteen; he was two years older. For his sixteenth birthday, she gave him an expensive pipe to add to his collection.

"Ralph was born and finished at age sixteen," says June, married today and living outside Chicago. "He was molded and done. He was firm in his ideas about fashion, who he was, and how things should be. He molded my ideas. I had to be an extension of him. It was too smothering.

"I don't know if he had imagination, but he had vision, a capacity to fill out a picture. My brother, who was six feet tall, would go to the door when Ralph came to the house, grab him by the lapels and say, 'Hey, Ralphie, what are you doing, why do you look like that?' And Ralph would be shy and embarrassed. Our dates were very private. We didn't go out with crowds, and on New Year's Eve we'd get together with a few of his friends and listen to Frank Sinatra records. On dates he only ate kosher. He would only have cheese on his pizza, for example. He really wasn't much of a kid. He was finished by then."

In the summer of 1956 Ralph went to Camp Roosevelt in the Catskills, where he worked as a waiter. It was the first time he was exposed to people who had grown up outside the Bronx, and this world, more sophisticated than his, fascinated him. It fed his fantasies of how people with money lived, the clothes they wore, the colleges they attended. Here, Ralph Lauren, who would always consider himself the outsider except in those worlds he created himself, would have an opportunity to measure himself against older, self-confident camp counselors, and as he did he found himself very much wanting to be like them.

"It was a very preppy environment," says Ralph. "A lot of the older kids were already at schools like Colgate or Syracuse, so it was much more diversified than what I was used to. A waiter was the lowlife at the camp. You're working, the rich kids are the campers, and you'd only get to go on the basketball courts when the kids or the counselors were gone. I went every summer from that point on, and I eventually became a counselor. We used to have what we called color wars, where the camp would be divided into two groups, one who wore blue, the other gray. You played sports, put on shows, sang, and were awarded points. Each team had a boy's general and a girl's general, and being picked to be one was a great honor. It meant you were highly thought of, that you were the top counselor. When I was nineteen or twenty, I was picked. It was a very big thing in my life. I'd started nowhere, at the bottom, not knowing anybody, and I worked my way up to being the top counselor. It sounds like nothing now, but at the time it was very important to me."

What to do when high school ended? Ralph wasn't sure. His parents couldn't afford to send him to an Ivy League school, and he didn't win any scholarships. The only money he had he earned working part-time at Alexander's, a nearby department store.

Ralph Lauren wanted a better life, but so did all his friends. The 1957 graduating class of DeWitt Clinton listed their aspirations in the *Clintonian*, their yearbook. One wanted to be a pharmacist, another a scientist, a third a physician.

Ralph didn't put a profession beneath his picture. Instead, he chose the single word that best summed up everything he wanted in life.

The word was "Millionaire."

After high school Ralph Lauren followed his older brother Jerry to the City College of New York. Part-time, at night, studying business. The CCNY campus was at Lexington Avenue and 23rd Street. It was an hour's subway ride from Ralph's home in the Bronx, and it had nothing to do with fun or romance or quadrangles crowded with kids throwing Frisbees at each other. Students went to this school because it was their only option. For those who worked hard, it provided a solid education. For those who dreamed of life on campus, it was considerably less satisfying. Ralph dreamed of life on campus. It was fall 1957.

Although Ralph didn't go to school in New Haven, he dressed as if he did. In high school Ralph had discovered the fine men's stores like Brooks Brothers and Paul Stuart. Jerry Lauren was a ladies' man and he spent hours working on his wardrobe. Younger brother Ralph looked, listened, learned. He may well have been the only night student at CCNY who was also a regular customer at Paul Stuart. Where did he get the money? "I don't know," says Ralph. "I worked. I had a part-time job at Allied Stores. I just got it."

Brooks Brothers and Paul Stuart were the retailers who specialized in soft shoulder traditional suits and jackets, clothes associated here with the English aristocracy. Fairhaired Englishmen with boyish smiles and incomprehensible accents wore these tweedy jackets and gray flannels when they took their after-dinner constitutionals around Grosvenor Square or stumped their way over rolling Scottish hills. These were the customers, too, secure in the knowledge that not only had they studied at Cambridge, but that their fathers and grandfathers had studied there before them. They wore soft woolens and cashmeres and oiled cottons, and in this country, their clothes became synonymous with an image of life played out in ballrooms and on estates and cricket fields in Kent.

Americans saw these clothes for the first time during World War I, when they passed through London by the thousands. Later, a booming stock market in the late 1920s enabled them to return as tourists. And like good tourists anywhere, they shopped, learning how to dress in the process. So influential was the Prince of Wales during the 1920s and 1930s that he is said to have revived the Panama hat, Fair Isle shetland sweaters, and tab-collared shirts.

The stores that sold such clothes here peddled the image of Old England for all it was worth. Merchants positioned themselves as more than clever salesmen; rather, they were selling the world of gentlemanly clubs, good service, and fine breeding, and the customers who shopped at Brooks Brothers or Paul Stuart shared and enjoyed the fantasy. Ralph Lauren did, and yet, as classy as the clothes were, he decided they weren't quite right. They needed more flair, he thought, more tailoring. Maybe an extra side vent or slashed pockets, or more buttons and wider lapels.

Since Ralph didn't see what he wanted, he designed it himself. There was a mood, a feeling, a sensibility he thought Brooks Brothers and Paul Stuart had somehow missed. Ralph didn't fantasize about becoming a fashion designer; he became a designer to fulfill his fantasies. Later, he would say that he had been inspired by Hollywood movies of the 1930s and 1940s.

No wonder, then, that as a customer, Ralph Lauren was a terrible pain in the neck.

"I seemed to have all the customers who were the most demanding," says Clifford Grodd, the snappy, suspender-wearing, president of Paul Stuart. Grodd has built a business based on service and fit, in an atmosphere as austere as nearby Brooks Brothers is collegial. "Ralph always had ideas of what he wanted executed, and he drove me nuts. Ralph was always quizzical, always asking why something wasn't done this way, always fantasizing about what he perceived as the world according to Ralph Lauren."

Ralph broke the rules because he didn't know them. He'd order a suit from superfine gabardine (a twill-weave fabric with a diagonal rib effect), not understanding that tailors hated this cloth because it tore so easily. Clifford Grodd would grit his teeth and try to have it made. Why go to the trouble? Because nobody was as interested in style as Ralph. Together, he and Grodd talked about clothes the way others talked about plays and books. "I put up with him where I probably wouldn't with somebody else because he was earnest, so honest, so appealing," Grodd explains. "He had charm, although on one level I cringed when I saw him walk in the door. He kept me on my toes."

Clifford Grodd would not be the only important influence on Ralph's taste and style. Later Ralph would be befriended by some of the city's finest tailors, including Morton Sills at Sartor & Co., the late Roland Meledandri, and Jimmy Palazzo, who today runs the largest men's wear factory in New York. Together with Brooks Brothers and Paul Stuart, Sills, Palazzo, and Meledandri specialized in the "Eastern school look," or tweedy, soft shoulder jackets, Irish brogues, camel topcoats. All were Anglophiles, and all were influenced by English fabric design, neckwear patterns, wool shetlands, paisley patterns, and Harris tweeds. Not only did they understand and make fine men's clothing, but they knew how to talk about it. Theirs was a world of color, a world of soft, sensuous fabrics, a world as orderly as it was elegant.

Compared to that, the City College of New York seemed stale, stifling, and ordinary. Ralph's grades weren't good, and after two years he dropped out.

"It was murder," he says. "I went afternoons and nights and summer school. I was on the trains, it was hot, and I wasn't inspired. My marks were mediocre. I got an A in psychology, my one A. I was bad in math, always bad in math. And that was that. I felt school was not what I wanted, so I went back to work."

Ralph Lauren was twenty years old, and he couldn't get a job because the armed forces draft was still in place. It didn't make sense to train somebody who would be peeling potatoes in six months.

Jerry Lauren's friend Neal J. Fox was working at Brooks Brothers. Maybe Ralph should be selling clothes instead of buying them, Jerry said, and maybe Neal could help. Brooks Brothers, founded in 1818 by Henry Sands Brooks in Lower Manhattan, was one of the first to carry ready-to-wear clothes, as well as hand-tailored suits. Later, Abraham Lincoln shopped there. So did the Duke of Windsor and F. Scott Fitzgerald. In the late 1950s the clientele was Park Avenue, it was Madison Avenue, it was the prep school kids, it was high society. Those were the customers who appealed to Ralph Lauren. Understanding what they wanted, how they lived, and where they lived would be a lifelong preoccupation.

Here Ralph Lauren would get his first lessons in how to

sell to the upper middle class. He would also see that the customers expected personal service, and that they were willing to pay for that service. Those were the lessons CCNY could never have taught him. Brooks Brothers would have perhaps more influence on his taste than any other store in New York.

Ralph stayed at Brooks Brothers through February. Soon afterwards he was marching in the Army Reserves, serving six months at Fort Dix. (The National Personnel Records Center in St. Louis has Ralph Lauren's service history. It is not public. When I asked Ralph to send for a copy, he shuddered. "Are you crazy?" he asked. "No way. Maybe they'll want me back again.")

Discharged, Ralph moved in with his parents. A clerk in an employment agency took one look at the suit he was wearing and sent him for a job at Meyers Make, Inc., a manufacturer of men's and women's gloves. Soon Ralph Lauren was posting orders in the back room. "I mailed the packages, stamped them," he says. "I'd open the salesmen's order books, write down how many orders there were and where they were to be shipped. . . . It sounds like another life."

Ralph was eager and friendly, and the boss, Jerome Fox, liked the sharp way Ralph dressed. The kid obviously had taste, and when Ralph asked him for a chance to sell the line, Fox sent him out to hound the hundreds of buying offices that then dotted New York.

"Basically I was selling women's gloves that buttoned up to the elbow," says Ralph. "Then I'd sit in on the sales meetings, with some real old-timers, and I'd learn. It was interesting, but it was a dying industry."

The job required patience and strong legs. It meant getting into his office early, learning which buyers were in town, and then hustling the rest of the day to make the sales. Ralph Lauren shuttled from door to door with his little box of gloves, and eventually he learned how to show a line. What he lacked in experience he compensated for in energy and enthusiasm.

His own wardrobe left others shaking their heads in wonder.

"He may have been making forty or fifty dollars, but he dressed like a million bucks," says Frank Arnold, who worked at Meyers Make with Ralph and still earns his living selling gloves. "He was easygoing, a warm guy. But it was obvious that he wasn't cut out for what he was doing. You could see his thoughts were elsewhere. He was really interested in men's wear in general, in fashion. This is 1961 or 1962, and he would buy a suit for two hundred dollars. Today that's like a thousand-dollar suit or more. Ralph used to tell me about his dreams, and how his traditional look was going to be big. 'Frankie,' he would say, 'you really don't understand what I'm talking about.' "

Before Meyers Make went out of business Ralph left to work for Ed Brandau, a friend from Brooks Brothers then managing the New York showroom of Daniel Hays Co., Inc., a glove maker. It was now the summer of 1963, and the salary Brandau offered was barely enough to cover Ralph's daily expenses. To help pay the bills, Ralph soon added a perfume line called Zizanie.

"He had a tendency to be a dreamer," says Brandau. "He wasn't really . . . well, how interested in gloves could you be? He was always dreaming of the future and what he could do."

Despite selling the gloves and the perfumes, Ralph needed more money. Finally Ed Brandau called a Boston tie maker he knew. Abe Rivetz had often said he wanted to hire a New York salesman, and now Brandau suggested Ralph Lauren. Let him sell the gloves, the perfumes, and Abe Rivetz's line of conservative ties, and maybe Ralph could make a decent living. Abe Rivetz agreed, and on January 23, 1964, *Daily News Record,* the men's wear industry trade paper, gave Ralph Lauren his first short plug. "R. Lauren joins A. Rivetz & Co." read the headline.

Abe Rivetz had noticed something about Ralph Lauren that he liked. It was the way he dressed, the way he smiled, his self-assurance. Ralph was going to be something special, he told the other salesmen.

Nobody at that company ever believed him.

Ralph Lauren was joining a chummy industry dominated by a handful of plain-spoken men whose fathers and even grandfathers had been friends. Everything was done by the book. There was a right way and a wrong way to show a tie, write

an order, color a tie. This was a snobby little world and what
it didn't understand it ignored. Fashion meant tradition, consistency was a virtue. In this club, the A. Rivetz Company was
a member in good standing.

The company was based in Boston, but often Abe Rivetz
and his son-in-law Mel Creedman did business in New York.
They rented a suite at the old Vanderbilt Hotel, showing their
line during the day and sleeping over at night. A. Rivetz &
Co. made conservative rep ties (ties with a diagonal twill weave),
English foulards (soft, satiny silks with fine twill), madder prints
(ties colored with vegetable dyes), stripes, and solid blues and
olives. The customers included Brooks Brothers and Bloomingdale's.

Change in this business was measured in eighths of an inch.
The buyers took weeks to make their decisions. Rivetz's top
New York salesman, Izzy Gamer, had been with the firm for
more than three decades. When Gamer died, he was replaced
by ruddy-faced Phineas Connell, who had worked for Rivetz
nearly as long. So stable was this industry that in 1986, seven
years after A. Rivetz had been sold to new owners, Connell
was still on the job, taking buyers out to dinner and selling the
same accounts at age seventy-five. This was a company whose
salesmen knew everything there was to know about making,
coloring, and selling ties.

Not Ralph Lauren. He was a glove man.

He was also twenty years younger than anybody else and
he wore the damnedest clothes to work. This meant spread
collar shirts and flare-bodied suits, which the other Rivetz
salesmen, mostly conservative New Englanders, considered
weird and strangely high spirited.

"I was a young hungry guy who lived in the city and said,
'Listen, this is what's happening,'" says Ralph Lauren. "I was
very Ivy League but I was also wearing side vent suits, two-
button coats. It was the Duke of Windsor. The guys at Rivetz
didn't understand it. It wasn't Boston."

People outside the office began to talk about Ralph and
his clothes. A reporter for *Daily News Record* hunted Ralph
down, and a few days later, on May 21, 1964, a full page appeared in the newspaper about Ralph Lauren's wardrobe.

The piece was headlined "The Professional Touch." *DNR*

sketched several of Ralph's outfits, describing each in detail. There were corduroy riding pants, a shaped suit, which meant the jacket flared out from the back and had broad lapels, and a double-breasted navy blazer with rounded shoulders and a straight lapel.

The crew at Rivetz was dazed. Since when did Ralph Lauren give interviews? More to the point, who cared what Ralph Lauren thought about clothes?

"Ralph was different," says Mel Creedman, Abe Rivetz's son-in-law. "If everybody was clean shaven, Ralph wore a beard. When the industry was selling skinny ties, Ralph had to wear a wide one. I'd constantly be telling him to clean his raincoat."

Abe Rivetz didn't care. He liked Ralph and he believed he had talent. Rivetz even started to dress like him. If Ralph owned a Burberry raincoat, Abe Rivetz would wear a Burberry raincoat. If Ralph had his suits made by hand, so would he. Abe Rivetz might have been in his sixties, but he had heart and imagination.

Everybody who saw the two together knew Ralph Lauren was going to play a major role in the company's future.

"Abe understood me," says Ralph. "He had that little extra, that hunger. He said, 'I'll go to your tailor. I want to wear that.' And he did. We were close."

The only thing that troubled Abe Rivetz was Ralph Lauren's car. It was a Morgan, a two-door English sports car. It was pale yellow and it had a black roof, a red leather interior, windows that clamped on, and wooden seats. There was a walnut dashboard, and an ivory speedometer with black numerals. What it lacked was a trunk. "Somebody will steal our line," complained Abe Rivetz. "There's no security. Get rid of it. Get a salesman's car, a car with a trunk that locks." Abe Rivetz was now talking about sending Ralph Lauren to the Fashion Institute of Technology, but he wanted Ralph to show he was committed to building the business.

One July weekend Ralph drove up to Phineas Connell's summer home in Niantic, Connecticut. With him was Ricky Lowbeer, a slim, blue-eyed blonde receptionist he'd met at his eye doctor's office. Ricky, born January 21, 1945, was nearly six years younger than Ralph. With her blue eyes, trim figure, and ash blonde hair, she looked every bit an English country schoolgirl.

That summer afternoon Ricky and Ralph sailed Long Island Sound on Phineas Connell's thirty-foot Atlantic, a sleek open-cockpit boat designed for racing. As they did, Rich Connell, Phineas's son, drove Ralph's car through his neighborhood. After dinner, Rich Connell bought it for $1,150.

Abe Rivetz wanted Ralph Lauren to show he could be practical. Now Ralph was going to justify Abe's faith in him. The following Monday morning, Ralph bought a car with a trunk that locked.

It was a classic 1957 Thunderbird.

Later, the car was stolen. But Ralph had made his point. He was willing to go along — but he'd do it his way.

Ralph was decisive about other things, too. He and Ricky Lowbeer went to discos in New York and Italian restaurants for dinner, and the more they talked, the more they found they had in common. Ricky's parents were Jewish, they were Austrian, they knew what it was like to leave the country where they had been born and start again. Ricky was down-to-earth and sensible. Ralph found not only that he could talk to her about his dreams, but more, that she believed in him. Six months after they met Ralph asked her to marry him. Later, he would insist it was love at first sight.

"When I met Ricky, I took her to the disco in the Gotham Hotel," says Ralph. "I knew what was happening. That was the beginning of the whole fashion explosion. That disco was European, the Beatles were happening. Ricky and I spent some of our earliest dates there. It was chic, and very, very glamorous. I was a New Yorker. I wasn't an outsider sitting back sucking my thumb. I was aware of interesting things."

Soon they were looking for an apartment they could move into after they were married. Ralph wanted to live in Manhattan and eventually he found one he liked. It was a studio, small but made attractive by its brick walls, fireplace, and loft bed.

"Let's take it," he said to Ricky.

"No, let's ask our parents first," Ricky replied. Ricky was then nineteen and living at home.

Ralph insisted. The rent was only $135, which he thought he could afford. Ralph signed a lease, paid two months' rent in advance, and gave one month's rent as a security deposit. This was every cent he had except for a few hundred dollars he'd saved for their honeymoon.

A month later, Ralph went back to make sure that the walls had been painted and that the apartment was clean. Instead, he found another family living there. He got into a shouting match with the landlord and demanded his money back.

The landlord told him to get lost.

"Finally I went to arbitration," says Ralph. "The landlord had four cases that night with different people. He was a real pro. He brought his superintendent, and by the time I left I'd lost everything. That guy lied to me and then he took my money. I walked out and I said, 'Jesus, there's no honor in life.' I was poor and they took everything away from me. This guy bullshitted, and he just took it. I was so honest and straight. So all I had left was my honeymoon."

Ralph and Ricky Lauren were married on December 20, 1964. Instead of moving to Manhattan, they took a rear two-room apartment at 4545 Knox Place in the Bronx, several blocks from Ralph's parents. It was hot, it was noisy, and the kitchen was a tiny niche in the living room. It was also the worst apartment in the building. Despite this, the landlord wasn't certain he wanted Ralph for a tenant.

"Frankly, I was worried whether he could pay the rent," says Isidor Schachter, who owned the building. "He was a tie salesman. But I'll say this: he never missed a payment."

Abe Rivetz died on the same day Ralph and Ricky Lauren married. When Ralph returned from his honeymoon, he would miss Abe Rivetz's friendship and encouragement.

But he hoped that Mel Creedman, who quickly took over the business, would give him the same opportunities Abe had talked about.

"When Abe died, I went back to Mel and said, 'Mel, I'd like to design the ties,'" says Ralph. "I went to Boston with

Mel, I slept over at his house. I'll never forget, he was driving me back to New York and I said, 'Mel, I want to design the line.'

"And he said, 'There's no such thing as a designer in our business.'

"I said, 'Mel, I don't care about the money. I know I can do it.'

"So he said, 'We'll think about it.'"

Creedman thought about it, but not for long. Abe Rivetz believed in Ralph Lauren.

Mel Creedman thought Ralph was an amateur.

"What I saw was a young, quite immature, ambitious salesman," says Creedman. "Ralph and I didn't get along. He was very green, and what he wanted to do was not commercial. It wasn't viable. I had a business to protect. I used to tell him to get his hair cut."

What bothered Creedman most was that he thought Ralph spent too much time talking about clothes instead of selling ties.

"He was supposed to be a neckwear salesman for us, but I found he was spending a lot of his time talking to people like Roland Meledandri, a tailor. Ralph could spend hours talking about the location and dimension of belt loops on trousers or the size of pocket flaps. Why the hell is the kid talking to somebody about belt loops? Let him sell neckties. So I would go back to Boston and tell Ruth, my wife, 'I've got to get rid of that little kid. I don't know what the hell he is doing.' Then Ruth or Phineas Connell would say, 'Come on. He's doing a good job; he's going to get better. Give him a chance.' So I'd go another week and another week. It just goes to show you. Who knew?"

Call it culture clash.

Creedman was right about one thing: nobody designed ties in the early 1960s. The basic shapes and widths were the same from year to year, and the fabric houses decided what fabrics and patterns would be available from season to season.

What separated one tie manufacturer from another was how he colored his line.

Coloring a line meant deciding whether a silk tie had a

blue background with a red stripe, or a red background with a blue stripe. It meant choosing whether the little dots inside the paisleys should be blue or yellow, red or green. And it meant guessing whether the background colors should be bold and bright, or muted and somber.

"We sold two major items," says salesman Phineas Connell. "Stripes and foulards. [Foulards are lightweight twills or plain-woven silks printed with small designs.] Sometimes the stripes are bolder, sometimes they are more subtle. Ralph wanted to choose which colors we used."

Ralph was so persistent that eventually Mel Creedman said, "Enough, do it, leave me alone." Not because Creedman needed or wanted Ralph Lauren's help, but because he wanted to do the kid a favor. "Color some ties," Creedman told him. "But nothing kooky, understand?"

Ralph said he understood. Mel Creedman wasn't so sure.

Rivetz was then doing business with a company called Greenhut Fabrics. An order came in for a group of striped silk shantungs, and Ralph went to Mel Creedman and asked if he could do the coloring.

Creedman was leaving for Europe, but he gave his approval on the condition that Phineas Connell signed off on Ralph's choices.

Ralph said that was fine. He understood. He didn't have much experience. Creedman was probably right to want somebody to oversee his work. If Mel Creedman wanted Phineas to give his blessing, that was okay with Ralph.

Creedman went to Europe. A week or two later, Ralph called Phineas Connell and told him he had finished coloring the line. They agreed to meet at Greenhut's office, where Ralph would show him his work.

Connell carefully looked over each of Ralph's designs, and when he was done, he looked Ralph straight in the eye and told him the work was terrible. Unusual. Too far out for the customers.

"Ralph, I won't be responsible for these," he said.

Then, thinking Ralph was so upset that he might break down, Connell desperately turned to Jeff Greenhut, who owned the business, and said, "Jeff, what do you think?"

"I have to agree with you," Greenhut replied. "I didn't want to say anything."

That was it. Final. The work was thrown out and Ralph had to do it again.

"The other guys in the company didn't understand what I did," says Ralph. "They were hardnosed. They lived in the little world of Ivy League. They sold the little stores that started when they started, and they didn't know how to budge. I scared them. I'd color some ties, and they'd say, 'Who you going to sell that to, the fags on Third Avenue? Why are you doing this? You're killing our image.' "

Ralph didn't see it that way. In 1967, his fourth year with Rivetz, Ralph set out to earn more than his $13,000 salary. He colored the line, he filled in at the showroom, he opened new accounts. He also became fascinated with wide ties. Ties three-and-a-half, four, four-and-a-half inches across. They were making ties like that in Europe, and Ralph had seen them in the window at Meledandri's. So now Ralph began to press Creedman to produce wide ties. "Let me do it," he pleaded. "Wide ties are new. Let me sell them to Bloomingdale's." To put an end to his pleading Creedman finally let Ralph make up one or two small groups, but that was Creedman's limit. Ralph was over the top. Wide ties looked absurd. A man might as well wear a bib to work.

The breaking point came when Ralph told Mel he wanted a bonus that year.

"I thought I was making a contribution," says Ralph. "I think Mel started to rely on me a little. Maybe he didn't. Maybe he thought he was making me feel good. Anyway, I thought at that point I deserved more. I did everything above and beyond selling. So I asked for the bonus."

Tie salesmen were never given bonuses. It was a tradition. And the tie industry was a very traditional business.

Creedman turned Ralph down. If he gave to Ralph, he said, he'd have to give to all the salesmen. The company couldn't afford it.

Frustrated and angry, Ralph began looking for a new job. As he did, he booked a major order for rep ties at Abraham & Straus, a division of Federated Department Stores. Not only did he color those ties, he put them in the store himself. Then, a few days later, he quit.

Ralph hadn't been gone a week when Mel Creedman got a phone call.

It was the buyer at A&S, the buyer who'd given Ralph that big order . . . and now regretted it. If Creedman didn't remove every one of those damned ties from his store the next day, the buyer warned, the Abe Rivetz company would never do business with A&S again.

"He said the colors were too bright for his customers," says Creedman. "It was a total fiasco. I had to send Phineas Connell's kid to pick them up right away. A&S was furious."

As far as Creedman was concerned, that proved it.

As he had often told anybody who would listen, the world just wasn't ready for Ralph Lauren.

▶ ▶ ▶ 3

Mel Creedman wasn't the only one who doubted that the world was ready for Ralph Lauren. Ralph was now searching for potential backers, telling them he intended to make wide, elegant ties reminiscent of the 1940s. Why investors? Because Ralph didn't have enough money to start his own company. His parents couldn't lend it to him; neither could his brothers. What Ralph did have was boyish charm and enthusiasm. Maybe people didn't understand why he wore flared jackets with wide lapels, and maybe people didn't want to dress that way themselves. But when Ralph Lauren came into a room, everybody noticed. And if somebody nodded at him in approval, Ralph would round his small mouth into a smile and beam. Ralph absolutely glowed goodwill. At a time when Timothy Leary was urging people to turn on and drop out, the sight of Ralph Lauren standing proud in his hand-tailored wool suits was as welcome as it was reassuring.

Ralph's low-key style helped him sell the Rivetz line, too. He didn't strut into a store and slap his ties down on the counter the way most salesmen did. Rather, Ralph laid those ties down carefully. Then he picked each one up and caressed it, running his hands slowly along the length of that tie like a child feeling silk for the first time. As his hands moved, he talked about those ties with the same conviction realtors used selling empty lots to anxious home buyers. Ralph was a natural salesman. He knew buyers wanted to believe their ties were special, and when Ralph talked about his rich stripes or his bold colors, the customers believed they were special. Ralph made his listeners see his ties the way he did, as more than ordinary pieces of cloth. He didn't sell his line on the basis of a particular style, a delivery date, a price. Ralph sold himself. His taste level. His personal commitment. Years later, men who'd worked as salesmen their entire adult lives would marvel at Ralph's ability to romance a line. Ralph Lauren wanted others to share the image of the world as he saw it, and for those few minutes, when he talked, they did.

At least some did.

Others thought Ralph Lauren was too cocky, too sure of himself. He was selling ties, not Burmese rubies. And maybe Ralph should show more gratitude to the company signing his paychecks.

Put Buddy Blake, a top New York tie maker, in that camp. When Ralph groused to his closest friends that he wanted to launch his own company, a mutual acquaintance phoned Blake and asked him to meet with Ralph as a favor. If Blake thought Ralph had talent, maybe he and Ralph could work something out. Blake was experienced and knew the market, and Ralph might have a little talent.

Send the kid over, Blake said.

After introducing himself, Ralph got to the point. "They won't let me do enough styling," said Ralph, referring to the Abe Rivetz company. "I think I can do more. I'm ready."

Blake doubted it. In fact, after talking to him, Blake thought Ralph was naive, and perhaps deluding himself about his abilities.

"Look," Blake counseled. "You've got a hell of a good job where you are. Stay there."

Ralph Lauren was not discouraged easily. Call him a dog with bark. Not only did he ignore Blake's advice, he also insisted on always saying what was on his mind. This meant his jaunty self-confidence sometimes left others fuming.

Look what happened to Marty and Elliott Gant. The Gant brothers were successful manufacturers of preppy, button-down shirts in New Haven, Connecticut. Gant Shirt Makers had started in business in 1949, competing with names like C. F. Hathaway, Embassy, and Troy Shirt Maker's Guild. By 1967 the Gants made some of the most popular shirts in the country. Business was so good the Gants began to think they should make ties to sell with those shirts. They had a famous label, they had money, and they knew the top retailers across the country.

In the world of men's wear manufacturers, the Gants had respect.

The last thing they expected to hear from Ralph Lauren

was a lecture telling them how they should run their company.

But that's what they got.

"You're starting to lose it," Ralph warned them. "I don't wear your shirts any more."

Ralph then outlined the direction the Gants should take. The customers were ready to pay higher prices for better quality clothes. Use finer cottons, bolder colors. Build value into the shirts and raise the prices. Give men more styling, not the same traditional looks year after year. Be aggressive. The customers would pay for the best when they were given a chance to buy it.

The Gants sat in stony silence.

They were not amused.

The next day Ralph excitedly called his friend Richard Jacobson, a piece goods dealer who had set up the meeting. Everything had gone great, he said.

"What did you say to them?" Jacobson interrupted. "They called me and wanted to know why I sent them a cocky, wise-guy kid."

Even today, Ralph finds their attitude hard to understand.

"Let me tell you, if a kid came into my office and said that to me, I'd hire him in a second," says Ralph. "I was never disrespectful. What I had was enthusiasm. I believed in what I was saying, I told them what I felt. They didn't want to hear it."

The Gants, though, had reason to be skeptical. Wide ties had been reintroduced a few years earlier. Mod, those ties had been called, short for Modern Youth. Mod meant Carnaby Street, Kings Road, wild colors, bold patterns. It meant Mary Quant and sport jackets without any collars. It was new and different, but as American manufacturers learned, it didn't mean salable. Modern Youth in this country decided they preferred their chinos, and the makers and sellers of Mod clothes lost a fortune.

"Mod was the English look," says Ralph. "It was the Beatles, it was very kooky, it was very wide, and it bombed. My ties were wide but they were different. My ties were very elegant. They were all handmade from old fabrics, little pieces of odds and ends. I wanted to change the prices, too. Ties were then inexpensive, three dollars, four dollars each. The ties I wanted to sell started at seven fifty."

The deals came, the deals went, this one was going to help him, that one was thinking about it, nobody could make up his mind. Finally Ralph Lauren found a sympathetic listener. Ned Brower was then president of Beau Brummell, a well-managed tie company based in Cincinnati. Beau Brummell made a conservative tie, ties men wore to the office without attracting a second look. But Brower read the trade papers, and he saw that the industry was changing. The customers who shopped at Bloomingdale's, the trendsetters, wanted fresh, more exuberant clothes. Since the demand was there, somebody was going to fill it. Already the doings of Pierre Cardin, Hardy Amies, and John Weitz were being reported almost daily in *Daily News Record.* The industry was truly shaken, however, when Bill Blass signed a men's wear license in February 1967. Blass was one of the most famous women's wear designers in the country. He had clout, he had taste, and the customers knew his name. Until Blass came along, most men's wear companies referred to their designers as tailors or stylists, and kept them in the back room. Now Brower saw that this would all change.

That was why Brower was willing to listen to a kid who dressed as if he owned Park Avenue. Besides, Beau Brummell was successful enough to take the small risk now and then.

"What I want to do is start my own company," Ralph told Brower over late-afternoon drinks at the Plaza Hotel. "My ties are more expensive, but they're worth it."

Ned Brower didn't think anybody could sell neckties for $7.50. But as he talked he balanced the pluses against the minuses. If Ralph was right, the customers were ready for four-and-a-half inches of raw Indian silk spread across their chests like holiday bunting. Most likely these weren't the same customers who bought Beau Brummell ties, which meant Brower didn't have to worry about cannibalizing his main business. If Ralph Lauren was wrong, the losses could be held to a minimum.

"We'll start a new division, and you'll run it," Brower finally decided. "You'll do the selling, and if our sales force has the time to help, fine. Otherwise, you're on your own."

Maybe the world was ready for Ralph Lauren after all.

Several days later, Ralph walked into Mel Creedman's office and told him he was quitting. "When Ralph finally came to me and said he was going with Beau Brummell I was happy because I wasn't going to have to fire him," says Creedman. "But I'll say this: the SOB had integrity."

In April 1967 Ralph Lauren joined Beau Brummell. Now that he was running his own business, he needed a company name. Jerry Lauren, his brother, suggested Polo Fashions. Polo was a rich man's game, and it conveyed money, style, and exclusivity, the same qualities Ralph wanted his ties to have. Ralph thought Polo was a terrific name.

Beau Brummell's New York offices were in the Empire State Building. "They gave me a tiny office and I kept my ties in a drawer," says Ralph. "That's how I worked for six months. No windows. Then I needed more space, so they put me in the back half of another office, where I had a desk and a chest of drawers.

"The guy who was the bow tie king was in the front half of the office. He was a real character. He'd tell me, in a Jackie Mason–type voice, 'Ralph, I have a tie for you . . . a deal for you . . . you'll be a king.' "

Ralph never bought the bow ties.

He didn't have the space.

Ralph was president, chief executive, and if he wanted to be, chief operating officer. He was also the packer, the shipper, the distributor, and the top salesman. He was selling wide ties that retailed from $7.50 to $15.00 at a time when ties were at least an inch narrower and almost never cost more than $5.00.

More than the price was different. Ralph made hand-blocked prints in bright colors, he made windowpane diagonal checks, he used any wild, exotic fabric he found in the remnant shops that lined the Lower East Side of Manhattan. Ralph was in a hurry, and if he used the everyday, ordinary fabrics, nobody would have paid attention.

"I'm promoting a level of taste, a total feeling," Ralph told *Daily News Record* that year. "It's important to show the customer how to wear these ties, the idea behind the look." Ralph dressed for that interview in an electric blue shirt with a navy grenadine tie, a jacket with four-inch-wide lapels, and pleated pants finished with deep cuffs. *Daily News Record* was impressed.

"Lauren rises above the detail looking luxurious," commented the paper. "He looks like the man he has described — the man of the twilight zone between fashion and tradition." That was as good a description as any. Sometimes it was hard even for the fashion press to understand Ralph Lauren. Tagging him as a resident of the twilight zone may have seemed a reasonable starting point.

The first customers were Clifford Grodd at Paul Stuart and Roland Meledandri. They didn't give Ralph big orders, but the cachet of having his ties in those stores helped Ralph with the smaller stores. "We just tried a little in the beginning, enough to give him support," says Grodd. "It was a selling point to say he was in Paul Stuart."

Each of Ralph's ties was hand slip-stitched, which meant the shell and the interlining were sewn together in such a way that the tie could stretch and yet pull back into shape. It took longer to make ties that way, which meant the ties cost more. However, since Ralph never flinched when it came to buying his wardrobe, he assumed his customers wouldn't flinch, either.

"The way he did business was to order maybe two dozen ties at a time," says George Bruder, who made Ralph's first ties. "I couldn't make any money on orders that small. It was a pain, but I liked Ralph, so I did it. You needed a lot of patience to work with him, too, because on top of everything else he'd sit there and actually quibble over a one-sixteenth of an inch. He'd look at me and he'd say, 'George, it's not quite right.' Neckwear was then narrow, but he was asking for ties four inches wide, five inches wide. Then he would argue over a fraction of an inch so tiny nobody else could possibly see it." Even the shape of Ralph's ties was different. Instead of flaring out gradually into the traditional wedge, Ralph's ties sprang full-bodied from the knot. They were ties that were wide at the throat as well as at the apron, and their sheer bulk commanded attention.

"We became friends," adds Bruder. "Ralph was a nice person, a likable person. He was humble, he had humility. But I don't know how he got his ideas. He was really different. If he saw your coat and liked it, he'd say, 'Let's make a tie out of it.' "

Where did Bruder find the patience to work with him?

"I was younger then."

Ralph Lauren may have been soft-spoken, but he was also part showman, and he understood that to build his business he needed more exposure than an occasional article in *Daily News Record*. Look how well Henry Grethel was doing designing shirts for C. F. Hathaway. Indeed, Grethel was such a hit with the customers that they often asked retailers for the same ties they'd seen in Hathaway's magazine ads. This made Henry Grethel a very important person in tie circles, and Ralph badly wanted to meet him.

Instead of calling directly, Ralph asked Clara Hancox, a reporter for *Clothes* magazine, to set up a meeting for him. One afternoon, while Hancox and Grethel were having lunch, she mentioned that Grethel should see Ralph's wide ties. Later, as Grethel headed back to his office, he realized he wasn't sure if he remembered the young man's name.

Finally it came to him.

He was supposed to meet a Mr. Polo.

Much to Grethel's surprise, Ralph was waiting for him, dressed in a wide-lapeled suit, a Black Watch tartan Viyella shirt, and a wide knit tie. After Grethel stopped gawking, Ralph introduced himself, and Grethel invited him in.

Soon Ralph was showing Grethel his line, and as he did he eagerly solicited Grethel's opinions.

Grethel didn't know what to think because these ties were so much wider than anybody else's on the market. They were either the homeliest, ugliest ties Grethel had ever seen, or very special.

Finally Grethel decided.

"I like them," he said. "I think they're terrific."

"No," said Ralph. "It's really very important. Do you really like them?"

"Yes, I really like them," replied Grethel.

"Why?"

"Why are you so surprised?"

Ralph paused.

"Because I don't like your shirts."

"What do you mean, you don't like my shirts?" Grethel said. Grethel was astonished. Every tie maker in New York swore he made the best shirts in the country. Grethel knew he was being flattered, but in fact he thought he did make a pretty good product.

"They're ordinary oxford button-down shirts. I'm beyond that stage now," Ralph continued.

Actually, Ralph thought some of Grethel's shirts were fine. But as he'd waited for Grethel to return from lunch, Ralph had browsed through some of Grethel's swatch books. The books were mostly bare, because Grethel had already matched most of his fabrics to ties made by other manufacturers. By the time Ralph saw the books, they were practically empty.

What was left he didn't like. And he said so.

This put Henry Grethel on the defensive.

"Let me see some other fabrics," Grethel called to his secretary. "Give me some of the swatches we've already reserved for other tie manufacturers."

A few minutes later, Grethel found himself nervously soliciting Ralph's opinions.

"Now, that's the kind of stuff I really like," said Ralph after a while.

Grethel nodded. But he had a problem. Those swatches were committed to other tie makers. He didn't think he could change his mind now.

"That's all right, Henry," Ralph said. "I'll wait until next season."

Grethel stared at him. "Ralph," he said. "Are you telling me you don't want to put your ties on our shirts?"

"Not this time," Ralph replied.

"Well, what if I gave you these fabrics," Grethel asked, pointing toward several swatches he'd promised to somebody else.

Ralph smiled. He said he thought that was a great idea.

Henry Grethel became one of Ralph Lauren's strongest supporters. When retailers dropped by, Grethel would mention

Ralph's name and send them down to Ralph's showroom in the Empire State Building. A few hours later, those same buyers would call asking if Grethel really thought the ties would sell.

That is how word-of-mouth builds a business.

Ralph's next goal was to place his ties in Bloomingdale's or Saks Fifth Avenue. The big stores were intimidating, though, especially for somebody who didn't know the buyers. What Ralph needed was a mentor, somebody who knew his way around and could make introductions for him.

Unlike his father, Ralph found one.

His name was Joe Aezen, and he was a salesman for Rooster Ties. The two had met at a trade show when Ralph was still working for the Daniel Hays company. Ralph had walked up to Aezen, introduced himself, and told him how much he admired the Rooster ties with their square ends and their prints of lobsters and sailboats and horses. Aezen thought Ralph Lauren was one of the sharpest dressers he had ever seen, English from head to toe, a lesson in advanced Brooks Brothers.

They became friends. Aezen was then in his thirties and he'd grown up in Philadelphia, a bantam-weight chain smoker. Aezen was loud, he was compulsive, he knew all the jokes. There was even a little jingle, too, to help people remember him: "Aezen as in raisin as in Rooster as in chicken." Aezen would beg, plead, shout, and sell in a series of dramatic flourishes, complete with a repertoire of raised eyebrows, pained smiles, and looks of approval, dismay, and astonishment. Nobody thought Aezen was perfect, but that's what buyers liked about him. Aezen was human. He cajoled, he gossiped, he suffered. This made the pushing and selling and craziness bearable.

Since he believed in Ralph Lauren, he wanted everybody else to believe too. Ralph's ties didn't compete in price or style with Rooster's, so when Aezen made his rounds from store to store each week, he handed out Ralph Lauren ties to the buyers, the assistant buyers, anybody who would take them.

Aezen was especially persistent at Bloomingdale's. He talked about Ralph Lauren to Franklin Simon, the men's merchandise manager, to Jack Schultz, divisional merchandise manager, to Gary Shafer, the men's buyer, and to Steve Krauss, an assistant to the buyer. He'd talk, they'd listen, and he'd talk some more.

"Joe Aezen would take Frank Simon and me to dinner, or bring us brownies when we worked late, and all the time he'd be telling us that we had to have these Ralph Lauren ties," says Jack Schultz, now president of B. Altman & Co. "Then he'd pull some ties out of his briefcase and say, 'You've got to wear these.' Bloomingdale's probably wouldn't have recognized Ralph Lauren's talent without Joe Aezen's help."

Not that Bloomingdale's bought the line.

Gary Shafer, the store's tie buyer, prided himself on styling ties for Bloomingdale's Sutton East label. Finally, as a favor to Joe Aezen, he agreed to buy some of Ralph's ties if Ralph would narrow them by an inch and put a Bloomingdale's label on them.

It was a generous offer. Selling Bloomingdale's would have given Ralph Lauren credibility with the other major retailers in the Federated Department Stores group, it would have increased his sales at a time when he badly needed more volume, and it would have shown Ned Brower that Ralph knew what he was doing.

Ralph said no.

The way he saw it, if he narrowed his ties and took off his label, he wouldn't stand for anything. He believed in wide ties, and wide ties were what he was going to sell.

"They'll come around," he told Ned Brower, explaining why he turned the order down.

"It's your company," Brower replied. "But we're here to make money."

Ralph wanted to make money too. But he wanted to do it his way. This meant selling a concept, or what Ralph called his point of view. It was the Duke of Windsor, it was Fred Astaire, it was gentlemanly dressing for people who had money and taste.

Not everybody understood. Soon after he turned down Gary Shafer's offer at Bloomingdale's, a buyer at Saks Fifth Avenue rejected Ralph. In fact, as Ralph started to show his line the buyer yawned and looked out the window.

"My ties were expensive, and I had a look," says Ralph. "The tie buyer at Saks had his buddies, and he didn't need me."

The small specialty stores believed in him, however. These were the stores like Roland Meledandri, Paul Stuart, Eric Ross in Beverly Hills, and Louis of Boston. Neiman-Marcus, too, became a customer. Neal Fox, who had helped Ralph get his job at Brooks Brothers, was now trying to coax Texans into believing that their $100 Stetsons looked best on $250 suits.

"Send some swatches down to our buyer," Fox urged Ralph one day. "I like what you're doing and we don't have anything like it."

Ralph went to Dallas himself. He flew round-trip in one day to save the cost of a hotel room. Nobody understood his ties the way he did, or could sell them the way he could either. When he dragged himself home late that night he had an order for 100 dozen ties.

"People don't buy our services, products or ideas," wrote Spencer Johnson in *The One Minute Sales Person*. "They buy how they imagine using them will make them feel." Ralph understood that principle as well as anybody in the fashion industry. When people put on his ties, they felt special. Maybe it was the quality of the silk, or the hand-finished edges, or simply the fullness of the knot. Maybe it was the shock of having spent so much on a tie. But if they bought one, they usually bought a second.

"Wearing a Ralph Lauren tie in those days was like belonging to a fraternity," says Berny Schwartz, who stocked Polo ties in his Eric Ross store in Beverly Hills. "No matter who you saw and where you saw them, you were identified as a fraternity brother. It could be on a plane, in an elevator, in Europe, but when you saw somebody wearing one of his ties you smiled. It was an entrée into a world.

"Those ties spoke of a certain type of guy, a guy who had longer sideburns, a guy with longer hair. He was with it. Ralph was dramatic, he was theatrical, he was fresh in his business. He was not a conformist. Ralph reflected a patrician point of view. And there was a reason for everything in his line. He's a very thoughtful person. It's a way of sharing his world, his dreams, his fantasies, an illusion, and bringing it to the marketplace. He feels like that kind of person, a man of stature, a man of mystery, aristocracy, wealth, and he can go ahead and do his job. You dress the part, you act the part."

Altogether, Ralph Lauren opened only two dozen accounts his first six months. If he was disappointed, he didn't show it. Certainly Michael Farina didn't notice any self-doubts. Farina was a fashion illustrator for *Daily News Record* who had grown up in Canarsie, a tough Brooklyn neighborhood. After a friend suggested they meet, Farina called Ralph and invited him to lunch at La Grenouille, an expensive French restaurant on the East Side noted for both its fresh flowers and such customers as John Fairchild, publisher of *Women's Wear Daily*, Jacqueline Kennedy, and Bill Blass.

"When we sat down Ralph insisted on facing the door," says Farina. "He always expected somebody would walk in and make him a star. He knew. He had that attitude. He wanted to be sitting where anybody could see him."

Afterwards, Farina took several of Ralph's ties back to the office. This was the start of an important friendship for Ralph, one which resulted in press coverage at a time when Polo couldn't afford advertising.

"Ralph spent hours talking to fashion editors," says Mel Creedman. "They spread the Ralph Lauren gospel. They said he was a young fellow who really understood and that retailers should go see the product. I don't know how he had the insight or wisdom to make himself known to those people and befriend them, and do it in such a fashion that they accepted him, but he did. And they gave him a lot of credibility. He got a lot of coverage very early."

One of his earliest boosters was Robert L. Green, an energetic former radio show personality from Washington, D.C., who had moved to New York in the late 1950s and emerged as an influential men's fashion editor at *Playboy*. Green not only understood that fashion would eventually change the men's wear industry, but he knew how to promote and package it. He was unique in that regard, and he was quick to let others know it. Green had a commanding presence and took such strong positions on the latest trends that he was soon making guest appearances on the Merv Griffin and Johnny Carson shows. Green was also receptive to young designers, and he often included their work in his *Playboy* fashion layouts.

"Ralph called me, and he was very young," says Green. "He was this nervous little voice on the telephone, a voice so nervous that I became immediately sympathetic. I mean it was . . . 'Hello, hello . . . my name, my name is. . . .' And I thought, Oh dear, how terrible that anybody should be so afraid of making this kind of telephone call. And so I was very reassuring and said, 'I admire your directness and you obviously should be seen.'

"He wanted me to look at his neckties. I said, 'I'll tell you what I'll do. On my way to something I'll drop in. I don't want to spend a lot of time. So if you lay out your things, I'll tell you right away whether I have any interest.'

"Now you have to understand that at the same time in London there was a boy named Michael Fish. Michael Fish worked for Turnbull & Asser. He'd come up with wide neckties. And they became known as fishes because they were wider than the current existing tie that was popular. When you laid them out they were rather like a fillet. I was prepared for the wider tie, you see.

"So I went over. What Ralph had done was take fabrics not associated with neckwear design and make them into ties. Suddenly you were looking at extraordinary madders and paisleys, almost landscape designs. Well, I went berserk. I said to myself, 'Now you have to relax because you have something here that is very important.' I was completely surprised.

"Anyway, he had a charming smile, an open quality which you discovered was a pattern probably set deep in his childhood which he probably still uses. He would ask your opinion as though he couldn't make a move without that opinion. If you ask twenty-two people and you're a good editor, you will get a hell of a good direction for yourself. Everybody will contribute a little."

Playboy would become the first national magazine to feature Ralph's ties on the same pages as men's wear designed by Bill Blass and Pierre Cardin. Others noticed, and slowly Ralph began to build a following among a very small, but influential, group of customers. By early 1968 business was so good Ralph told Ned Brower he needed help. Design this, sell that, inspect, pack, ship. It was overwhelming, Ralph said. Joe Aezen had introduced him to a salesman he wanted to put on staff. Hire him, Brower replied.

That's how Phil "Pinky" Feiner became Polo's first employee. Feiner was a good-looking salesman from Philadelphia who knew the men's wear business. The nickname Pinky came from Pinya, Yiddish for Philip. Feiner was a Damon Runyon character in Brooks Brothers clothing, a popular customer's man with a penchant for gambling.

"Ralph's concept then was the natural shoulder, the Brooks Brothers look, but updated," says Feiner. "You could see he had talent. It was like going to acting school. One guy becomes Al Pacino, the rest are still on the street. Ralph knew the look. He was into cuffs before anybody even thought about cuffs. Same with wide lapels. He was a perfectionist, too. I remember the only disagreement we ever had. He said, 'Phil, this tie is supposed to measure four inches. It's off.' And it was, a fraction of an inch. That's how precise he was . . . When Ralph finally got into Bloomingdale's, it was a Thursday night I think, he was so high — even then Bloomingdale's was the ultimate."

Bloomingdale's bought Polo ties because Steve Krauss stepped around Gary Shafer. Krauss, once Shafer's assistant tie manager, had been promoted to manager of the men's department in the Fresh Meadows store. Normally department managers don't do their own buying. But Krauss wanted Ralph's ties, and when his boss Frank Simon didn't discourage him, Krauss quietly placed an order.

"After we put Ralph's ties in, the business exploded," says Krauss. "I was getting ten dollars for linen ties and I couldn't believe it. The prices were crazy for those days. But when I saw what was happening I moved into better priced jewelry, too, and then I moved into more expensive categories across the board. Six months later, Frank Simon promoted me again."

Krauss's enthusiasm was contagious. One afternoon Simon spotted Ralph in the store and called him over.

"Tell me, how are we doing with you these days?" asked Simon.

Ralph shook his head. "Nothing," he said. "You aren't going to buy it. You want your label on my ties and I won't do it."

The only designer label then carried in the Bloomingdale's men's department was Christian Dior. Bloomingdale's didn't believe in promoting designers. But Simon knew how well Krauss had done in Fresh Meadows, and on the spot he decided to change the policy.

"Ralph," he said. "Let's talk."

The following Father's Day, Bloomingdale's Lexington Avenue store put Ralph's ties in a four-foot case and on a small standing rack. The ties included English twills and Indian madrases and Indian silks.

Ralph was so excited he went to the store and polished the case himself.

"Those ties were wide and controversial, and they looked wonderful to me because they represented a new direction," says Simon. "They were out of the mainstream, but the fabrics were of the finest material. Ralph insisted on quality. He also insisted on the prices, which I thought were too high. I told him that even Bloomingdale's, in one of the most affluent neighborhoods in the city, couldn't sell Polo ties at fifteen dollars.

"I was wrong."

That was the start of a marriage between Ralph Lauren and Bloomingdale's that would last more than twenty years. It has been a relationship with its share of fits and starts, but as marriages go, it's been a good one.

In fact, it has outlasted the marriages of many of the customers.

April 1968 would mark Ralph's first year in business, and *Daily News Record* took note by sending a reporter to interview him.

On the same page that reported that the government's decision to negotiate with North Vietnam "with no conditions whatever" had lifted the Dow Jones Industrial Average nearly eight points to close at 843, Ralph Lauren talked about what was on his mind.

After complaining that retailers were more interested in a good price than they were in the latest fashions, Ralph said, "My long-range wish would be to design all kinds of men's wear, not just ties. It's gratifying that people who come here and like my look will ask why I don't design handkerchiefs, scarves, even shoes . . . I would call the look old-time Brooks Brothers. You must understand oldness to be a fashionable dresser. This is traditionalism. There is a real beauty in an old seersucker suit that bags."

Ralph also believed the customers were ready to spend as much as $15 or $20 on a tie. This meant he never quibbled over price when it came to buying piece goods. Ned Brower, accustomed to spending a dollar or two a yard for fabric, worried that Ralph was investing too much money in inventory. Brower was even more upset after he learned that Ralph had turned away Wallachs, one of the fastest-growing men's specialty store chains on the East Coast.

"Wallachs came and said they wanted to buy the line, but I didn't want to sell them," says Ralph. "I didn't think they were the right image for me. They didn't have the customers I wanted to sell. They were commercial, and I thought it would kill the mystique, it would kill the exclusivity. I was the consumer, and I understood exclusivity. Exclusivity, individuality, being special, relating to certain images. If you buy expensive products you don't want to see them all over the place. You want to know what you are getting is a rarity. I still believe that."

That was how Ned Brower learned he was in the mystique business.

"Ralph didn't drive us crazy. But he had no business organization experience and we didn't think he was keeping things in proper perspective," says Brower. "Anybody can buy piece goods. What you have to do is move merchandise. Most designers will drive businessmen a little berserk."

It was one thing to like Ralph Lauren.

Understanding him was something else.

This is when Norman Hilton, third-generation suit maker, came into the picture. Back in the late 1880s four Hilton brothers opened a tailoring shop in Patterson, New Jersey. Many years later, the firm would open a large showroom at 1290 Sixth Avenue in New York and acquire a 70,000-square-foot factory in Linden, New Jersey. By the late 1960s the Hilton company was among the top makers of natural shoulder clothing in the country, counting among its accounts Saks Fifth Avenue, Bergdorf Goodman, and Jordan Marsh.

Norman Hilton was aggressive and demanding. He drove his people as hard as he drove himself, and he pushed the department stores even harder. Norman Hilton knew he was tough, but he paid well and he let his salesmen buy his best suits for as little as $25. He also liked to gamble on his instincts.

In the spring of 1968 Norman Hilton's instincts told him something new was happening in the men's industry. His friend Alan White, who ran a men's store in New Haven, walked into his office one morning wearing one of the ugliest, widest ties Norman Hilton had ever seen. It wasn't a tie, it was a death sentence.

Jeez, White had a sense of humor.

Then Hilton began seeing those same wide ties all over town. Buyers wore them. Sales reps wore them. Bloomingdale's was selling them.

"Pete," he said finally, calling over Peter Strom, his vice-president. "Pete, go find out where those ties are coming from. I'm interested. Whoever is making those ties should be making them for Norman Hilton."

Peter Strom, born Peter Strom Goldstein on May 31, 1929, was Norman Hilton's alter ego. Where Hilton shouted, Strom soothed. Where Hilton could be emotional, Strom was steady and reserved. In manner Strom was as much a listener as he was a salesman. Strom knew something about the men's clothing business, too. His grandfather, and then his uncles, owned Max Goldstein & Sons in Passaic, New Jersey, a men's clothing store where Strom worked on weekends and holidays. Strom liked to say a good salesman had to have lint in his blood. Strom felt he had it the first time he put a roll of herringbone worsted over his shoulder in the Hilton factory, where he started as a floor worker when he was twenty-eight. Later, when Hilton brought Strom to New York as a salesman, the two became close.

In fact, in Norman Hilton's mind, the two were inseparable. Peter Strom was one of the most reliable people he knew.

"We want to do a total look," said Norman Hilton, after Strom introduced him to Ralph for the first time. "We'd like you to make the ties for us."

"You've got the right idea," said Ralph. "But I don't want to make your ties. I want to be in business for myself. What I'm looking for is a fifty-fifty partnership. I don't want to work for anybody."

The meeting soon ended. Neither would budge.

That summer, Ralph and Peter Strom rented houses in the same New Jersey shore community. The two became friends. Strom would talk to Ralph about Norman Hilton, and to Norman Hilton about Ralph Lauren, and gradually Hilton decided he could live with Ralph Lauren as an equal partner. One percentage point didn't mean much when it came to dividing the profits. Eventually Hilton told Ralph that he was willing to open a separate company called Fashion Design & Development and through it lend $50,000 to Polo Fashions. Better still, Hilton said he would make the suits and sports jackets Ralph now said he wanted to design.

"I went to Norman Hilton because I wanted to get into the clothing business," says Ralph. "He offered me the opportunity to make suits. I wanted to do it all, something which had never been done here before. I wanted to do an entire concept, and design it myself. I expanded because I wanted to do more things. I wanted shirts, I wanted suits, I wanted sports

for our magnificent tie. Its distinctive geometric pattern and subtle multi-coloring bespeak an age of masculine elegance; its full knot and expanded width mark it as the tie for today's fashion. Done in sumptuous silk from Switzerland, it is hand-made and bar tacked at both ends. $15."

"That morning I remember getting a phone call from our Stamford store," says Bloomingdale's buyer Gary Shafer. "They'd already sold two of the ties and they couldn't believe it. You have to realize that fifteen dollars then was the equivalent of seventy-five dollars today. But Ralph's timing was just right. Wall Street was booming, and men had money in their pockets."

There were other changes, too. Phil Feiner, Ralph's first employee, resigned and was replaced by Anthony Edgeworth, a lean, sardonic salesman who was then working for Norman Hilton.

"By the time we moved into the new offices, Ralph couldn't meet the demand," says Edgeworth, now a successful New York fashion photographer. "He was literally turning away customers. Even that vile tapestry tie Bloomingdale's featured in that big ad sold. You can't imagine the excitement.

"There were these two brothers who'd drive in from Brooklyn in a Rolls-Royce. They were so pushy Ralph once asked me, 'Do you think we should sell these guys any more?' Then he'd say, 'Let me deal with them,' and he'd push another hundred dozen down their throat. They had to have them. That was the beauty of it. He was really hot. There was nothing like his ties in the business. Everything was J. Press or Saks's men's department. There wasn't any men's fashion." Indeed, at Bloomingdale's the customers were buying them five and ten at a time.

As the business increased, Ralph decided he needed more sales help, somebody who knew how the stores worked and spoke their language. He also wanted somebody who believed in Polo and understood the image he was trying to convey. Finally he hired Steve Krauss, the first Bloomingdale's employee to buy his line.

"Ralph was humble to begin with, extremely humble," says Krauss. "Sometimes, after work or on weekends, he'd call and we'd go to a movie. He was a little unsure of himself. He'd show his ties and suits like they were his children, and then he'd hold his breath waiting for people's reactions. He took it as a personal hurt if somebody passed an item, if the store didn't buy what it did the previous year."

Ralph had now established the fashion direction he would follow for the next twenty years. It would be the classics cut from the best fabrics, a look he liked to describe as "timeless." Ralph Lauren didn't invent Fair Isle sweaters or Harris tweed jackets or khaki pants. But he had the wit to make them new again.

Look at the spring 1970 collection he showed in October 1969. Sprinkled among his jackets with the wide, notched lapels were white linen slacks, white flannel blazers, and even white flannel suits. "If Lauren's look is 1930s, it's F. Scott Fitzgerald's 1930s, not the Duke of Windsor's," observed *Daily News Record.*

Think of it . . . white flannel blazers. At a time when many were protesting the Vietnam war and John Lennon was singing "Give Peace a Chance," Ralph Lauren was resurrecting *The Great Gatsby.* His clothes reflected faith in society and respect for tradition, and as such they constituted a political statement from a man who had little interest in politics. Ralph's only concession to popular taste was a wild, multicolored, Italian silk tapestry shirt. Even that cost $125.

No wonder Ralph Lauren's favorite book was Ayn Rand's novel *The Fountainhead.* You remember, Howard Roark, rebel architect, sacrificed his career and the woman he loved because he refused to compromise the quality of his work. Howard Roark was an idealist. He would build *his* way, or he would not build at all. He had principles, he had vision, he had taste, and only a handful of wealthy, self-made men appreciated his concept.

Eventually, Howard Roark became famous, won the big contracts, and got back his girlfriend.

And in the movie, he was played by Gary Cooper, one of Ralph's favorites.

Ralph didn't know much about making suits, but he was eager to learn. Suits designed by Oleg Cassini, Pierre Cardin, and

Bill Blass were featured in the advertising pages of the *New York Times* and in the windows of the Fifth Avenue department stores. Tie designers, in contrast, came and went like circus acts.

Ralph wanted to build a business and he wanted to do it fast. He had ideas. What he lacked were the technical skills, skills those who worked in the Hilton factory had developed over a lifetime. Michael Cifarelli was head man there, and in many ways he represented the old guard in the men's wear industry. Cifarelli knew his business, he took pride in his work, and he understood that his name would never be known to Norman Hilton's customers. He didn't complain, because that was how the system worked, and as Norman Hilton's top pattern maker and designer, Cifarelli was an important part of that system. Cifarelli dominated the factory floor the way a French chef commands a three-star kitchen. His word was law, his eye unquestioned. He approved every bolt of fabric, every pattern, every cutting. He came from a family of master tailors in Italy, and he made what he thought were the best suits in the country.

Michael Cifarelli did not want to discuss the finer points of tailoring with somebody who wore ties made from upholstery fabrics.

"Names didn't mean so much at the time," he says. "Names were created because of business. Ralph came and we made the first labels for Bloomingdale's. The labels said *Designed by Ralph Lauren*. I saw that, and I said to Ralph, 'I'll start you out. This will be your department over here, and you will have to take care of it.' He says to me, 'I don't know anything about this.'"

Artists are allowed to have temperaments, and Cifarelli considered himself an artist. The way he saw it, Ralph Lauren wanted the credit for Michael Cifarelli's work.

"Later I said to Norman, 'Don't you think we aren't saying the truth to the world when we say *Designed by Ralph Lauren?*'" continued Cifarelli. "'The retailers know me, I don't care, but it's not nice.' So we changed the label to *Made by Ralph Lauren*. Anybody could say *Made by*, and it sounded better to me."

Theirs was a stormy relationship. Ralph wanted Cifarelli to make a shaped suit, a suit that flared out from the hips.

Cifarelli didn't understand it. Neither did the other Hilton factory people, who were happier making traditional, three-button suits. Hilton thought the problems could be worked out. What mattered, he tried to explain to Cifarelli, was that the company would attract younger customers, thus expanding its market. "I thought we'd make our traditional suits and Ralph's new suits and we'd be in high cotton again," says Hilton.

But there were moments when even Norman Hilton realized it would never work out that way.

"One day Ralph was in our factory discussing a suit with Cifarelli," says Hilton. "The suit was on a dummy. Ralph was making these points, and Cifarelli was making other points. It wasn't terribly heated, because I don't think Ralph ever gets too excited. Cifarelli took the jacket off the form, carefully. Then he began to jump up and down on it with his feet . . . So you can see it was a little difficult."

Ralph wanted a jacket with extremely soft natural shoulders, shoulders known in the trade as shirtsleeve shoulders. Also, Ralph said, his jackets would have a front dart, a low-button stance, and a flared skirt. The Hilton factory only made suits with a square shoulder, and when its tailors tried to accommodate Ralph Lauren the suits didn't fit. Ralph insisted on doing it his way, the factory its way, and the bickering continued until the first group of suits was shipped to Bloomingdale's.

Not surprisingly, they were a catastrophe.

The pants were too long, the rise too high. Some of the jackets arrived with arm lengths that appeared to have been fitted on Little Leaguers.

Frank Simon, merchandise manager, called Peter Strom to complain, and then sent the suits back. Ralph Lauren blamed Norman Hilton, and Norman Hilton blamed Ralph Lauren. Nobody was happy.

Not that Norman Hilton wasn't generous. He wanted Ralph to learn, to grow, to broaden his education. One day in the spring of 1969 he asked Ed Brandau to take Ralph with him to Europe on a buying trip. Brandau said sure, he'd be happy to take Ralph.

Several weeks later, on a Saturday afternoon, Brandau had

a car drive him to Ralph's apartment at Third Avenue and 74th Street. After several minutes, Ralph came down and sat inside the car, very upset.

Ricky was pregnant, and Ralph said he didn't want to leave. (The Laurens would have three children: Andrew, born May 7, 1969; David, born October 31, 1971, and a daughter, Dylan, born May 9, 1974.)

Ralph then got out of the car, and went back upstairs.

"He was very upset at leaving her," says Brandau. "He really didn't want to go. Finally I convinced him. It also turned out that he was very frightened of flying, something he told me when he was on the plane. Ralph never drank, but I got us something to calm him down."

Rome was the first stop. Ralph was more than a tourist. He wanted to expand his business into coats, socks, sweaters, jewelry, shoes, and luggage. This visit would give him an opportunity to shop the finest Italian stores. He would see for himself what the Italians did best, and what he liked he would buy and bring back to New York.

He never stopped looking and shopping, even at dinner.

"One evening we went out to eat at a chic underground restaurant, da Meopatacca," says Brandau. "Ralph called the waiter over. This waiter didn't speak English, and Ralph didn't speak Italian. But Ralph made himself understood. What he wanted was the white laundry coat the man was wearing. And he finally got it."

A house photographer took their picture that night. Ralph and Ed Brandau are sitting at the end of a long table. The table is covered with a red-and-white check tablecloth. In front of the two men are a carafe of red wine, and Ralph's Marlboro cigarettes. Ralph has one hand casually draped along his glass, and he is leaning against a brick wall. His face is full, his hair starting to gray. He is wearing a dark jacket with wide lapels, and a dark tie so wide that the knot alone measured more than two inches in length. He looks satisfied, and with good reason. That waiter's jacket would inspire his next line of men's suits. Ralph always liked clothes that flowed with the body instead of constricting it. The waiter's jacket, which lacked padding and heavy interior seams, wore like a favorite shirt.

When Ralph returned to New York, he went to work on a new collection he referred to as unconstructed jackets and suits. Frank Simon at Bloomingdale's wanted a Polo suit line priced at $125. Too many of Bloomingdale's middle-class shoppers admired the Polo look but couldn't afford the $250 price, Simon said. Ralph, too, wanted to attract Bloomingdale's young strivers, the core customers whose aggressive shopping habits helped make the store famous.

The unconstructed look, however, flopped. The customers didn't understand why their jackets were supposed to fit like shirts, and nothing Bloomingdale's said changed their minds. Eventually the look disappeared.

Then Ralph met Leo Lozzi. Like Michael Cifarelli, Leo Lozzi also had been born in Italy. But unlike Cifarelli, Leo Lozzi instinctively understood what Ralph wanted. Lozzi was then a partner in Lanham Clothes, a men's wear company that operated a factory in Lawrence, Massachusetts. Stubby, charming, and never more gracious than when a woman was nearby, Lozzi was at once sincere and worldly. He also had the skills to make Ralph's soft shoulder jackets.

"Norman Hilton made good clothing, but Ralph wanted perfume," says Lozzi. "One day he came by with Joe Barrato [Polo's first sales manager] and I showed him a jacket I just finished. Joe put it on. Ralph saw it, said it was exactly what he wanted, and that was it, good-bye. Finished. He came with me to Lanham. We worked together for years.

"Ralph Lauren is a man who talks very little. He is not a clothing man, he's a man with vision. You have to understand it. When Cifarelli made his suits, he made Hilton suits. The shoulders were too square. Ralph wanted a soft, round garment. He was complaining, he was fighting, they said he was crazy, what does he want? But they didn't understand his point of view. I am not a genius but I understood Ralph right away. Ralph and I communicated without talking. He explained to me in a few words.

"Ralph wanted a garment to look such a way . . . without explaining how, because he couldn't, but he made gestures with his hands . . . rounder, softer, a longer lapel, high pockets, shaped . . . he makes the motion and you have to understand the motion. I understood what he wanted. His motion was very interesting to me. He was moving with his hands what it has to look like. I understood in my own way. The conventional suits that everybody makes are like a woman when she gets up in the morning before she puts on her makeup. That's the difference. I captured the feeling. I understood his movement. And Ralph has no constant motion. No, he has abstractness. One day do this, one day do that. In between the changing something comes out. If you don't change your mind, nothing happens."

In mid-July, 1970, Ralph decided to leave the Hilton factory and have his spring 1971 line made by Leo Lozzi at Lanham.

Norman Hilton argued against the move, but Ralph was adamant. Norman Hilton might own half of Polo Fashions, but Polo was going to make its suits at Leo Lozzi's factory.

Not long after, Ralph Lauren won his first Coty Award.

These prizes were the invention of Eleanor Lambert, publicist. Back in 1943 Lambert had persuaded the Coty cosmetics company to create the Coty American Fashion Critics' Awards to honor top American women's wear designers. The prestige of associating the company with such an event, she promised, would boost the company's image. Coty was then sold in chain drugstores, and the brand had all the status of a Sears nightgown.

Lambert was right. The Coty Awards became the equivalent of the movie industry's Academy Awards. As American designers gained in prominence and status, some of that cachet rubbed off on Coty.

By the late 1960s, attending the awards show had become mandatory for all of the top designers. (It didn't hurt that there were lots of winners each year, either. The Coty Awards were operated on a theory much like that of a rich kid's birthday party: it's impolite to send guests home empty-handed.)

Part of the skill in managing such a contest is knowing how and when to add new categories. By the late 1960s everybody was talking about the number of women's wear designers who had licensed their names to men's wear manufacturers. Just a few years earlier, the men's wear industry never used the word designer. Fashion guys were called stylists. The big guns were the highly paid tailors who worked anonymously in the factories. The virtues of modesty were still prized; any man who wanted to wear a "designer" label would have been suspect. Then came Pierre Cardin, Hardy Amies, John Weitz, and Bill Blass, and attitudes changed as the customers changed.

This turn of events was perceived by Lambert as a terrific opportunity to give out yet more prizes, to old friends at that, and the Coty people moved fast. In 1969 Bill Blass won the first men's wear award.

A year later, to everybody's amazement, it was Ralph Lauren's turn. Remember, Ralph had been in business for himself not quite two years. "When Eleanor called to tell us we'd won the Coty, we went crazy," says Joe Barrato, Polo's former sales manager. "It was like a dream. It was that exciting." Winning meant Ralph Lauren had been recognized as a top designer, it meant that the press would call more often, and it meant that the big stores would have to pay more attention. Compare it to a lawyer's passing a bar examination.

The twenty-eighth annual black-tie Coty American Fashion Critics' Awards ceremony was held on September 24 at Alice Tully Hall, Lincoln Center. Each winning designer — Ralph, Herbert Kasper, Chester Weinberg, Giorgio di Sant'Angelo, and Bill Blass yet again — presented a brief fashion show, or scene, as it was described in the program. (Ralph won as best men's wear designer. The others won for other, less well-defined reasons, such as fostering creativity, or expressing the "New Chic.") Ralph divided his presentation of tartan pants, wide ties, and paisley-printed dinner suits into three parts: in-town and out-of-town suits, country weekends, and evening wear. Society singer Bobby Short played the piano, wearing one of Ralph's first tuxedos. Afterwards, Ralph invited his family, friends, and supporters to a champagne supper at the "21" Club.

"I arrived at the party late because I had to get all the clothes together," says Barrato. "The first thing Ralph did was kiss and embrace me. We had a dinner. Don't forget we were a poor company. It was a great honor, but it was also very costly. We had to be discreet how we spent the money. We had to participate in model fees, we had to supply the clothes, have special things made, there were tickets to buy. These were major expenses for us. But it was a beautiful night. It was Ralph's launch into the big time."

It also helped him with a fight he was then having with Bloomingdale's. Ralph wanted Bloomingdale's to open a Ralph Lauren shop. Ties still accounted for more than half of Polo's sales volume, but Ralph wanted to show his entire collection together. This meant the suits, the shirts, and a line of pants. There were also Ralph's imported raincoats, outerwear, sportswear, luggage, and belts, all of which he had made in Italy.

Designers didn't work like that in 1970. They made either suits or ties or sportswear. A fall collection meant one line, not a group of varied lines linked together by a uniform, cohesive look. Nobody merchandised a line that way. Ralph did because he thought the customers wanted choices that reflected the way they lived. Since Ralph dressed one way at work, one way at home, and one way on weekends, he assumed the customers did, too. Call this the start of life-style marketing.

"When men went to a party on Saturday night, they wore blue blazers and gray flannel pants and a rep tie, the same clothes they'd been wearing all their lives," says Ralph. "That was their weekend uniform. I gave them something different.

"In 1969 and 1970 there wasn't any real sportswear. One guy would make a jacket, or chinos, or shirts. There were casual clothes, but no sense of development. Most retailers only understood suits and jackets. They carried some sweaters, but there was no roughwear, no active. Those were my things, and I went to different people and had them make them for me. I was aiming at quality, the high-level consumer, the consumer who wanted change and understood it and was well traveled. It wasn't aimed at the masses. There were other people doing flamboyant clothes, but they were not as classy. Even though something might have been wild, it was still made from beautiful fabrics and tastefully cut."

He needed a shop, Ralph told Frank Simon at Bloomingdale's, because he was selling an image of a way of life. He didn't have the money to advertise, which meant he could only tell his story through his own store.

Simon thought this was a dumb idea. The customers don't

care about shops, he said. Grouping Polo together in one section would hurt Polo sales in other areas of the men's department. Forget it, Simon advised.

"Finally Ralph said that if we didn't build him a store, he'd go somewhere else," says Simon. "That's Ralph. He's a good, cool negotiator, and he's consistent. He doesn't come in with one idea one day, and another idea the next. He even knew which home furnishings he needed to surround his merchandise. He had the dream, but he wasn't big enough yet to do that himself. That's how we helped him."

Ralph wanted an environment that was traditional without being stuffy, a shop as respectable and inviting as an old Fifth Avenue men's club. This meant he wanted wood paneling, oriental rugs, even an English riding saddle. His boutique would be more than a place to sell clothes: it would be a reflection of how he thought his customers wanted to live. It was Brooks Brothers, but it was a sporty, lively Brooks Brothers, a snappy, cool Brooks Brothers.

"I sold the English look, but what got me on the map had nothing to do with those clothes," says Ralph. "I didn't bring the customers button-down shirts and rep ties. I didn't bring them spread collars. I didn't do that. You have to understand the balance. There is a foundation of taste that has flair. What I do is feel things. I like classics, like a beautiful chair built in the 1930s, but I also love flat black industrial looks. I love Porsches as well as the Bentley. I love flat black things as well as wood dashboards and old mahogany. I saw the world as a much bigger world, not a narrow regimented world. I did what I felt was exciting for the time. And I felt change was needed. I dressed nothing like the people who influenced me. I sold to them. They bought my clothes. They didn't say, 'Ralph, we have it.' Morty Sills bought my stuff. Roland Meledandri bought my stuff. Paul Stuart bought my ties, they bought my clothes. Why would they buy it if they had it? In other words, they influenced me but I didn't look like them. That was the difference."

The Ralph Lauren shop opened that fall in Bloomingdale's. It was the first time the men's department had given a designer his own boutique, and some at Bloomingdale's still felt ambivalent about it.

"We don't really believe in 'designer' clothing," Frank Simon told the *New York Times* soon after the boutique opened.

"I don't believe in it myself," added Ralph, in the same article. "I make clothes I like to wear."

For the second time in his brief career, Ralph Lauren had gone eye-to-eye with Bloomingdale's.

And for the second time, Bloomingdale's blinked first.

By the start of 1971 business was so good that Ralph Lauren was talking about buying a Rolls-Royce.

The customers expected glamour, he said.

He could afford it, too. At the age of thirty he owned half of a company doing nearly $4 million a year in sales. Polo's profits were also growing. For the fiscal year ended March 31, 1970, the company showed $210,000 in after-tax earnings; for the year ended March 31, 1971, earnings would jump almost 50 percent to $299,000. Not only did Polo sell the best men's specialty retailers, but such department stores as Bloomingdale's, Higbee's, and Neiman-Marcus were steady customers.

What better way to symbolize Ralph's growing stature than a Rolls-Royce, a car synonymous with tradition, good taste, success?

"I want to be a star," he told *Gentlemen's Quarterly*. "I don't want to go to a party and have to promote myself. I want to be recognized. But I want to be myself, too. You must try not to lose yourself."

This, then, was his dilemma. What would such a car mean to his image?

There was something charming about a thirty-year-old fashion designer who said he didn't give a hoot about the fashion world.

Put him behind the wheel of a Rolls-Royce, however, and Ralph might appear as though he were starting to take that world seriously. For the first time, Ralph had brushed up against the realization that it was sometimes easier to have a dream than to live it.

Finally he decided against the Rolls-Royce because friends convinced him that it was the wrong image for him at that

time. Aristocrats and other establishment types drove Rolls-
Royces; Ralph was supposed to be a maverick.

Ralph agreed. And then he found a car he liked better.

Michael Farina, the *Daily News Record* illustrator, had bought
a new Mercedes 250 sedan that year. One evening Farina drove
into the city to have dinner with Ralph and Ricky. Later, after
the meal was finished, Farina turned to Ralph and said, "Come
on. I'm going to take you for a drive. I want to show you what
this car can do."

Out they went. Farina's car was wine red in color with a
lush tan leather interior.

They got in and Farina drove down a two-way street. One
of the things he liked best about the car was its incredible
turning radius. The car didn't turn, it glided.

Now he had somebody he could impress. Ralph Lauren
was almost as obsessive about automobiles as he was about old
movies and basketball and clothing. Ralph even collected miniature models of the famous classic cars from F. A. O. Schwarz.

"Watch this," Farina said, making a sharp U-turn across
traffic. The Mercedes responded effortlessly.

"My God, that's fabulous," Ralph said.

Farina smiled.

"I bet you haven't seen this before," he said. Farina pointed
to a small indentation on each side of the steering wheel. A
German engineer had noticed that when a driver rested his
hands on the wheel he would feel more comfortable if there
were small groves for his fingers.

Ralph, who loved the details of fine workmanship of any
kind, was enthralled.

"Let me drive," he said.

Several weeks went by. The next time the two talked, Ralph
said he had something to tell him.

"I just happened to be walking by the Mercedes showroom on Park Avenue," he said. "They had this convertible,
and God, it was beautiful. I don't have a car, and. . . ."

Ralph was calling because he needed advice. He loved the
car, a Mercedes 280 SL, but the color of the showroom model
wasn't right. What he wanted was a silver-colored Mercedes
with tan leather seats and a tan-colored roof.

The salesman had explained that Mercedes didn't make a tan roof for the car Ralph wanted. However, if Mr. Lauren was willing to pay a little extra it might be possible to . . .

It took more than three months for the car to arrive. In the interim, every time Ralph talked to Farina he asked whether Farina really liked the colors he'd chosen.

Farina said the colors sounded fine.

Good, said Ralph. But what did Farina really think?

He didn't stop asking until the car arrived.

Ralph Lauren was running a business.

But everything was personal.

Look at his relationship with Berny Schwartz.

Schwartz was a Los Angeles retailer with a Fidel Castro–style beard and a nonstop rap, which included frequent references to dope, politics, and the Byzantine sexual practices of various Hollywood stars. Schwartz was a one-man drum and bugle corps. He radiated charm and goodwill like a sunlamp. Ebullient, creative, and gifted with energy, Schwartz in 1966 parlayed a manager's job at the super-preppy Lew Ritter store in Los Angeles into Eric Ross, his own fine men's store near Rodeo Drive. Schwartz, an Anglophile, decorated his store with wallpaper covered with hunting scenes, added the appropriate English knickknacks, and attracted a clientele that included Steve McQueen, Rock Hudson, and Tony Curtis. He sold forward-looking Ivy League, soft shoulder clothes, hip, but not too far-out.

Schwartz had also been the first and only retailer in southern California to buy Polo, a relationship which dated back to the days when Ralph did business in his tiny Empire State Building showroom as a division of Beau Brummell. Schwartz was not Ralph's most important account at Beau Brummell, but he was among the first. After placing his initial order, Schwartz went back to Beverly Hills and marked down the rest of the ties he had in stock. The Eric Ross store, he announced, would sell only Polo neckwear.

Schwartz, then, was a believer at a time when believers in Polo were hard to find. He was also a teacher, a kindred spirit.

He appreciated the finest fabrics, and he knew where to find the best tailors. Schwartz was an acknowledged trendsetter; some went as far as to say he was one of the better men's wear designers in the industry, an opinion with which Schwartz agreed.

He was also a skilled businessman. Before placing his first order with Ralph, Schwartz asked for, and received, the exclusive rights to sell Polo Fashions in Beverly Hills. It was an easy promise for Ralph to make in 1967; the other retailers there weren't interested.

By 1971 Ralph's situation had changed. He was a Coty winner, he had his own shop in Bloomingdale's, the big stores were placing larger orders. Ralph, in turn, wanted Schwartz to give his clothes the support and promotion they needed. Instead, Schwartz seemed more intent on building his own reputation and developing the Eric Ross label.

Berny Schwartz had always been an asset.

Now Ralph began to see him as a liability.

Schwartz sold the clothes, but he was not committed to establishing the Polo image, which meant to Ralph a separate department and English antique furnishings. Schwartz's attitude became a problem, because Ralph believed that building the right image was as important as using real horn buttons and the best piece goods. His generation was the first whose tastes and buying habits were dominated by what they saw on television. Many manufacturers sold well-made clothes. Ralph Lauren was the first to address how customers imagined themselves living. Where others were selling shirts or suits or ties, Ralph was selling the ideal of a different life, a more privileged life. Whether he succeeded would in large part be determined by whether he created and communicated the right images.

What he needed was retailers who understood that.

Eventually he found one. Rather, one found him.

Jerry Magnin then owned a small boutique on Rodeo Drive in Beverly Hills. Unlike Berny Schwartz, Magnin didn't consider himself a designer. As the grandson of Joseph Magnin, founder of the San Francisco–based Joseph Magnin department store chain, Jerry Magnin was born to be a retailer. Jerry Magnin first bought Polo ties in 1967, when he worked for

Joseph Magnin as the men's wear merchandiser. When Joseph Magnin was acquired in 1969 by Amfac, the Hawaiian-based conglomerate, Jerry Magnin was given a five-year employment contract. He resigned within a year, choosing instead to open his own men's store, featuring the clothes of such designers as Pierre Cardin and Roland Meledandri.

Magnin wanted something fresh, something new. He intended to be a trendsetter in Beverly Hills, not a shopkeeper. Then, on a trip to New York, he saw a display of Ralph Lauren sportswear at Bloomingdale's. Magnin had previously bought some of Ralph's ties as a buyer at I. Magnin, as well as one of Ralph's earliest suits. He was stunned, however, by the sportswear he saw at Bloomingdale's. It was the most exciting collection he'd ever seen.

"We were then selling what was called high fashion," says Magnin. "At the end of the 1960s and in the early 1970s, the men's wear revolution was just starting to take place. It was in its formulative stages. Two things bothered me about my store. First, my heart was really with traditional clothing, which was the kind of thing Ralph was doing. Second, I knew we were excluding ninety-nine percent of the market by being in the forefront."

A few days later Magnin was in the office of Joe Barrato, Polo's sales manager. Magnin knew how to make a case, and for nearly three hours he tried to convince Barrato of the wonders of being on Rodeo Drive. He loved Ralph's clothes . . . he understood Ralph's concept . . . the two would make big money together. Finally, when Magnin was finished, Barrato told him Polo had given an exclusive for Beverly Hills to Berny Schwartz. It was an important relationship, a long relationship, and Barrato didn't see how Magnin and Schwartz could share the line. Sorry.

Magnin said he understood and left.

Two days later he called from Beverly Hills.

"Joe, I know you have a problem," Magnin said. "But would you consider selling me if I gave you your own Ralph Lauren retail store?"

"I don't know," Barrato replied. "Let me talk to Ralph first."

Barrato was as surprised as he was excited. Nobody had

ever offered to open a Ralph Lauren store before. As soon as he put down the phone, he ran down the hall into Ralph's office. The next week, he and Ralph Lauren met with Jerry Magnin and Magnin's wife, Erin, at La Caravelle.

There Jerry Magnin painted a picture of what it would mean to Polo to have a store on Rodeo Drive. Not only would it give Ralph Lauren status on the most prestigious shopping street in Los Angeles, but the store itself would become a major customer of Polo clothes.

How would Magnin feel if Ralph Lauren designed the store to his specifications?

No problem, said Magnin.

What about staff? Ralph thought the store's manager should project the Polo image. He knew a male model, Bill Loock, who was one of the handsomest men in New York. Loock played golf, he knew how to talk to people, he would be terrific for Polo's image.

Whatever Ralph Lauren wanted, replied Magnin.

Finally Ralph had heard enough.

"It sounds good, but I've got a deal with Berny Schwartz," he said. "What do I do with Berny?"

Magnin shrugged. This was business. Magnin was talking about investing hundreds of thousands of dollars in a new store that would be directly adjacent to his current store. He would have it designed and decorated as Ralph wanted. Magnin would not pay Polo a licensing fee, but he would stock it exclusively with Ralph Lauren merchandise, except for those categories that Ralph did not yet design.

Dealing with Berny Schwartz was Ralph Lauren's problem.

Ralph nodded. Somehow it would all be worked out, he decided. It was too big an opportunity to turn down.

On the way back from lunch, they saw Bill Loock modeling some clothes for a John Weitz ad.

Ralph pointed at Loock and said, "That's the look I want. He's our manager."

Loock, who until that moment had never thought about or wanted a job that required that he stay in one place for longer than a week, smiled pleasantly and said it sounded interesting. A few days later, he called Ralph to see if Ralph had been serious. Indeed he was, and eventually Loock and his family moved to Los Angeles so he could manage the store.

Time passed. Plans moved forward.

Yet Ralph Lauren could not bring himself to tell Berny Schwartz. Neither could Joe Barrato.

"We were afraid," says Barrato. "We knew there would be a scene, and we didn't want to confront him. We were giving him a raw deal, and we couldn't face that. We were kids. We knew this was the right thing for our future, yet explaining it to Berny, our friend, would be very difficult."

Berny finally got the message on a flight to Milan.

Jerry Magnin gave it to him.

Magnin and Schwartz knew each other because Magnin was an Eric Ross customer. After Magnin had opened his own shop, the two men remained friends. There were enough customers in Beverly Hills for everybody.

After the usual chitchat, Magnin turned to Schwartz and said, "I guess you know I'm opening a Polo shop."

"No," said Schwartz. "I don't know anything about it. Tell me."

Magnin told him.

Schwartz was dumbfounded. He was the first retailer west of the Hudson to stock Polo. He bought the line when nobody else knew who Ralph Lauren was, and he bought in quantity. Schwartz had gambled on Polo and that gamble had paid off. Now somebody else was going to capitalize on Schwartz's hard work.

"I almost fell out of the sky. Literally," says Schwartz. "When I met with Ralph in Milan, that's when he told me. Of course I was very hurt, yes, and it caused me to step back from Ralph for a couple of years because I felt it was something that could have been worked out. We didn't come to blows, but I was angry. I was even more disappointed and hurt that he didn't say he would take care of me at the same time he was opening up Jerry. I wish he had but he didn't. I would have continued buying the ties.

"The reason he wanted the shop was to showcase his suits. His clothes were in the embryonic development stage at that point. I wouldn't make a statement with his clothes and suffer from mistakes in construction and design which were there. Nor would I allow my customers to wear anything that wasn't perfect. What Ralph was doing in those days I had my own makers doing much better. I wanted to promote the Eric Ross name."

Berny Schwartz had once been an important customer.

But Ralph Lauren wanted his business to grow, and Berny Schwartz wasn't willing to invest the money or the energy in building the Polo name when he could do the same for Eric Ross.

So Berny Schwartz would have to go.

It was nothing personal.

It was business.

▶ ▶ ▶ 5

Jerry Magnin was willing to build Ralph Lauren a store because he believed in his clothes and Magnin thought the two would make money together.

Magnin knew there would be problems. Designers tended to be finicky, indecisive, insecure. But Magnin had worked with designers before. He knew how to be patient, he knew when to press, and he knew how big the payoff could be if everything was done right.

So Magnin waited. Because as much as Ralph Lauren wanted a store, he didn't know what that store was supposed to look like. What he did know was that it had to project a mood that was young and yet traditional, elegant without being overdone.

Nobody knew what this meant.

Including Ralph. He was a fashion designer, not an interior decorator. What he needed was somebody who shared his taste level and could translate his dream into four walls, fixtures, and carpeting.

Over lunch he explained his problems to *Playboy*'s fashion editor, Robert L. Green. Green suggested Tom O'Toole. O'Toole's only decorating experience had consisted of designing a showroom for *Playboy,* but Green was so impressed he subsequently hired O'Toole to do his Greenwich Village townhouse.

Green told this to Ralph and then invited him to take a look for himself. Green would even call O'Toole, and the pair could visit Green's house together. Ricky could come too, if she wanted.

Following Green's call, O'Toole swung by the Polo office and picked up Ralph and Ricky in a cab. O'Toole had been a decorator at Bonwit Teller before deciding to launch his own business. A tall, thin, elegant dresser, O'Toole always looked as though he'd stepped directly from the shops on Saville Row.

Ralph was impressed. O'Toole, he decided, was the embodi-
ment of the Polo Man. He understood the clothes, he understood the life-style, he understood the concept.

Before the cab reached Greenwich Village Ralph said that
the job of designing and decorating the Beverly Hills store was
O'Toole's if he wanted it. Ralph would look through Green's
house as a courtesy, but he really didn't care what Green had
wanted, or what O'Toole had done for him. That was for Green.
Ralph had his own ideas.

"What he was trying to represent with his clothes was the
look of the East Coast," says O'Toole. "I felt the Beverly Hills
store, which was a former jewelry shop, resembled a barn. So
I created a greenhouse exterior, using raw brick. Then I put
a little whitewash on the brick, and added a lot of honey-colored
wood for the interior. I added mirrors and skylights and lots
of plants. For furniture I used wing chairs, a sofa, and lots of
stripped pine. I also put in antique Persian rugs. The total
effect was warm, almost like a weekend house.

"The image we wanted to create was one of casual sportswear, and casual old money. It was to have a contemporary
look, and yet it was to have a sense of tradition." One of the
walls was covered in heavily textured plaster, much like the
walls at Orsini's, one of Ralph's favorite New York restaurants.
Another wall was bare brick. The interior partitions were covered with gray suede.

Jerry Magnin had hired Tom O'Toole on Ralph Lauren's
say-so. He hired Bill Loock as store manager on Ralph Lauren's say-so. And he hired Joel Horowitz, the son of Sidney
Horowitz, Polo's production man, to work as a salesman on
Ralph Lauren's say-so. O'Toole was hired because Ralph
thought he had great personal style. Loock was hired because
he looked like Cary Grant. Horowitz was hired because Ralph
considered his father almost family.

Ralph was building a business, but it was a personal business.

"Ricky's parents introduced my mother and father to each
other," says Joel Horowitz. "That was the connection. As a kid
I remember going to Ricky's house in the Bronx. My father
worked for a major company in the neckwear industry. The
way he tells it, he was at a party at Ricky's house when he was
introduced to a Ralph Lauren, the son-in-law. Ralph had heard

that my father was a professional in the tie business, and he said, 'I'd like to have you work for me.' My father laughed. Here's this young kid offering him a job. He didn't take it seriously. Then my father had a major heart attack, and when he recuperated he said, 'I'm not going back to that hellhole.' So he called Ralph, and Ralph had a job waiting for him.

"What Ralph liked was that there was a family relationship. Ralph didn't know my father, but because he was connected to Ricky and Ricky's parents, Ralph felt confident in him. My father was the kind of guy who gave his life's blood, and I'm sure Ralph saw that right away."

Joel Horowitz joined Polo in 1969 after dropping out of the University of Miami in Ohio. On his first day of work, Horowitz wore the only good clothes he owned, his Bar Mitzvah suit. He had long hair and a mustache.

After talking to him the first morning, Ralph gave him some advice.

"Shave," he said.

"What for?"

"You'll look better."

Horowitz wasn't happy. But Ralph wasn't finished. He went into the showroom and came back with six suits.

"Wear these, cut your mustache, cut your hair, and come in looking the way I want you to look."

Nobody had ever given Joel Horowitz six suits before.

He shaved.

That summer Joel Horowitz quit to travel through Europe. When he returned he went back to work as a Polo salesman, but he was bored. Finally he turned to his father and said, "What else is there for me to do?"

"They're talking about opening a Polo store in California, and they are looking for people. How would you like to go?"

Joel thought about living in Southern California and decided it sounded great. Ralph, too, liked it. Ralph thought Jerry Magnin was an honorable guy and that Bill Loock's good looks would project the right Polo image. But sending Joel would almost be like having a brother there, somebody Ralph knew he could trust. Joel went.

A few weeks later, on a Sunday evening, Ralph Lauren,

tailor Leo Lozzi, illustrator Michael Farina, and Joe Barrato
flew out for the Beverly Hills store opening. Also in the group
was Buffy Birrittella, a former reporter for *Daily News Record*
who had joined Polo as a full-time design assistant in April
1971.

"It was the first time I'd ever been on a Boeing seven forty-
seven," says Barrato. "Ralph would do nice things for you. He
tried to share and to give to people he was close to. We had
first-class tickets, took the late-night flight, had dinner, the whole
works."

Later they went into the lounge, where people were introducing themselves to each other as though they were at a party.
Ralph motioned over Barrato, Lozzi, and Farina and reached
into his pocket. He then gave them 18-karat gold dog tags
from Cartier with the word *Polo* engraved on them. Ralph also
gave a gold I.D. bracelet to Buffy Birrittella. The message was
both subtle and convincing. If Ralph Lauren was going to do
well in life, so would those around him.

Jerry Magnin greeted them at the airport. Then he made
a tactical mistake. Instead of checking them into their bunga-
lows at the Beverly Hills Hotel, he drove directly to the store.
It was still under construction, and because it was Ralph Lauren's first store and he didn't have any experience with what
a store looked like when it was still raw, he panicked.

"He didn't like the brick, and he didn't like the color of
the stucco, and he wasn't even sure he liked the stucco," says
Buffy Birrittella. "He didn't like the stain on the floor, and he
wasn't even sure he liked the widths of the planks on the floor.
He was real upset. When you look at a shop in construction,
and you are just looking at the floor, you can pick apart a lot
of things about that floor. But when the shop comes together,
you don't worry whether the planks are four inches wide or
four-and-a-half inches wide.

"Ralph pulled me aside and said, 'You've got to change
this. I'm not coming in again until it is ready to open.'

"So I talked to Tom O'Toole. First Tom assured me that
I couldn't make any changes. Two, he insisted it was going to
be fine. After we talked I felt comfortable with what was going
to happen, and that's what I told Ralph. And of course, by the
time everything was ready, it was."

The opening party Jerry Magnin gave Ralph Lauren in September 1971 was restrained by Beverly Hills standards. About three hundred came, including actor Hugh O'Brien. Guests were served champagne and hors d'oeuvres. Men were given sterling silver collar stays in small wooden boxes that said *Polo*. Women received burlap bags with leather trims from the Italian manufacturer who made Polo's belts and shoes.

Ralph dressed for the occasion in a navy pin-stripe suit and a pair of English velvet slippers with golden woven wolf heads on the toes.

All eyes, however, were quickly drawn to the most outlandishly dressed person at the party . . . Berny Schwartz.

Schwartz was an uninvited guest. He knew that nobody wanted him there, but he didn't care. He had discovered Ralph Lauren, he had brought Ralph Lauren to Los Angeles, and Berny Schwartz was going to Ralph's party regardless. He marched over straight from work, wearing a khaki bush hat with a soft brim, a surplus U.S. army shirt, camouflage pants from Milan, and heavy lace-up army boots. Attached to his belt was a *sabretache*, a pouch worn by English soldiers in the Boer War.

There is a photograph of Berny Schwartz and Ralph together that evening.

Ralph is leaning against a display of ties and shirts. He is wearing his dark blue pin-stripe suit, a wide tie, and a shirt with a white deep collar. He has his hands in his pockets, and because he is slouching he looks both uncomfortable and short.

Schwartz, holding a cigarette in a hand adorned with two rings and heavy silver bracelet, towers over him, a beaming, jolly revolutionary.

"Ralph has this quizzical expression on his face like, 'Okay Berny, you did it, thanks a lot.' But he was very friendly," says Schwartz. "I didn't feel strange. It was a look I wore every day. The expression on his face is priceless. He looks like I smell."

After the opening, Jerry Magnin hosted a private party at nearby La Scala, an expensive Italian restaurant favored by Hollywood celebrities and politicians.

Maybe eighteen people were invited, some of whom didn't know each other. To make them feel comfortable, Jerry Magnin stood in front of the table and personally seated everybody. As he did he said, 'I want so-and-so from such-and-such to sit next to so-and-so from such-and-such because they should know each other. He does . . . she does . . . they do . . .'"

It was a tactful, mannerly thing to do. People didn't know where to sit or whom to talk to. This way everybody had something to say to the person next to them. Ralph Lauren was impressed, and he paid attention. Months later, at a different restaurant, he would do the same thing himself.

Jerry had one last surprise in store for that evening. Before the dinner was over he gave Ralph a small but expensive work by Raimonds Staprans, a California figurative painter whose work is often compared with that of Richard Diebenkorn and Wayne Thibaud. "He'd admired it earlier, and I wanted to give him something special," explains Magnin.

For the first three months, business was fabulous.

Then the store started to have delivery problems like those of many of Ralph's other retail accounts. The difference was that Jerry Magnin was almost 100 percent dependent on Polo for his merchandise. If Polo didn't ship, Jerry Magnin didn't have anything to sell. This is why the store had a poor first year.

What happened was that the good merchandise sold immediately. The dogs stayed on the hangers and ended up on sale.

For Bill Loock it was boring beyond words.

"It was a beautiful shop, but we didn't have enough merchandise," says Loock. "It got very frustrating because of the inactivity. Beverly Hills is a funny place. Nobody moves till noontime, except on Saturday, and then they come in his-and-hers tennis clothes.

"I also found dealing with the stars a pain in the ass. They never had any taste, and you had to tell them they looked like the greatest thing since herbicide a thousand times. The one thing you can say about Ralph's clothing is that you can put it on anybody and he looks better than he ever has in his life. Whether you like the cut is another thing, but the fabrics are wonderful. Sometimes the customer didn't understand it, and it made me frustrated.

"What drove me away, and I wish I could have done a

better job, was the inactivity. I just couldn't stand it. Having been on the move all my life I found working in a shop devastating. I couldn't adjust. It wasn't anybody's fault but my own . . . Jerry and Ralph did everything for me. I couldn't handle the waiting. And I'm not a manager. Hell, I can't tell people what to do. I have enough trouble telling myself, surviving. I drank more martinis than the law allowed just to keep awake. After a year I quit, and Joel Horowitz replaced me."

Despite the delivery problems, the store, as Jerry Magnin promised, was good for Polo's image.

What nobody realized, though, was that the store would push Ralph Lauren beyond shirts, suits, and ties. He designed his first shoe collection for Jerry Magnin, his first belts, his first sweaters. He had to design these products: Magnin had empty shelves.

As for Berny Schwartz, he later won a Coty Award for his design talents. Then Berny's fashion tastes began to change, and eventually he sold his store. In early 1987 he was talking about buying into a tee shirt business in Washington.

When asked to express his feelings about Ralph Lauren, Schwartz said he understood why Ralph had made the decisions he'd made . . .

It wasn't personal.

It was business.

Ralph Lauren would hire many fine designers to work with him over the years. Few, though, would be more talented than Jeffrey Banks. Banks can only be described as a fashion prodigy. When his friends were playing ball or chasing girls, Jeffrey Banks was pondering the significance of rep ties, oxford button-down shirts, and cuffed pants. At twelve years old he was a regular customer at Britches of Georgetowne (a preppy men's store). At fifteen he was on the Britches payroll as a salesman, working for Rick Hindin and Dave Pensky. He was surely the only high school student in Washington, D.C., with his own subscriptions to *Daily News Record* and *Women's Wear Daily*.

By his senior year in high school Banks was wearing Polo

shoes, Polo belts, and Polo raincoats. So when Ralph and Joe Barrato flew down for a charity event and a fashion show, Banks was chosen to pick them up. Banks took the day off from school, borrowed the Britches station wagon, and promptly had a flat tire.

"I finally flagged somebody down to help me change it," says Banks. "Fortunately, their flight was a little late. They came down with this beautifully framed silk scarf as a present for Dave and Rick. The airlines, though, wouldn't let Joe take it on the plane. Instead, they made him put it in baggage. And then they broke it. Joe was furious. That was all he could talk about, because the glass had torn the scarf. Ralph, though, was really cool. I was flustered and tongue-tied, but he was great.

"Anyway, that year Ralph had done a burgundy double knit sweater blazer with peaked lapels. It sounds awful, but it was made in Italy and it was beautiful. He was really ahead of his time. I wore it with gray flannels and brown suede kiltie Polo shoes, and a jacquard burgundy tie. And Ralph loved it, because he'd brought a sweater jacket with him. He loved the idea that this sixteen-year-old was wearing the same kind of thing. So we talked about clothes and about Gary Cooper and Cary Grant, and I showed him how I put together the clothes and what my favorite looks were.

"Finally he said, 'What are you going to do after you graduate?'

"'I'm going to go to Pratt or Parsons and study fashion design.'

"'When you come to New York to look at schools, come talk to me about a job.'"

Jeffrey Banks and his mother arrived in New York on St. Patrick's Day. He went to see Ralph the following day. The spring of 1971 was moody and indecisive, 40 degrees one day and 65 the next. That day it was 65, and Jeffrey Banks was wearing a camel hair blazer, Harris tweed Polo pants, and a wool-lined Polo raincoat. Banks was dying, he was so hot, but it was the only Polo outfit he'd brought. He had to wear it.

"Joe Barrato came down and he took me around the offices and then I spent some time talking to Ralph," says Banks.

"The funny thing was Ralph hired me without looking at my sketches. What we did was talk about clothes. Joe was wearing a round-collared shirt, an 1890s shirt with a white collar and a striped body, and I loved it. Ralph and I discussed the shirt and the polka dot tie with it, and it was a meeting of the minds."

Banks got special permission from Pratt to move into a dormitory before the school year started, and that August he started his new job. A few weeks after that, he and Ralph Lauren went to Brooks Brothers. In the window were handturned cable socks priced at $7.50 a pair, shetland socks in reds and blues and yellows, and they were as beautiful to look at as they were comfortable to wear. Each bought a pair, marveling at the skill that had gone into making them. The salesman must have overheard, because before they left, he blurted out that Brooks Brothers wouldn't be carrying those socks any more.

Ralph told Banks he couldn't believe it. Luxurious, quality clothes were the foundation of the Brooks Brothers franchise. These were the products that attracted the customers. If Brooks Brothers wasn't going to fill that need, it meant somebody else could step in.

"He loved the kind of thing that people didn't want to make any more," says Banks. "It's the old way of making something, the right way of making something. It's cross-stitching the buttons, it's having the buttons be real horn or real pearl. The customer may not know the buttons are pearl, but he knows there is something about that shirt he loves, something he can't put his finger on."

Jeffrey Banks was in school, but he did most of his learning at Polo. Ralph Lauren would take him into the stores and walk through the different areas of the men's departments, asking Banks his opinions about collars and jackets and fabrics, and exposing Banks to a different world. Ralph also made him a member of his family. Jeffrey Banks would eat dinner with Ralph and Ricky Lauren, stay at their house, baby-sit for their kids on Saturday nights. Working at Polo was more than a job. It was a full-time commitment.

"Ralph was like a father to me," says Banks. "My father had no interest in clothes whatsoever. He wore lace-up Florsheim shoes, expensive Florsheim shoes, but he wouldn't wear a slip-on shoe, and he didn't know from tassel loafers. He felt a dress shirt had to have a pocket so he could put his pen in it.

"Ralph treated me like a son. I never felt like I was an assistant. I always felt a part of his family. There were extremes to that too, in terms of long-suffering devotion. You worked there and it was your life. It was his life and it became your life, and everything else was subordinated.

"But you also had many other experiences with him. Ralph made me have my first drink. It was at Catch of the Sea, and we'd gone there for dinner. I was seventeen, it was my first summer in New York, and I'd never had a drink, not even a glass of wine.

"Anyway, we're sitting there and the waiter comes around and asks for drinks.

"I said, 'I'll have a Coke.'

" 'Enough of this Coke stuff,' said Ralph. 'Have a drink. Have you ever had a drink?'

" 'No.'

" 'Marguerita, with salt.'

"And that was my first drink. He made me drink it, too."

Ralph Lauren was building a business. But it was a personal business. He worked ten- and twelve-hour days, and he expected the others to do the same.

Look at Banks's schedule. He went to Pratt from 8 A.M. to 10 P.M. on Tuesday and Thursday. Monday, Wednesday, and Friday he worked full days at Polo. Homework? At night, after the office closed. Since Banks didn't get back to Brooklyn until 9 or 10 P.M., that often meant staying up until 2 A.M.

"We'd sit in these crazy design meetings with Ralph until midnight, trying to decide whether we should do navy blue or royal blue," says Banks. "On the way out Ralph would take the swatch and ask the cleaning lady what she thought.

"The worst feeling in the world was when Ralph said you were wrong about something. You felt like a piece of garbage. He made you insecure about your own feelings about whether something should be wide or narrow, red or black. He just had this way, this hypnotic way of making you feel, 'I don't know anything. This guy just has it all.' I was so young and impressionable. If he told me black was white I believed it."

Ralph, age thirteen, in Bronx schoolyard. The Indian on his leather jacket was the symbol of Public School 80, the junior high school next to the apartment building in which he grew up. © Polo/Ralph Lauren Corporation

RALPH LIFSHITZ
C.C.N.Y.
Lunch Room Squad, "Clinton News," Dean's Office Squad, Health Ed. Squad

Millionaire

Ralph as he appeared in his 1957 DeWitt Clinton High School yearbook. Courtesy of DeWitt High School

Ralph, standing fourth from left, as camp counselor at Camp Roosevelt in 1958. He was eighteen. Courtesy of Alan Zaitz

Ralph as a twenty-two-year-old preppy. He has draped a shetland sweater around his neck and is wearing tweed trousers and a white button-down shirt. © Polo/Ralph Lauren Corporation

ll 1972. The first sportswear
ollection for women. He is wearing
brown Harris tweed jacket with
een corduroy safari pants; she
in a brown Harris tweed suit.
1972 by Mellon

Fall 1972. Ralph's first gray flannel suit for
women, photographed in his office at 40 West
55th Street. The blue-and-white ginger jar on
the fireplace mantel is still in place today, as is
the Indian rug. © 1972 by Mellon

Facing page: Ralph with Beverly Hills retailer Berny Schwartz at the
opening of the first Polo shop in September 1971. Schwartz, who until
then had carried the line exclusively, crashed the party given by store
owner Jerry Magnin. Courtesy of Berny Schwartz

Spring 1973. The start of the "Great Gatsby" look. She is wearing a shaped regimental blazer with a narrow waist and white silk shantung trousers. He is in a white flannel blazer with navy corduroy pleated trousers. © 1973 by Mellon

Fall 1973. He is in what Ralph called a "Vanderbilt" jacket complete with patch pockets and back-belt; she is wearing Ralph "Duchess" suit cut from beige herringbone © 1973 by Mellon

Facing page: Fall 1974. She is in a worsted wool "Duchess" suit; he is wearing a pin-striped worsted double-breasted jacket and vest with gray flannel pleated trousers. Shot in front of the Plaza Hotel. © 1974 by Mellon

Facing page: The first national ad in which Ralph appeared. The photograph has been positioned to appear as though he and the two models are being seen from the side mirror of a truck. "They couldn't understand why I wouldn't wear the outfit that they wanted to sell on the fourth floor," says Ralph. "I said, 'This is what I'm like. This is what I want to wear. This is who I am.'" September 1975. Courtesy of Saks Fifth Avenue

Peter Strom, president and partner, Polo/Ralph Lauren Corporation. When Strom joined at the end of 1974, the company and its licensees did $7 million a year at wholesale; for fiscal year ended March 31, 1988, the company and its licensees generated $925 million at wholesale. © Mark Jenkinson

Ralph Lauren's image of you, the American independent. Reflect it in his haberdasherer's classics, now at S.F.A.

If there's one thing you know, it's sportswear. America's gift to fashion, Ralph Lauren's gift to you. His mood, his interpretation of country classic English haberdashery is pure American. Clothes that last, clothes you love year after year. Ralph's genius, your good fortune. Reflecting the very best in American design, reflecting the very best in you. Left, Harris tweed wool checked overshirt with hood, brown, $134. Matching button-front skirt, $112. Shetland wool crew neck sweater with three-button shoulder, heather green, $50. Center, Ralph Lauren, the great haberdasher himself. Right, guncheck hacking jacket, brown wool, $230. Shetland wool crew neck sweater, beige, $50. Classic trousers with watchpocket, wool covert cloth, tan, $104. Sweaters for 30 to 36 sizes, everything else for 4 to 14 sizes. Ours exclusively in Collection Sportswear.

Our new store hours. In Chicago, Monday through Saturday, from 10 to 6.
In Skokie, Monday and Thursday, from 9:30 to 9; Tuesday, Wednesday, Friday and Saturday, from 9:30 to 5:30

Saks Fifth Avenue, Chicago, 669 North Michigan Avenue • Skokie, Old Orchard at Skokie

Ralph walking down the stairs to receive his 1977 Coty Award. Note his Texas string bowtie.
© Jade Albert

Ralph and Ricky with daughter Dylan (*left*) and son David in East Hampton, 1976.
© 1988 by Barbra Walz

Ralph and Ricky with Ralph's black Porsche 911 Turbo.
© 1988 by Barbra Walz

Ralph and Ricky, circa 1976. © 1988 by Barbra Walz

The hours were exhausting. As long as he was at Pratt, however, Banks was able to juggle his schedule. But in his junior year he transferred to Parsons, and then it began to unravel. Banks lost thirty pounds in three months, his grades suffered, and finally his teachers told him he would have to choose between Polo and school.

Banks chose school.

Ralph was furious. Banks would never get such a good job again, he said. Banks didn't need school. He was already learning the things he had to know. Quit school and work for him full-time.

"Part of me said he was right," says Banks. "I loved going to work more than I did college, and I was certainly learning a lot more going to work. But I also felt if I was that good, if I was as good as he thought, Ralph could hire me back when I finished. And if I wasn't that good, eventually he'd fire me anyway."

Ralph was angry and hurt and upset, and it showed. He shouted that Banks was making a big mistake, a terrible mistake. The words hurt all the more because Ralph never shouted.

Banks sat in his chair and started to cry.

"He was angry with me the way a father is angry with a son," says Banks. "I kept second-guessing myself because I really loved being there. Here I was, making real good money for somebody twenty, I loved what I was doing, these were the clothes I loved, it was everything. But I left.

"Then we didn't see each other. That was it. They cut me off."

Ralph was building a business, but it was a personal business, and Ralph took the loss of Jeffrey Banks very personally.

Every year a handful of might-have-beens go broke on Seventh Avenue while equal talents survive. The ones who make it talk about hard work, good timing, smart business managers. Stories about virtue rewarded sound swell, even when virtue has very little to do with the reward.

Then there are the stories the losers tell about the crooked contractors, the easy drugs, the rents that doubled. Every failed son-in-law has an explanation. If the buyers had liked solids, not prints, if the skirts were longer, not shorter, if the piece goods had arrived on the first, not the thirtieth. . . .

Listen long enough and the word *luck* seems to go a long way toward explaining why so many fail, while others drive Chrysler convertibles.

Ralph Lauren was lucky.

In November 1969, on a trip to San Francisco, he told a writer for the *San Francisco Chronicle* that he had been approached to design a women's collection but that the idea didn't appeal to him.

"My heart just isn't in it," he said.

Eighteen months later, the idea appealed to him a lot.

"What happened was that we had piece goods in inventory that we weren't moving," says Joe Barrato, Polo's former sales manager. "At the same time, we were producing a nice men's tailored shirt. Rose Wells, an executive at Federated Department Stores, used to grab me by the lapels, shake me, and say, 'Tell that little SOB to make a lady's shirt like he makes a man's shirt.' I mean, she would bang the hell out of me, and I would then tell Ralph what she said.

"Finally, he said, 'Okay, we have nothing to lose. But we'll make our ladies' shirts different. We'll use white collars and white cuffs.' "

This is how Ralph started in the women's wear business.

Here were folded shirts cut expressly for women, single-stitched to ensure quality and made from luxurious imported cottons and wool blends. There were tattersalls, there were navy-and-white pinstripes, there were wine-and-white pinstripes, and there were brown-and-white pinstripes. There was also a group of four different striped silks. Some came with ascots, some not, but all were priced at $24. These were sexy, shaped shirts, and the fact that they were tailored by a men's designer expressly for women made them that much more desirable.

Joe Barrato stuffed the new line in a suitcase and flew to I. Magnin in San Francisco. The following day he sold 200 dozen. Fabulous. Next, Bullock's Wilshire in Los Angeles bought almost as many. Then Neiman-Marcus in Dallas wanted 200 dozen, too. Barrato was so excited he called Ralph at every stop.

The label inside Ralph's men's wear read *Polo Fashions*. But if he was going to compete in the women's business, Ralph thought he wanted something softer and more personal. He saw that other designers were using their names, and he decided his label would read *Polo by Ralph Lauren*. Then he added a witty accent almost as an afterthought. He put a little polo player on the white cuffs.

That is how empires get started. Business books are full of homilies about hard work, ambition, and perseverance.

Luck counts, too.

Stitching that polo player onto his woman's shirt was one of the savviest things Ralph ever did. "The polo player became the new status symbol for women," says Raleigh Glassberg, who bought Ralph's first women's shirts for Bloomingdale's. "To me, it was a way for women to identify with what their boyfriends or husbands were wearing. Ralph's shirt was also a nicer product than any other folded shirt around."

Madison Avenue spends millions each year researching what motivates customers to buy. One of the more interesting areas of study involves semiotics — the philosophy of communication through the use of signs and symbols. Companies use signs and symbols (brands) because they break language barriers and they have immediate emotional impact. Symbols are part of every childhood. A skull-and-crossbones means poison and danger. A square red cross means medical assistance. Then there are other symbols, cultural symbols, that over the years have become associated with status. A Rolls-Royce, for example, symbolizes wealth and position. This is why an advertising agency which wants to signify that its hotel client is aiming at the luxury market may photograph a Rolls-Royce in the front driveway. If the car is there its owners are inside and, since they drive the best, they probably expect the best in service. Call it rub-off marketing.

Ralph Lauren's polo player worked the same way. It communicated an image of sophistication and financial success, and as a selling tool its value would prove inestimable. Wearing a shirt with a polo player on it became chic. Everybody knew polo was the outdoor sport of choice of high society. The fans and players lived in Palm Beach or Palm Springs or Greenwich, and beginners took classes at places like the Rangitiki

Polo School in England, where they played at Windsor Great Park by permission of the Queen. Polo had more class than big-time wrestling, even if it never developed stars with the same appeal as Hulk Hogan.

Joe Barrato didn't have the time to run the women's business himself; instead he turned it over to Ken Giordano, a Polo salesman. Giordano knew something about women's wear from earlier jobs, he was handsome, boyishly friendly, heroically polite, and the buyers, especially women, loved him. Giordano had sex appeal.

"At the very beginning of women's wear we were invited to an industry luncheon, together with designers like Bill Blass and Oscar de la Renta," says Giordano. "I went as a representative of Ralph Lauren and was seated next to designer Anne Klein. She turned to me and said, 'Who are you with?'

"I told her I worked for Ralph Lauren.

" 'Who's he?'

"A men's wear designer.

" 'And now he's going to do women's wear?'

"Right.

" 'Well, I think he's crazy.'

"You might say there was a lot of skepticism, because until then designers had first established themselves in the women's business and then made the move into men's wear," continues Giordano. "We were doing the opposite. And there were a lot of things we didn't know about women. For example, a man's shirt buttons left over right. A woman's shirt buttons right over left. Who knew? What we gave them was the best cotton we could buy, a man-tailored shirt with removable collar stays, a safety button on the sleeve placket, all nicely folded.

"Also, Ralph really only cared about one thing. He wanted to dress Ricky. As long as the clothes fit her, he was satisfied."

This was a problem because Ricky was a petite woman. So, too, was Buffy Birrittella, Ralph's design assistant. Birrittella might have been a quick study, but she didn't have the body of an industry fitting model. (A fitting model spends most of her day standing in her underwear taking on and off sample clothes. There are dozens of women on Seventh Avenue earning $60 an hour who do nothing but count calories and utter observations like "too tight," "too loose," "I can't button the buttons." They are worth every cent.)

Ralph wasn't interested in fitting models.

Buffy Birrittella was a woman, she knew what women liked, she understood the way Ralph thought, and since she was there, Ralph fit his clothes on her. This was a mistake. Dante may have been inspired by Beatrice, but he didn't quote her.

This is why the only women who ever felt comfortable in one of Ralph Lauren's shirts wore size six — Buffy Birrittella's size.

"I'm the culprit," says Birrittella. "I was a thin little person at the time. We had a shirt with very high armholes, and therefore a very tight fit. He wanted his women's shirts to have the same tailoring and crispness as the men's shirts, but he wanted them to be very feminine. At that time in Europe, everybody was wearing these shrunken little shetland sweaters, these shrunken little Fair Isles, and blouses with a very tight French fit."

Women with more ample figures suffered.

"They had to buy at least one size larger than normal," sighs Joe Barrato. "It wasn't good for them psychologically, but they wanted the shirts."

Frank Simon asked for a Bloomingdale's exclusive in New York and opened a Ralph Lauren women's shirt shop on the third floor near the escalators. Response was so good that Simon decided to run a seven-column ad bragging about the shirts in the *New York Times*. And what better time than Christmas to really boost the sales? Get your inventory ready, he told Raleigh Glassberg.

Glassberg didn't have to be told twice. She was a worrier from the get-go, and the problems she saw with Ralph's production team only made her more anxious. As the weeks passed and the day the ad was to appear approached (December 12), she became convinced that good ole Ken Giordano at Ralph Lauren was not going to deliver the goods.

Giordano didn't make it any easier for her.

Since he prided himself on telling the truth, Giordano confided to Glassberg that delays looked inevitable. Making a woman's shirt to Ralph's specifications wasn't easy. Sure, Ralph owned a factory in Mount Vernon, but there were only so many hours in a day. Ken would do his best, but he couldn't promise.

"One day I told her we were going to be late, and she said, 'How can you do this to me? You go to hell.' " said Giordano. "I'll never forget it. My God, I was shocked.

"I went in to see Ralph and I said, 'Ralph, I just can't take much more of this. I'm getting killed out here.' So he made me laugh, and then he told me to fix it."

Giordano tried.

On December 11 he sent Jeffrey Banks up to Mount Vernon to pick up the shirts. Banks didn't get there until 4 P.M., and even then the shirts weren't ready.

"I literally sat there while they folded and pinned and packed them," says Banks. "I brought them to Bloomingdale's that evening. The store was having a strike, and I walked through the front door with these shirts. It was like breaking the line. People were screaming at me . . . it was really intense. Raleigh had gotten some shirts in stock, but she'd sold them all before the ad was about to run, and she didn't have anything else. She was screaming on the phone."

The next morning, readers of the *New York Times* saw what the commotion had been about. The ad read:

"And now . . . Polo by Ralph Lauren for the girls. The most liberated shirt in town! Free of every bit of confusion . . . It's that fabulous man's world shirt tailored with separate but equal perfection by Ralph Lauren. Assured stripes, thoroughbred solids, many collared and cuffed in white . . . all wearing the symbolic polo player on the cuff. Polo in wellbred cotton, 6 to 16, $24. Mail and phone. Polo Shop, third floor. New York and all stores."

The shirts were priced $10 higher than any made by the competition. The customers didn't care. The shirts sold out.

"When Ralph was just starting, he was very involved in everything," says Raleigh Glassberg, today a buyer for Marshall Field in Chicago. "You'd sit in his office, you'd go through things together, he'd listen to ideas. It was very much of a partnership. You didn't influence his style, but you'd talk about what would be commercial and what wasn't in terms of timing or certain shapes.

"He had two floors, and people were bobbing in and out. You'd go for the afternoon kind of thing to look at preliminaries and work on the line, and it was as much a family relationship as you can have in business.

"At first, Ralph's clothes were sold as part of the blouse department. Then, maybe nine or ten months later, Bloomingdale's built him his department. His timing was right. There was a resurgence of the man-tailored look for women, and he was in sync with what was happening. Ralph did unusual things in those days, such as mixing tweeds and velvets for work. Or he put velvet with silk or tweeds with silk madders. Then he came up with the Duchess of Windsor suit, and Hepburn pants. Also, he single-handedly brought back linen blouses for women, as well as lace. People copied him.

"As a designer sportswear buyer I used to be appalled by those women lawyers or bankers walking around in their suits with their little ties. Ralph's look wasn't that look. It wasn't a power way of dressing. Women who are secure don't have to go to work in a suit, especially a rigid suit. His clothes were tailored, but he didn't dictate that rigid sensibility. He had a more feminine approach.

"He also surrounded himself with people who understood his concept and were able to take care of it on all levels. You can't do it single-handedly. All the people in his business really believed in the product. They were, and still are, ingrained Ralph Laurenesque people. You need that to pull off a business like his."

One of those people was slender, whispery-voiced Sal Cesarani. Ralph was not a women's wear designer by training. But he knew how he wanted women to dress. Sal Cesarani had the necessary technical skills to transform those ideas into products. Cesarani was a graduate of the High School of Fashion Industries and the Fashion Institute of Technology, and he knew how to sketch, how to drape, how to cut patterns. He had also designed women's collections for a handful of Seventh Avenue companies. He knew the fabric shops, the button suppliers, the zipper suppliers, the belt makers, the pad makers. Cesarani was a tailor. He was also impressionable, easy to motivate, and a romantic. Cesarani always put his job ahead of his personal life. What he sought in return was a nod, a word of approval, an "Attaboy." Sometimes he appeared so devoted to Polo that he seemed almost to worship Ralph Lauren.

"We were young kids when I joined the company," says Cesarani. "I wanted to make his dream come true. People didn't even know who Ralph was at that time.

"The first skirt we made was a total disaster. It was gray flannel with a button-front fly all the way down. The pleats opened up because we didn't allow for hips. We only made eighteen and they didn't work. People were producing them up for us, thinking they were salesmen's samples, not knowing it was our entire line. We also had a white-belted khaki chino skirt with a little sailor's pleated pocket on the front — that was big. I didn't create the women's wear division. What I did do was implement the designs."

In May 1972, Ralph showed his first full women's wear collection. It consisted of sexy, fitted jackets, skirts, suits, and pleated pants, men's clothes adapted for a woman, and the press thought it was a snappy idea.

"With all the talk about classics, someone was bound to bring back the mannish tailored suit. Fortunately, it was Ralph Lauren, who knows something about tailored," wrote the *New York Times.* Those suits would be the start of the "dress for success" look. Ralph may not have been the first to see that women were serious about working in the office, but he was the first to offer them a professional wardrobe. The prices ranged from $200 to $250.

Ralph knew his show was good. And he was so relieved afterwards that he called his small staff together and said, "I just want you to know, this is it. I want to quit women's and leave on top. I had a good show and I don't think I can go anywhere else because I don't know how to do anything else."

"We would talk and design on the run," says Sal Cesarani. "Oh, there were moments when Ralph frustrated me, when he'd say, 'I don't know what you are trying to say. I don't understand that idea.' Then he'd say to me, 'I have a great idea,' and there was the idea. He always dreaded the fact that he couldn't sketch and that when I started, I sketched for him. But he knew how to take the concept forward."

If Ralph Lauren didn't know how to sketch or drape or how to cut fabric, how could he call himself a designer?

Ralph didn't need those skills as long as he could communicate his ideas to others, says Cesarani. Ralph could hire sketchers and drapers and sewers. The concepts, though, were his. His approach worked, too, because he was patient. Ralph didn't worry about deadlines, and nobody could rush him into making a decision. Even when he made a decision he was just as likely to later reverse it. What satisfied him? Nobody was ever really sure. Ralph would explain his idea, it would be interpreted, he would explain again, and finally the dress or the suit or the pair of pants would leave his workroom. Sometimes he would give Sal Cesarani a crude sketch of a pocket or shoulder detail, and then Cesarani would execute it for him. Or Ralph would say, "Look at this pocket on this shirt. Why don't we put it on a skirt?" And Cesarani would say, "Let me make a sketch and show it to you." Or Ralph would say, "I want a velvet-collar Harris tweed jacket. Add a suede skirt." And Sal would sketch those. Ralph approved the fabrics, the buttons, the pockets, everything. Even if he didn't know what he wanted when he started, he knew it when he saw it.

Compare it to building a house. Ralph picked the paint, the wood, the carpeting. He didn't hammer the house together, but it was his house.

Ralph developed one other skill: he became a terrific motivator. He knew how to generate intense loyalty and how to make others feel important. Maybe it was his soft voice. Maybe it was his intensity, his need for approval. Whatever. It worked.

"Ralph would get out the best from people," says Cesarani. "It wasn't a question of forcing an issue. It was, 'This is what I need, you've got to do it for me, it's got to be there for me. I won't take no for an answer.' And if I didn't get something accomplished, he'd shake his head, say, 'God,' and sigh. That was enough."

Cesarani could see the business doubling overnight. There were times when he'd go into Bloomingdale's and not find a shirt from a delivery the day before. That Polo might be expanding too fast was the last thing on Cesarani's mind. Sure, there were the days when he and Ralph would go to a mill, and a salesman would complain that he hadn't yet been paid for the last shipment. Then Ralph would look at Cesarani, shake his head, and say, "We didn't pay that bill? I can't believe it." Sal never worried because Ralph didn't worry. People were always late, he thought, why should Polo Fashions be any different? It was more important to find the perfect belt for that jacket they were working on. Somebody else was responsible for keeping track of the money.

Cesarani, though, did more than design. If Ralph had an important lunch with someone, Cesarani would be sure to send that person a shirt the next day with a note attached. Ralph didn't have to ask; Cesarani wanted to do it. Not that there weren't frustrations. When Cesarani helped design the first spring/summer women's collection, he had to share a small office with Buffy Birrittella. Buffy got the desk. Cesarani worked on a ledge.

"We didn't have any space," says Cesarani. "It was work on the ledge or work in the bathroom. I was furious. I hated every minute of it. There was no room for me and I was there to do a job. I remember those moments with tremendous anguish. I had to create a miracle . . . We didn't have a production man, either, so I oversaw the making of the first women's patterns. I made the prototypes so we could see what the clothes would look like. The fittings were done on Buffy, not a fitting model. Ralph didn't understand fitting models because Ralph came from neckwear. I also knew the company couldn't afford fitting models. I said, 'I can't work this way,' but I did."

Cesarani would hear all the complaints. The armholes on the women's blouses were too high. The sizing was off. The sleeves were so narrow the customers couldn't close the buttons. The rise on the pants was so high women couldn't walk when they put them on. He understood, but when he tried to make changes, Ralph would shake his head. A hairline, that is how much change Ralph would make after he liked something. A fraction of an inch so tiny most people couldn't see it. Ralph would say, "That's fabulous. That's the look I want to achieve." When Cesarani would complain that the blouse or jacket or skirt wouldn't fit, Ralph would say fine, change it. But it always seemed that Ralph's idea of change was a smidgen of an inch.

Still, Cesarani was happy. At Christmastime Ralph would give his staff presents from Gucci, Cartier, Tiffany. Even the smallest gesture would create emotional ripples. One year Ralph gave Cesarani a signet ring, which he still wears. With the ring came a note, which read, "The only two people I have given this gift to are my wife and my brother."

That was enough to leave Sal Cesarani dreamy-eyed for another six months.

"I lived morning, noon, and night at Ralph Lauren," he says. "I didn't have the time to breathe. I was obsessed with what I was doing. My wife knew it was the most exciting thing in my career and that I was part of something. Also, Ralph was under so much stress. Once we went to a club in London for dinner. He got dizzy and said he was going to faint. I said, 'Ralph, don't faint.' I took him downstairs to the men's room and he washed his face. Later I asked the waiters to take away our food. I remember saying to myself, 'God, don't let anything happen.' "

Cesarani noticed many things about Ralph Lauren. There was Ralph's warmth, his enthusiasm, his patience, his taste level.

There was something else, too, something Cesarani thought almost everybody else seemed to overlook.

Ralph Lauren had to win at everything he did.

"One evening we went to a friend's for dinner in Rye," says Cesarani. "Afterwards, we went downstairs to the basement to play Ping-Pong. Every game Ralph played he won. The others wanted to win. But nobody wanted to win more than Ralph."

Nothing in his men's business had prepared Ralph Lauren for the frantic pace of women's wear. Men's buyers spent days picking through spring and fall collections. The women's wear business was chaotic in comparison. There was a spring collection, a summer collection, a fall collection, and a holiday/resort collection. Some manufacturers even make an early-spring collection, which they start shipping in January. Every collection meant new fabrics, new styles, new colors. The tension was nonstop.

This meant Ralph needed a bigger staff. After naming Ken Giordano executive sales director in July 1972, Ralph later hired Liz Serman and Carol Nolan as salespeople and added Kelli Questrom. (Kelli is the wife of Allen Questrom, the former vice-chairman of Federated Department Stores.) Kelli Questrom, who earlier had worked at *Mademoiselle* magazine, often dressed like a man. She wore her husband's shirts and recut his old pants with large pleats. Or she would wear one of his shawl-collared cardigans with one of her snake or lizard belts.

"Ralph had already come up with the idea that women would like to wear men's tailored clothing done in a woman's fashion," says Questrom. "He was intrigued by the way I dressed, and we used to talk about it."

Others also gave advice, especially the late Katie Murphy, a fashion director at Bloomingdale's.

Take Ralph's trousers.

Ralph cut his women's pants as though they would be worn by men. This meant the waist contained a good quarter-inch of lining and interfacing to prevent it from twisting. Quality workmanship, said Ralph. Wrong, replied Murphy. Women wanted their waists to look as thin as possible.

Then there was the matter of not finishing the ends of his trousers. Freedom of choice, said Ralph. One leg might be a tiny bit longer than the other. Maybe the customer wants them to break heavily over the shoes.

Wrong, said Murphy. Since he was the designer, women wanted him to decide whether the pants should be cuffed or not. Besides, women hated paying the extra $15 the stores charged to finish them.

"Ralph always envisioned certain kinds of bodies, certain kinds of personalities, as his perfect client, his perfect customer," says Questrom. "He would say to me, 'I dream of dressing Audrey Hepburn. But my client is never Audrey Hepburn, it's Irma.' He was trying to make clothes for a streamlined body. He liked thin women, not extremely well-endowed women. To this day you never see a woman with cleavage in a Ralph Lauren ad. His woman was the well-bred Englishwoman, not the American woman with the Coke-bottle figure. So he'd pick a rail like me to see how the clothes would look on the customer he envisioned. But those customers seldom bought his clothes. Katie Murphy would say, 'Ralph, your stuff looks great on your models, but our customers have narrower shoulders and a bosom and they can't button their jackets.' "

As public relations director, Questrom would also arrange Ralph's store appearances. Sometimes he showed up. More often, he would agree to go somewhere and then refuse to get on the plane. Ralph didn't like meeting new people, and he felt uncomfortable making small talk. Rather than do it badly, Ralph preferred not to do it at all. Besides, once he made appearances for one store, the other accounts would insist that he make appearances for them as well.

"He once stood up Howard Goldfeder, the former head of Federated Department Stores," says Questrom. "Bullock's Wilshire was putting on a big wingding in Ralph's honor, including a fashion show and a big party. Ralph was in New York, and at the last moment he decided he wouldn't go to California. This was just before I left his company because my husband had gotten a job at Bullock's.

"Now, I'd never met Howard Goldfeder. But the week my husband, Allen, joined Bullock's, Howard entertained us. At one point he said, 'Kelli, I understand you worked for Ralph Lauren. If you haven't severed your relationship, I wish you'd call and tell him for me that that was a dreadful thing he did, not making the appearance.' Actually, Howard put it in worse terms than that. He was very angry because he'd hired an orchestra and invited five hundred important customers of his store. For the designer not to show up . . ."

The days blurred. Choose the piece goods, attend the fittings, check the books, hire more people. And just when it seemed impossible to add as much as one more suit, Bloomingdale's told Ralph he had to start designing a line of low-priced men's wear.

The money was rolling into Polo Fashions like a tidal wave.

But as Ralph would learn, it could roll out even faster.

Meet now Robert Stock, born Robert Fegelstock on August 16, 1946, in the East Bronx. Intense, street-smart, Stock was a natural salesman, a pusher, a doer, a nonstop talker with a patter that blended Seventh Avenue–type derring-do with the easy let-it-be camaraderie of the late 1960s. There was a bit of the showman in Stock, and when it came to selling clothes or talking about life, Stock's rap was as good as anybody's.

At first glance, it would be hard to imagine somebody less like Ralph Lauren in attitude. Where Ralph was quiet and restrained, Robert Stock was gregarious; where Ralph was uncomfortable with strangers, Robert Stock saw in every new face a new opportunity. Yet Robert Stock had this in common with Ralph Lauren: he was ambitious and he understood fine traditional men's clothing. He was also quick to spot a new trend, and even quicker to jump on it. Everybody saw that Robert Stock was talented and cocky and a little bit wild.

Ralph understood that Stock, beard and all, was a character. That was okay. The customers who were going to buy the $10 jeans Ralph wanted to make were probably characters, too. Ralph had known Robert Stock a long time, as far back as the days when Ralph sold Abe Rivetz ties and Zizanie perfume to the Alvin Murray men's store on the Grand Concourse. Stock, who worked there as a salesman, liked Ralph's pale yellow Morgan, the brown leather bomber jacket he wore with a white scarf, even the way Ralph caressed his ties as he sold them. As the years passed, and Robert Stock went from salesman to self-taught designer, the two stayed in touch. So when Robert Stock and two partners opened Country Britches, a company that made tweed five-pocket jeans, Ralph knew it, and when that business began to fall apart, literally, Ralph saw that also.

"It was a great company until we began knitting our own fabric," says Stock, still bearded and given to snappy, snazzy clothes. "I got a call one day from the plant telling me the sewing machine needles were making holes in the seats. I said, 'Sew them up and ship them out,' because there was nothing else I could do. We just prayed the United Parcel man wouldn't bring us any returns. For the first few weeks, nothing happened. Then they started coming back in bundles. It got very tough, and that's when Ralph approached me. He was already doing a little shirt business, a little coat business, and people were beginning to knock him off. So he said to me, 'Why don't we start a new price division, you run it, and we'll be partners.' Not knowing anything, I said, 'Sure, Ralph.' He owned eighty percent and I owned twenty percent, but I didn't have to invest any money."

Why make $10 jeans? Because every time Ralph walked into Bloomingdale's he saw the Polo knockoffs. At half the price his pants cost. It was big business, Bloomingdale's told him, a business he should be capitalizing on himself.

There was a good marketing hook here, too. If Ralph got the $10 customers today, he could teach them to buy the $250 Polo suits tomorrow.

In March 1971 Ralph opened a subsidiary. He called it Rugby Enterprises because he wanted it to suggest country weekends, rugged sports, and the outdoors. Then the owners of the name Rugby Enterprises complained that they had copyrighted the name first. No problem. Ralph said good-bye to the playing fields of Eton and instead saddled up the most enduring of all American myths, the American cowboy. Ralph had always fantasized about the West, mostly because of the Randolph Scott pictures he saw as a kid. Hence the name *Chaps*. Not Chaps as in good fellows, but Chaps as in fringed jackets and riding pants and boots. (It would not be coincidence that Marlboro cigarettes flopped when first introduced in the 1920s as a women's cigarette. Only in the 1950s and 1960s, when the Leo Burnett agency created the Marlboro Man and Marlboro Country, was the brand positioned to become the largest-selling cigarette in the world. The American cowboy is probably the strongest image Hollywood ever created.)

Chaps was Ralph Lauren's answer to the slick Polo knock-offs.

Not that Ralph's focus changed. As far as he was concerned, Polo and Ralph Lauren still stood for the best English woolens, the $250 vested suits, the sportcoats with the belted backs. Ralph Lauren created Chaps because it made business sense. He would market Chaps because that was what the stores wanted. But as Robert Stock would learn, Polo would always be first in his heart.

"The second or third week I'm on the job with Ralph, he had a serious problem with Bloomingdale's," says Stock. "He'd promised to make them a denim suit with a corduroy collar and a flannel lining. There was bootlike stitching on the pockets and a jean pants, and it was a great idea.

"Ralph said to me, 'Listen, I've got to deliver these suits in three weeks. Leo Lozzi is making them, but he won't tell me when they'll be done. Robert, you have to go to Italy and check out these suits.'

"I said, 'Ralph, I don't know anything about jackets. I know about pants. And I've never been to Italy.'

"But he had a way of convincing you, and so I said, 'Ralph, I'll do it.'

"The next day I leave for Italy. I get over there, and I had to page Leo Lozzi at the Excelsior Hotel, where he was staying. At the time I was a casual guy, and because the temperature was a hundred degrees, I was wearing sandals, a pair of shorts, and a tee shirt. So I walk into the Excelsior, and everybody is wearing beautiful linen suits and the Italians are carrying their little pocketbooks and the hotel pages Leo Lozzi for me. Everybody is looking at me. Suddenly I feel somebody poking me in the back.

" 'Who is looking for me?'

" 'Are you Mr. Lozzi?'

" 'Who are you?'

" 'I'm Robert Stock. I'm here to see you.'

" 'Come with me.' And Lozzi takes me outside. 'How can you dress like this?' is the first thing he says.

" 'I'm here to see the factory. Give me a break.'

" 'Meet me later, we'll go out for dinner.'

"So later that night, Lozzi and Norman Hilton, who had a partnership in the factory, take me out for this unbelievable dinner, the longest meal in my life. It lasted four hours and was on the roof of a hotel. Then they put me in a car and took me to the town called Montefiascone, north of Rome. It was so late the factory was closed.

"Leo says, 'Don't worry about the factory. You'll see it tomorrow.'

"So we stayed overnight. At ten the next morning we go into the factory, and I don't see our stuff. All I see is people sewing pants, but they aren't making any jackets. Leo takes me to the back and I see only a few pair of finished pants, and the order is for two hundred or three hundred. So I say, 'Leo, what's going on? This stuff has to be delivered in three weeks.'

" 'Don't worry, don't worry.'

" 'Leo, they aren't making any jackets.'

" 'What's the difference? I make-a-the-jackets. I show them how to make-a-the jackets.'

" 'Are you sure? I've got to call Ralph.'

"So I get on the phone that night and call Ralph.

"Ralph says, 'Everything okay?' He was a total optimist. Nothing could ever be bad. 'Everything okay?'

" 'No, Ralph.'

" 'What's wrong? What's wrong?'

" 'Ralph, number one, his factory doesn't make jackets. It's a pants factory. Number two, not even all the pants have been cut yet, and the jackets haven't been touched. I don't have to be a genius to know anything about coats or pants or jackets. I've watched the way these people work. They sew about a pair of pants a day. They are never going to make this delivery.'

" 'You've got to have it made.'

" 'What can I do? There's no way I can do it.'

" 'I sent you over there.'

" 'Ralph, I'll talk to them.'

"To make a long story short, the suits are never delivered. And Bloomingdale's ran a full-page ad promoting them. To this day Frank Simon doesn't talk to me. Every time he sees me he says, 'What happened to those suits?' "

Norman Hilton? He was a partner in the factory but not

the manufacturer. Adds Leo Lozzi: "I can't explain what happened. It was my job to give the factory the pattern, the specifications, and a sample. I did that."

Over a year's business, 200 or 300 blue denim suits doesn't mean much. Every company makes mistakes; Polo was no exception.

The idea was not to make the same dumb mistakes over again.

Ralph understood that. He also knew that unless he got some help, Polo would never amount to more than a small men's wear company with a handful of snooty salesmen.

What Polo needed was a business manager. Somebody who liked and understood numbers. Somebody who could take control of the day-to-day administrative problems. Ralph had gone as far as he could alone. As a businessman he'd done better than most; not only did Polo appear to be solvent, it was making money. Now he was exhausted.

Look at the numbers. Sales for the first fiscal year, ended March 31, 1969, amounted to $400,000. (Ralph and Norman Hilton started together in October 1968, which meant those revenues represented only a six-month period.) For the fiscal year ended March 31, 1970, sales were $2.4 million with earnings of $210,000, and for the fiscal year ended March 31, 1971, sales would be $3.4 million, with earnings of $299,000.

In other words, Polo was earning after-tax profits of nearly 10 percent, or about twice the industry average. Considering that Ralph was doing everything himself, it was an impressive performance.

But when it came to managing a company, Ralph Lauren was self-taught. He knew he didn't have the skills, or the time, necessary to oversee a $5 million business. There were no cash-flow projections at Polo, no systems in place to manage the growth. There was nobody in the company who understood how the bankers talked, and even more important, liked talking to the bankers.

What Ralph needed was a partner. Somebody he could trust. Somebody who could run the company.

"I handled everything in the beginning," says Ralph. "I'm a very cautious person. I don't sit and look at numbers every morning. But I feel it, I know it, I know my business, where I'm going, and it has nothing to do with looking at reports every day. The sales and earnings were good.

"But I couldn't handle it. I couldn't do all of it. I needed more sophistication to grow, I needed somebody there with me working . . . you can't get all your figures from an absentee accountant or a bookkeeper . . . I had a lot of loyal, loving people. Very nice people who watched me begin, sat with me, did all the right things. But things change and you have to grow.

"What I did was bring in a financial guy to run the part of the business that I didn't know how to do. I brought him in; nobody asked me to. I was willing to give him a piece of my business. I felt I needed him, and I did. That's how Michael Bernstein came to join the company."

Michael Bernstein was a friend from the old neighborhood in the Bronx. Michael Bernstein and Ralph Lauren had played basketball together when they were fourteen-year-olds; they shared the same roots. Bright, disciplined, anxious to succeed, Bernstein went to the City College of New York, working his last two years part-time at Max Rothenberg & Co., an accounting company. After graduating in June 1962 Bernstein was hired at $6,000 a year as an accountant, supervising and handling audits, counseling clients, and preparing tax returns. Two years later he was named office manager, supervising a staff of thirty-five. Eventually he became a certified public accountant. Bernstein was so talented, so hard-working that in February 1968 he was made one of seven partners and was given a 5 percent interest in the company. It was a fast climb, reflecting in part not only his ability but Max Rothenberg's affection for his protégé.

As an accountant, Bernstein specialized in working with companies in the garment center, both retailers and manufacturers. Learning this, Ralph Lauren hired Max Rothenberg & Co. to be his auditor in early 1970. Bernstein would be the partner in charge of the account. It was such a good relationship that Ralph soon asked Bernstein to join Polo as treasurer.

Bernstein said no, he was already a partner, he had a good future in the firm.

Over the next eighteen months Ralph repeated his offer. Polo needed a solid financial man, Ralph told Bernstein, somebody who understood how the garment industry worked. Somebody had to supervise the accounts receivable, check the credit-worthiness of the small accounts, oversee spending on piece goods.

In May of 1971, Bernstein decided that maybe Ralph Lauren was right. Polo would do $3.8 million in sales in its next fiscal year. The company also owned a men's shirt factory in Mount Vernon, a fledgling women's wear business, and Chaps. Bernstein would be responsible for managing the financial growth of these businesses, and he would be an important figure in the executive team Ralph said he intended to develop.

The two sealed their deal at the end of May during a breakfast meeting at the Plaza Hotel. The contract Ralph showed Bernstein called for a $35,000 salary and a $50,000 term life insurance policy for Bernstein's family. Another lure for Bernstein was an option to acquire 10 percent of Polo Fashions at a later date. Without that promise, Bernstein most likely would not have left Max Rothenberg & Co., where he already owned some equity in the business. As breakfast ended, Bernstein and Ralph shook hands on what they both expected to be a partnership that would last years.

In fact, Ralph so believed in Michael Bernstein and his financial skills that he named him in his will "to take care of my kids."

Running Polo Fashions was a business.

But it was a personal business.

Bernstein went back to his office and told Max Rothenberg that he was leaving to join Polo. There were risks, he said, but they were risks worth taking. Max Rothenberg had taught him how the garment industry worked. Now Michael Bernstein would show just how good a student he was.

Bernstein reported to work on the first Monday in July 1971 as Polo's treasurer and chief financial officer. He assumed his responsibilities would be strictly financial. Ralph Lauren was then president, chairman, and chief operating officer. Norman Hilton and Peter Strom were both officers of the company, but neither played active roles. Polo was managed by Ralph and Sidney Horowitz, vice-president of production, who countersigned checks. Horowitz oversaw piece goods purchases, warehousing, and shipping. Horowitz also costed out the Polo line, which meant he decided the company's wholesale prices. Joe Barrato was in charge of sales.

Michael Bernstein, accountant, would be in charge of the company's bookkeeping department. But his job required more than pen-and-paper skills. Bernstein would also work closely with the First National Bank of Boston, which then factored Polo Fashions. In garment industry parlance, a factor is somebody who accepts retailer receivables as collateral for a loan.

Factoring works like this. On June 1, Polo Fashions ships Bloomingdale's 100 suits valued at $200 each wholesale. Instead of waiting 40 days for payment, Polo uses its $20,000 in receivables as collateral and borrows money from its factor. Usually a factor lends a manufacturer up to 80 percent of the full value of receivables. For that service, the factor demands 1 percent of sales. The factor also charges interest, as much as two or three points above the prime interest rate set by the major banks.

Factors sometimes loan money without receiving any receivables as collateral. A men's manufacturer, for example, might buy his fall piece goods in January or February. It may then take him six months to cut those piece goods into finished suits, sell them, and then bill the buyer. During that period the manufacturer needs money for overhead, labor, and other costs. Factors provide that money. The loans are called "unsecured" loans, and they make lenders very nervous.

Unknown to Michael Bernstein, Polo's unsecured loans to the First National Bank of Boston on the date of his arrival amounted to over $300,000, or more than Polo's earnings for the fiscal year ended March 31, 1971.

No wonder, then, that on his first day at work nervous bank officers from First National called and asked for a meeting.

As surprised as he was, Bernstein didn't panic. What he had to do was put together some sales projections for the next

six months. This was as much a public relations job as anything else. If the bankers walked in and Bernstein appeared
calm, competent, and serious-minded, chances were he could
settle them down long enough to work through the rough spots.

Bernstein also knew that a smile wouldn't be enough. He
was a professional; he understood the bankers wanted to know
what business looked like for the next season, how many yards
of piece goods Polo would have to buy, and what plan Polo
intended to format in order to start paying down its debt.

The problem was, Bernstein didn't know the answers.

Why should he?

He'd just started work that morning.

And by the time he left he was wondering whether Polo
would survive.

Bernstein knew he needed help. He had to base his numbers on something. How many suits did Polo sell last season,
how many pants, how many shirts? And what about going forward? Would the company's sales grow 10 percent, 20 percent, 30 percent?

He asked Sidney Horowitz, and the answers didn't satisfy
him. Neither did Horowitz's record-keeping skills. Horowitz,
Bernstein decided, might have known the tie business, but he
was not skilled enough for a full-line men's wear company.

So now Bernstein had two problems: Sidney Horowitz and
First National.

The bankers weren't sympathetic, either. Almost immediately they brought up the subject of chargebacks. Specifically,
the $100,000 in chargebacks Polo had suffered from January
through June 1971. (A chargeback is simply a credit issued by
a manufacturer when its goods are returned.)

Say Bloomingdale's orders $1,000 worth of suits. The suits
arrive but they're torn. Or they're made from heavy wool and
they don't arrive until March. Bloomingdale's then insists on
returning the suits, and it wants the $1,000 it has paid charged
back to its account.

There are always chargebacks in the garment manufacturing business. First National was concerned, however, because
it had loaned money to Polo against Polo's receivables. Now
Bloomingdale's wanted those receivables charged back to its
account.

This meant the receivables that First National had used as collateral for its loans to Polo were worth less. Later Bernstein would complain that when he joined Polo 13 percent of all merchandise shipped was later returned; the industry average was 3 to 6 percent.

Bernstein worked hard, and eventually he was able to work out Polo's problems with First National. But there were limits. Within three months he told Ralph he wanted to add an experienced controller. He also wanted a new production manager, and an experienced marketer. Ralph said no, the company didn't need those people. Besides, Polo's overhead was growing too fast. It was safer to keep the costs down.

There was reason to be cautious. For the first time since Ralph had gone into partnership with Norman Hilton, Polo was having money worries. Especially when it came to getting paid. Ralph Lauren had never wanted to do business with many big department stores; that would kill the exclusivity, he said. This meant Polo had to sell dozens of small men's specialty stores. Often these were companies founded by men with big dreams and little business know-how.

At the end of the month, after they paid their rent, they sometimes didn't have enough money to pay what they owed Polo. They would then call Ralph and ask him to let them go for another thirty days. Frequently he did, and as a result, Polo ended up carrying tens of thousands in uncollectible receivables.

Ralph Lauren saw the problems. And he had a choice. He could design the clothes or he could manage the company. Since he had delegated authority regarding the company's finances to Michael Bernstein, he would, with few exceptions, let Michael Bernstein make the big money decisions. That's what Ralph had hired him to do. Ralph would stick to what he knew how to do best, which meant designing.

And on the design front, he had reason to be satisfied. The Polo label was gaining in prestige in men's wear, the women's wear collection was developing a cult following, and Chaps was building a moderate-price business. Ralph didn't know much about making moderate-price clothes, but that was why he'd hired Robert Stock.

"Bob ran that division," says Ralph. "It was his world. I

brought in the concept of doing Chaps, I had the vision of
what I wanted to do. But I couldn't sit there and run it. He
did that alone."

Stock moved fast. By August he had shaped the first Chaps
collection, and hired Ivan Benjamin as his sales manager and
Larry Sussman as his assistant. Wholesale prices ranged from
$5 for basic jeans to $13 for chamois jeans.

"We started as a pants line with classic fabrics like tartans
and corduroys and made them into gentlemen's jeans," says
George Saffo, who joined Chaps for its second season. "Then
we broadened the collection to include clothing and knit shirts.
Everything was done with style. If Ralph had a fashion show
or a luncheon for the press, it was organized to the last detail.
The atmosphere at work . . . it was like going into a beautiful
apartment . . . it was always low-key, pressured but not frantic. I remember there was a Jewish holiday, and Ralph mentioned to me that he was leaving early that day but he never
said anything about the holiday. That's what it was like."

Saffo, soft-spoken, gentle, easy-going, would be the exception at Chaps. More in the Robert Stock mold was Ivan Benjamin. Benjamin had no illusions about the business he was in,
or his role in that business. Born in Philadelphia, Benjamin
had joined a coat manufacturing business when he was only
eighteen. First he pushed coats off the factory floor, sizing them,
shipping them. Only later would he be promoted into the
showroom. This meant Benjamin understood the grimy, stifling, backbreaking side of the business most retailers and customers never saw, and this understanding made him determined and knowing. Soon after quitting his job in the coat
business he went to work for Robert Stock at Chaps.

"My job was selling," says Benjamin. "I sold."

The team consisted of guys in their late twenties and early
thirties. Stock had an eye for color and fabric and style that
closely resembled that of Ralph Lauren. And because Stock
had once worked in sales, he valued sell-through as much as
he did aesthetics. This combination was a plus in an industry
that attracted its share of daydreamers. That Ralph Lauren
and Polo continued to gain status at retail could only rub off
in a positive way for Chaps.

Even the Chaps letterhead reflected the good things to come. At the top, printed in brown ink, was a man on horseback galloping past a group of cheering gold miners. "We open our collection September 13, 1971, at 40 West 55th Street," read an announcement Polo sent to its customers that summer. "The concept is classic good taste . . . Bob Stock has joined as head of Chaps, Ivan Benjamin is head of sales."

It was a modest enough beginning.

"People thought they were getting Polo at cheaper prices," says Robert Stock. "We put a pant line together, and then we had some suits and sportcoats. Then it got wild. The business started growing by leaps and bounds. Ralph did this, he did that, and nobody knew what was going on. I mean it was like we were all designers. Jeffrey Banks was there, we had Sal Cesarani, we had designer Gil Truedsson. None of us were business people, including Ralph, although Ralph had a very strong common sense level. The thing with Ralph is that when he was thirteen, he was forty. He was always older. He was an old soul. He had a good grasp of what was going on, but he never really wanted to know the financial side of the business. All we cared about was design, design, design. It got out of hand, the whole place. It grew too fast. Bad inventory problems. Things weren't shipped on time. Overhead was getting huge. I put on staff, Ralph put on a lot of staff. We weren't controlling any part of the business. We were just expanding because we thought anything we could do we could do well."

It looked that way. As soon as Chaps opened, Ivan Benjamin booked 70,000 pairs of jeans at $5 to $7 a pair. The customers included Bloomingdale's, Neiman-Marcus, Bonwit Teller, and Marshall Field. Fabulous business. Unbelievable. The letterhead had been prophetic: Chaps would be a gold mine.

The only thing left to do was make the jeans and ship them.

Somebody suggested a manufacturer in Massachusetts with a beautiful factory in northern New England. Knocking out 70,000 pairs would be easy, and they would do the entire job for only $1.75 a pair.

Chaps shipped its piece goods to Massachusetts and soon

the cut goods were ready for shipping to the factory. Add $2 for fabric, and total production costs amounted to $3.75, leaving a profit before expenses of $1.25 per pair. Not a big markup, but standard for the times.

Everything was terrific — until the manufacturer announced it now wanted $2.75 per pair to sew the jeans, not $1.75. If Ralph Lauren didn't like it, he could drive to Massachusetts, load those 70,000 fronts and 70,000 backs onto a truck, and find his own sewers.

That was a problem.

The orders were written; the wholesale price locked in at $5. If Chaps wanted to maintain its credibility with the stores it had to deliver as promised.

"The guys in Massachusetts were complaining that they were losing money," says Benjamin, "but what they were doing was what everybody was doing in those days. They saw this young guy, Ralph Lauren, a rising star, and they figured they'd pick his pocket."

Not even Ralph Lauren could pay $4.75 for a pair of jeans, sell those jeans for $5, and make a profit. All of those hours huddled over sketches, arguing over fabrics, planning inventories, had been wiped out by a failure at the production end.

There is nothing glamorous about production, nothing exciting about it. Most designers know absolutely nothing about it and care even less. Chaps would outsell and outperform its plan, and always it would lose money.

"It was a good concept," insists Benjamin. "It was very well received. Ralph Lauren's timing has always been excellent. This was a case in point. We had huge bookings."

Altogether Chaps would book orders totaling $685,000 that first season. There were the corduroys, the brushed denims, the brushed sateens and, as beautiful as they were, they were costing Ralph Lauren money.

"No doubt there was more talent than expertise," says Benjamin. "We were young guys with great ideas. We could conceive it, we could market it. But we didn't have any nittygritty. There are nuances to the apparel business which don't appear in a CPA manual. It's not like making bagels, where you press the button and they come out of the oven.

This is a business of timing. You have to peak the inventory
at a certain time of the year, bring your fabric in, be into the
bank early in the season because you are buying piece goods.
Later in the season you're long on cash and short on inventory
because everything has been shipped. These are the nuances,
and Bernstein didn't have a handle on them. Our financial
planning wasn't good and neither was our merchandise planning — we were often too long on the wrong stuff. We booked
more orders than we owned goods, and then we had to try to
cover those sales. Or, the goods would come in late.

"We could sell anything we wanted. But we couldn't get it
made, or we couldn't get it made on time. It wasn't so much
that stores wanted markdown money. It was more that we
couldn't get the product delivered on time. If your shipping
window is January 25 to March 25 complete, and you are still
shipping goods the first of May, some guys refuse to accept it.

"That's the kind of thing that transpired on a continual
basis. You have to understand that, unlike most companies,
Polo existed on design excellence. That was what Ralph Lauren was bringing to men's wear."

Benjamin was right about sales. Chaps's volume the first
year amounted to nearly $1.2 million. But it lost money be-
cause nobody paid enough attention to the overhead.

"Just because you have a hundred dollars in your pocket
doesn't mean you can afford to blow a hundred dollars," says
Benjamin. "You might have it today but owe it tomorrow. There
was nobody hip enough to realize this thing had the potential
of being great. Everybody was into the immediate gratification
of what they were doing."

By August of 1972 changes had to be made. Robert Stock
wasn't going anywhere; he owned 20 percent of the business.
That left Ivan Benjamin, director of sales. He was fired.

"We were all young," says Benjamin. "I made mistakes. I
had bad habits. I was doing my job, but it got complicated.
And the complications festered."

What went wrong?

Benjamin blames it on inexperience and poor management.

"Selling is more than laying a swatch on the table," he says.

"The sale starts not when you call the guy for an appointment. It starts when you write the order. Do you know how many things happen when you write an order in January to deliver in July? You have to get the orders booked, then made, then get it packed, then get it shipped. Then you have to get paid. All of these things are what constitute a sale. People get confused. They think an order is a sale. An order is only an order. A sale is when a check comes in after an invoice has been mailed out. . . . This segment of the business didn't exist properly at Polo in those days. Nobody could really execute the business like a business."

Robert Stock saw things were going bad but he didn't know how to fix them. The inventory was backed up. There were problems getting the bills paid. The company was making dozens of different products but having problems delivering any.

"It was a mess," says Robert Stock succinctly.

And there was nobody to straighten it out.

By early 1972 Ralph Lauren was one of the fastest-rising stars in the fashion industry. His comings and goings were chronicled by the trade press, his shows were covered by the big metropolitan dailies. The reviews were terrific. After he presented his men's collection at the "21" Club in March, the *Los Angeles Times* wrote, "The whole Polo concept easily could be the most prophetic fashion statement since Cardin's Edwardian Dandies of the 1960s . . . The refinement of the Polo collection reminds one of the English dukes and lords who come to London from their country estates every three years to buy a new suit." The lords and dukes who lived in Beverly Hills took notice. Ralph even overcame his fear of flying. He was so eager to express his point of view on how men and women should dress that he visited Chicago, Pittsburgh, San Francisco, Washington, D.C., often buzzing in and out in a single day.

Ralph was thirty-two. He didn't have time for self-doubts. His wife, Ricky, became accustomed to having him come home near midnight; he would try to make it up to her on weekends. There was a time for family, there was a time for work, and he was trying to balance them. The Laurens were on the move, too. The family left their two-bedroom apartment at 174 East 74th Street for a three-bedroom apartment in the same building. They then hired decorator Tom O'Toole, the same Tom O'Toole who had designed the Ralph Lauren store in Beverly Hills and the Polo showrooms.

The apartment was as handsome as it was eye-catching. First O'Toole created a hall entrance by blocking off the kitchen with a sliding door on which he hung an eighteenth-century Rajasthani cloth painting. Centered in the living room were a pair of sofas covered with white canvas. There was also a glass dining room table, French chairs, and a Welsh pine sideboard. O'Toole added floor-to-ceiling white shutters to cover the windows. The apartment was so impressive that the *New York Times Magazine* devoted two pages to it.

Ralph now began to dream even bigger dreams. He was no longer a kid from the Bronx with a line of luxurious ties and a cocky attitude. The big names from the women's wear industry, like Bill Blass and Geoffrey Beene, were designing men's wear, but they weren't giving it the detailing and excitement he brought to his clothes. For the first time, people were becoming interested in what Ralph Lauren had to say about fashion. He was approachable, he was fresh, he was good news copy.

He was also tired of being shackled to Norman Hilton. Ralph no longer made his clothes in the Hilton factory. He didn't ask Hilton's advice, and he didn't use the Hilton name to do business with the major department stores. The original $50,000 Hilton had invested in Polo had long since been repaid. Yet Hilton still owned half the business.

Norman Hilton stood for Norman Hilton clothing. Ralph Lauren stood for Polo Fashions, Ralph Lauren stood for Chaps, Ralph Lauren stood for his own collection of women's clothing. Ralph was an unknown when he first met Hilton. Now Ralph's clothes were on the front pages of *Daily News Record*, and in the small world of men's fashion he was a bit of a celebrity. Everything but his partnership with Norman Hilton had changed.

Norman Hilton would have to go. That spring, Michael Bernstein and Norman Hilton met for lunch at the Italian Pavillion, a New York restaurant just a few doors east of Polo's offices on West 55th Street. After the small talk, Bernstein came to the point.

How much, he asked, did Hilton want for his Polo stock?

About $750,000, Hilton responded.

Too much, said Bernstein. Polo's book value — its assets minus liabilities — didn't come close to that amount.

Hilton shrugged. He thought $750,000 was a nominal price to pay considering that he had put Ralph in business. Without him, Ralph might have spent the rest of his life selling ties for Beau Brummell. Hilton always acted on his gut instinct. That day his gut told him his stake in Polo was worth $750,000.

Besides, Hilton didn't want to sell.

After lunch Bernstein went back to Polo and discussed the offer with Ralph. Both felt Hilton's price was too high. What mattered was that both sides were talking. Norman Hilton didn't have a licensing arrangement with Ralph Lauren. He owned half the business. Forever. Nobody could force him to sell. However, once Hilton had time to think, he'd realize he'd have to sell eventually. Ralph wasn't worried about the price, either. Even without looking at the books, he knew Polo was doing good business. Every month new accounts shopped and bought the line, increasing both the company's distribution and its prestige. Polo was growing faster than he'd ever thought possible.

In a small, undercapitalized company, though, too much growth can be dangerous. More sales means buying more piece goods, more piece goods means taking more debt, more debt means more interest expense plus repayment of the principal. It leaves very little room for error — or for deadbeat accounts.

Polo Fashions, then, was at a crossroads. The future, based on past sales and earnings, looked good. But deciding how fast to expand and how much risk to assume was a critical issue. Ralph Lauren was growing as a designer and finding his customers. With the right promotion, the right marketing, and the right level of retail commitment, he could emerge as one of the industry leaders. Buying out Norman Hilton was certainly tempting. But the Hilton negotiations required energy and capital that might better have been invested elsewhere.

Ralph had other interests, too. He added staff, he traveled to Europe, he broadened his line. There were so many choices to make, so many judgments, that he didn't have time to think his way through each one. Everything was instinct. He looked, he said yes, he said no, it was gone, it was over. Sometimes he would look at a sketch or a swatch on Monday, say he loved it, and then decide two days later he hated it. Design assistant Jeffrey Banks learned the entire routine: "I love it . . . I love it . . . send it back."

Ralph's obsession with detail made Polo unique. It also meant that the company more often than not missed its delivery dates. Outsiders thought Polo Fashions was one of the hot-

test new designer companies in the industry. The insiders knew
better. Ralph Lauren's design talents didn't mean much if the
company couldn't produce and ship to the stores on time. Listen to Ron Cummings, who then worked in the Polo showroom.

"People don't realize what a nightmare it was. We would
sell beautiful concepts to the stores and they'd never be delivered, or they'd be delivered two days before Christmas. We'd
get returns, I mean, after all, what store is selling fall merchandise a week before Christmas? You'd have to be insane to
accept it.

"Sometimes if we delivered forty percent of what we sold
we were proud. There was a period when we had to eat more
than we sold. Let's say we sold a hundred suits; we'd have to
take ninety of them back because we couldn't deliver them on
time. The orders were cancelled. You can't make money like
that. When a store returns goods because they aren't delivered
on time, whose fault is it? Ralph spent so much time playing
around with the merchandise to make it perfect that it never
got delivered on time."

The late deliveries meant credits had to be issued to the
store accounts. It also meant Polo was stuck with old inventory
at a time it needed cash. Worse, the returns also damaged Polo's
credibility with Bankers Trust, now its factor. Bankers Trust
lent money on the basis of Polo's accounts receivable. If the
returns rendered those receivables worthless, Bankers Trust
had no collateral.

On paper, Michael Bernstein's job didn't require involving
himself with sales or production. Bernstein was hired as the
company's treasurer. But Polo was a small company, and
Bernstein was learning the business. The more he learned, the
more involved he became in all operations. Bernstein saw there
were problems. He also understood he had to learn what caused
them before he could fix them.

This meant there were constant fights over turf inside the
company. Few resented his interference more than Joe Barrato, executive director of sales and one of Ralph's first employees. Barrato didn't think Bernstein knew much about the
fashion business, and he didn't like being told how to sell men's
clothes.

"He was a guy in the wrong pew in the wrong church for the wrong reason," says Barrato. "He had no sensitivity to the business. But Ralph, because Michael was a boyhood friend and played basketball, really leaned on him."

Some of this resentment was sour grapes. Joe Barrato always believed that Ralph Lauren would one day offer him part of the company. Maybe not a big piece, but a piece. Something to show his appreciation. Bob Stock got a piece of Chaps, Michael Bernstein was going to get a piece of Polo. Yet somehow there was never anything left over for Joe Barrato. That rankled.

But more than Michael Bernstein bothered Joe Barrato. In Polo's early years, he and Ralph did everything together. They walked the streets after work, they shared dinners, they talked about their dreams. Later, as the business expanded, the atmosphere at Polo changed and Barrato began to think of some of the newcomers as toadies.

"There was an ass kissing thing that started to prevail there," he says. "Ralph and I were friends. I'd call him names in a loving way, because I had a tongue-in-cheek sense of humor with him that I regarded as very important to our relationship. If I saw something that I didn't like, I'd say, 'Ralph, cut the baloney. Will you please get down to the real world?'

"Suddenly he surrounded himself with people who were like Nixon in the White House. People began to protect him . . . It got strange. It was no longer a labor of love for me."

It showed. One day Bernstein decided he'd had enough of Barrato's attitude and fired him.

On the way out of Bernstein's office, Barrato saw design assistant Sal Cesarani.

"Sal, Bernstein just fired me," Barrato said.

"Joe, he can't do that," said Cesarani. "I'm going to go tell Ralph."

Ralph then called Bernstein and Barrato into his office and asked why they couldn't get along.

"It's just gotten impossible," said Barrato. "We can't work together."

"Look," said Ralph. "I need you both, and I want you two to work it out."

Like two kids, Bernstein and Barrato nodded their heads and said they would try. A few months later, though, Barrato resigned and went into partnership in a men's specialty store on Long Island.

"Michael and I never hit it off, and Michael knocked me out of there," says Barrato. "He was a strong personality, and Ralph didn't support me. I gave Ralph an ultimatum in so many words, and to this day, Ralph has never forgiven me."

Barrato's resignation rated only a small paragraph in *Daily News Record,* but insiders saw it as yet another sign of Michael Bernstein's increasing influence and power.

And in case they forgot, they could always read the memos he sent them.

• On September 22, 1972, Bernstein sent a memo to Barrato's successor, John Moore, reviewing all southeast accounts and analyzing whether an outside sales force which then covered that territory should be retained, or whether Polo should service those accounts with in-house salespeople.

• On October 9 he sent a memo to Polo's four production executives, Sidney Horowitz, Tom Kelly, Jerry Gold, and Al Weinberg, informing them that they were to complete an inventory within the next four days. Bernstein needed the inventory for submission to an accounting firm preparing a six-month audit.

• On October 23 he sent a memo to all Polo and Chaps personnel complaining that they were wasting money on messenger services. The company factory was on West 26th Street, its executive offices and showrooms were on West 55th Street, and there was constant traffic between the two locations. Thousands of dollars a year were being spent on messengers, and Bernstein wanted it stopped.

• On October 23 again, Bernstein sent out a memo to all company personnel regarding the use of expensive sample garments. Bernstein wanted somebody assigned to count and inventory samples as they came into the warehouse on West 26th Street to prevent them from disappearing.

• Also on October 23 Bernstein sent a memo to Sidney Horowitz, Tom Kelly, and Jerry Gold. This time Bernstein wanted to set up a meeting to discuss pricing current and future product lines for the men's and women's collections.

"When I brought Michael Bernstein in he had a job to do," says Ralph Lauren. "His job was to run this place. And the others had to work for him. I wasn't going to sit in on every meeting. I left that to Michael Bernstein. Whomever I like, I like. Michael Bernstein would come to me and say, 'I'm going to fire this guy, what do you think?'

"I'd say, 'I think he's good,' but if Michael said he was no good I would have to take his word. I had my feelings, and I would hope he'd respect my feelings, and we'd discuss it. But in the end that was his role."

Call it overload. Bernstein oversaw the staff, watched the sales, analyzed piece goods purchases, managed the company's finances. Those were demanding, full-time jobs, even for experienced professionals. What made it all the more demanding was that Polo's sales were in the process of increasing from $3.8 million for the year ended March 31, 1972, to nearly $8 million for the year ended March 31, 1973.

Nobody in the garment industry plans for growth like that. It's too much, too fast.

To make matters even more complex, the negotiations with Norman Hilton began to get serious in the fall of 1972.

The talks were tough because Norman Hilton held almost all the cards. He liked being partners with Ralph Lauren, and he didn't need the money. This meant he didn't have to set a reasonable price. Polo was turning out to be a pretty smart investment. What he really wanted to do was hang on and enjoy it.

Norman Hilton, seller, was a man who lacked incentive.

"I didn't want to go," says Hilton. "I never wanted to leave Ralph . . . but he wanted me out. I recognized that I owned half the corporation but I didn't own half of Ralph's brain. There was no law that said he had to work for that company. It was his talent. His talent was the whole thing. When he wanted me out, what was I going to do? I fought him as hard as I could, but if I fought him too hard, he could have walked off.

"I said, 'Ralph, I don't want to go.'

"And he said, and these are his words, 'It's torture being

a partner to somebody you don't want to be a partner with.'

"You have to understand something. I have nothing against him. Since we've split up he's been a gentleman. I like Ralph. He's got tremendous charm and all those things. But one of his major characteristics is greed. He is one of the greediest SOBs you'll ever meet in your life. I don't say it in a pejorative way. But he's got a tremendously acquisitive nature. He wants money. Now, that is greed. The seven cardinal sins are pride, anger, greed, lust, envy, gluttony, and sloth."

Finally, at the end of December, Norman Hilton sold his stock. He settled for $633,000 instead of the $750,000 he wanted.

Norman Hilton later used that money to build himself a vacation home on Sea Island, Georgia. This is the house Ralph built me, he would tell his guests, smiling. It was a hollow joke. If Hilton had remained a partner in Polo, today he could own thirty houses on Sea Island.

On December 28, 1972, the papers were signed and Ralph Lauren became the sole owner of Polo Fashions. The deal worked this way: Ralph paid Norman Hilton $150,000 in cash and signed notes for the remaining $483,000. Those notes called for quarterly payments of $40,000 plus interest of 7 percent.

The price reflected one half of the company's book value, then estimated at $980,000, plus a $150,000 premium.

Who determined Polo's book value? The two sides doing the negotiating. Polo's biggest asset was designer Ralph Lauren. The company owned a shirt factory in Mount Vernon, some pine furniture in the showrooms, and the value of its own good name. It was not worth anything approaching $1 million at the end of 1972.

Fact was, the company coffers were so bare that Ralph had to borrow the $150,000 in cash he needed from J. P. Maguire, a New York factoring company. Bankers Trust refused to advance Ralph Lauren another cent until it was repaid the $135,000 Polo already owed. Indeed, Polo's finances were so shaky that Ralph Lauren was fortunate Michael Bernstein found any backers at all. Certainly Bankers Trust was surprised, especially when J. P. Maguire also agreed to assume responsibility for all of Polo's unsecured debt.

"Bankers Trust was very concerned," says David Goldberg, the Maguire executive in charge of the Polo account.
"They probably thought we were crazy. You couldn't get into
this thing without thinking your way through what you'd be
liable for at the peak. It's one thing to take out an existing
loan, as we did with the hundred and thirty-five thousand owed
Bankers Trust. But we knew that loan, now our loan, wouldn't
be repaid unless we took Polo Fashions through several successful seasons. That meant we would have to finance inventory buildups, which would mean the loan was going to go up
before it came down. So we had to develop an operating budget based on cash flow so that we knew what we would be in
for before it was all over."

The way Goldberg saw it, Polo had problems, but they
were manageable problems. Bring in the right accountants, establish better controls, cut the overhead, and move Ralph Lauren out of manufacturing and into licensing.

"I don't want to say he would have gone under," says
Goldberg. "There were others who had interests that would
have been well served by keeping Ralph alive. Norman Hilton
had an interest, because he was holding Ralph's notes. Bloomingdale's, too, made it clear they were going to stand behind
him. Bloomingdale's support was important, because it showed
us that somebody in fashion cared about him."

Goldberg knew that the sales would be good. What he didn't
know was whether Polo could control its overhead, maintain
its margins, and start making its deliveries on time.

"It was a company out of control," Goldberg says.

Indeed, throughout 1972 Polo was late paying its federal
withholding taxes for its 200 employees. The sums weren't big,
no more than $20,000 for each three-month period. Yet Polo
was so desperate for cash that Ralph insisted on using whatever money was available to buy piece goods. The result was
that Polo was assessed penalties for late payments.

As a designer, Ralph Lauren had a banner year in 1972.
His men's wear earned good reviews, and his first complete
women's collection had been a smash with both retailers and
the customers.

As a businessman, though, he found the year a nightmare.

Polo booked more orders than it could ship, and it shipped most of what it made late. There were also massive returns, and inventories were out of control. Even the good news created problems. Norman Hilton had been bought out, but in operating terms that meant Polo had added more than $600,000 in debt, debt which had to be paid every quarter.

There was the image, and there was the reality. The image of Polo Fashions was that of a well-run business making expensive, tweedy clothes for the landed gentry. The reality was that Polo was a company losing control. Gradually, piece goods suppliers became leery about shipping more fabric on credit, favored contractors refused to do additional work without payment.

The only one who didn't seem to know how badly the situation had deteriorated was Ralph Lauren, owner.

▶ ▶ ▶ 8

It's said clothes reflect the way we think about ourselves as well as how we want others to see us. Ralph now owned all of Polo, and both his exuberance and his optimism showed in the men's collection he presented in March 1973. A year earlier, he had rented a room at the posh "21" Club to introduce his fall line. This year he was more modest. The invitations he sent requested buyers to drop by his showroom on March 21 at 12:30 P.M. He would serve lunch, and he would also show his first licensed shoe collection, a line manufactured by the Kayser-Roth company.

Ralph himself dressed in a pin-striped black suit, a white shirt, and a black tie. *New York Times* writer Anne-Marie Schiro seemed amused if not completely convinced. "How long has it been since designers dressed that way?" she asked her readers.

It had probably been twenty years, maybe longer. Ralph had turned back the history pages and found a mood and a sensibility he instinctively understood. He did not copy what he saw button-by-button; what he did was translate a mood. Ralph Lauren was fantasizing about black-tie dinners and a New York that existed only in the columns of Cholly Knickerbocker. Ralph even created a special night-on-the-town outfit: black trousers, a white piqué vest, a striped shirt, and a black sweater-jacket. Wear it while listening to Bobby Short play the piano at the Cafe Carlyle, he urged.

"The words he uses to describe his fall collection are 'dapper,' 'neat,' and 'traditional,'" wrote Schiro. "All those words apply to a double-breasted gray flannel suit with matching vest ('because double-breasted jackets usually don't look good when they're open'). The suit is shown with a white shirt, a pin-dotted tie and even a white handkerchief in the pocket, but there is nothing stodgy about the total effect. Bone buttons update the look, and so do the brown suede shoes.

"What really embodies the spirit of Polo '73 is an outfit Lauren calls the 'Vanderbilt.' The jacket, in Donegal tweed, has a back belt and bellows pockets. It's worn over a matching vest, with white flannel trousers. There's even a collarpin on the shirt. You just know that the gentleman wearing it belongs to a private club and drives a Rolls-Royce (or at least wants to give that impression). . . . For the Vanderbilt who has everything, there's even a leather slip-on with a gold buckle for monogramming." It was a bold, grand look, completely contrary to the dreary, unimaginative clothes other men's wear designers were making, and the critics applauded.

So much for the fashion side of the business.

From a financial standpoint, 1973 started badly for Polo and rapidly got worse. Sales for January and February fell behind plan because key contractors refused to make and ship merchandise unless they were paid cash. As a result, Polo's volume was $340,000 less than expected. Chaps was also doing miserably. Its sales were behind plan by $125,000. Even Polo's own factory mutinied. In March the Andrew Shirt Company refused to release 400 dozen shirts to four key accounts until its invoices were paid. This at a time when Ralph Lauren was showing "Vanderbilt" suits.

The situation deteriorated so quickly that Polo's board called a special meeting on March 12. Part of the agenda that day was devoted to commissions Ralph received on the sale of certain Polo items. Those commissions were in addition to Ralph's regular salary, and they amounted to $129,000 for the year ended December 31, 1972. Embarrassing as it was, Polo couldn't afford to pay Ralph the money. Instead of cash, the board offered him a promissory note.

Ralph wasn't the only one growing concerned. Polo's factor, J. P. Maguire, had invested on the basis that goods would be shipped and that deliveries would improve. Frank Beame, president of J. P. Maguire, wanted to know what was going wrong, and he asked for a meeting with Ralph to talk things over. Eight days after Polo's board meeting, Beame, Dave Goldberg, who managed the Polo account at J. P. Maguire, Ralph, and Michael Bernstein gathered for lunch at Jimmy's Restaurant.

Beame and Goldberg outlined the problems as they saw them. The clothes were being delivered too late. The quality control was terrible. Stores were sending back truckloads of merchandise, including 8,500 pairs of Chaps pants in the last five months. Worse, Ralph continued to ship accounts with bad Dun & Bradstreet credit ratings. This meant Polo's receivables were suspect because they were largely uncollectible.

Frank Beame wanted explanations, and he wanted action. If Ralph expected Maguire to continue investing in Polo, Ralph was going to have to show some good faith himself.

"We asked Ralph up to the table," says Dave Goldberg. "Ralph had to be committed and he had to show us the ways in which he was committed."

Stepping up to the table for Ralph meant handing over his personal savings passbook as collateral. (Maguire already had Ralph's personal guarantee. The passbook arrangement meant that the cash in that account was pledged specifically to Maguire and could not be attached by any other possible debtors.) In the account was over $100,000.

Polo Fashions was a business.

But the way Frank Beame saw it, it was a personal business. Beame would suffer if Polo filed for bankruptcy. He thought he'd sleep better at night knowing Ralph Lauren would bleed, too. Too often in the garment center owners declared bankruptcy and walked away, leaving their creditors to fight over the scraps. Beame wasn't interested in scraps.

Dave Goldberg also insisted on sending his own people into Polo's administrative offices on West 26th Street to evaluate what he suspected were major bookkeeping problems. So jumbled were the accounts that Goldberg later determined Polo had $600,000 worth of receivables on its books that were virtually uncollectible. In other words, Polo had shipped goods valued at more than half-a-million dollars to stores that couldn't pay for them.

Ralph was now feeling the pressure, too. Michael Bernstein had begun sending him memos detailing how creditors were squeezing the company. The memos made Ralph ill. Why send him memos when he didn't have the time or the know-how to fix the problems? Ralph didn't send Bernstein memos itemizing the problems he had choosing between swatches of light blue and royal blue. For the first time, Ralph began to have trouble sleeping at night.

Once the pressure started to build, it seemed as though

there was no relief. Until now, Ralph had concentrated almost exclusively on only what interested him personally. That meant buying the right fabrics, working with his design staff, building a reputation for high-quality merchandise. Those were his concerns. Financing, credit obligations, cash flow didn't interest him. Money was not an end in itself, so he didn't worry about it the way he worried over a silhouette or a pocket.

Things went from bad to worse, and by the end of March, nearly three-quarters of a million dollars of merchandise that should have been shipped was still sitting in contractor workrooms.

Again, nobody can plan for a company to more than double its sales growth. When a business gets that hot it becomes a runaway train, beautiful and dangerous. Everybody loves the speed but nobody knows if the brakes still work. In the middle of this, Bernstein began to negotiate a new two-year contract for himself. Ralph had promised him 10 percent of the business when he joined in July 1971; now that Norman Hilton was gone, Bernstein wanted his stock.

In early April, Ralph gave it to him. At a bargain price. Ralph Lauren still trusted Michael Bernstein, still believed in his abilities, still considered him a vital part of the company.

That is why he asked Bernstein for only $40,000 for his 10 percent stake. Remember, fewer than sixteen weeks earlier, Ralph Lauren had paid $630,000 for 50 percent of the company, establishing the company's worth, at least in his mind, at $1.2 million. A 10 percent share should therefore have been valued at $120,000, not $40,000. Bernstein's cost had been discounted by about two-thirds. Better still, Bernstein was also given a new two-year employment contract, which specified an annual salary of $60,000 a year, nearly twice the $35,000 he'd been paid less than two years earlier.

It was a gracious offer. With only $8,000 down and a promissory note, Bernstein bought the stock. Ralph knew that Michael Bernstein didn't have $120,000 in cash; what mattered was that Ralph had promised Michael the stock, and now Michael would have it.

Ralph Lauren and Michael Bernstein were friends from the old neighborhood. Now they would move into the new neighborhoods together.

At least that was the dream.

Part of the uncertainty at Polo was that nobody knew the exact state of the company's finances. In January and February there had been several discussions with the investment bankers Drexel Burnham Lambert about a private placement to raise additional capital. Drexel was then a client of Polo's legal firm, Marshall, Bratter, Greene, Allison & Tucker, and Ralph had formed a relationship with Mark Kaplan, Drexel's president. But before Kaplan could arrange a private placement he needed to know how much money Polo was making or losing.

Dave Goldberg agreed to put together a pro forma financial statement for the year ended March 31. He finished in May and sent a copy to Ralph.

The numbers Ralph saw told a story only a liquidator could love.

Polo, despite increasing its sales to nearly $8 million against $3.8 million in fiscal 1972, had lost $10,000 compared to a $35,000 profit the year earlier. Worse still, the company now had a negative shareholders' equity of $45,000. That meant all of Polo's retained earnings from the earlier years had been wiped out, as well as all the company's working capital.

Every penny Ralph Lauren had invested in the company was gone. Also at risk was the money in the savings book he had given to J. P. Maguire a few months earlier.

More frightening than the losses were the debts. Polo now owed well over $500,000, including the $433,000 due Norman Hilton. If any of the major creditors, including L. Greif & Brothers, a division of Genesco then making Polo's line, insisted on immediate payment, the company would have been forced to file for bankruptcy protection.

The day that Michael Bernstein saw Dave Goldberg's pro forma statement for the first time, he walked into Ralph Lauren's office looking, as Ralph would later describe, "white as a ghost." Chaps had lost $200,000, Bernstein said. It was a catastrophe.

The news shocked Ralph, because he had thought Chaps was going to make money that year. But what really stunned him was Michael Bernstein's astonishment at the losses.

"You're running the business," said Ralph. "I don't understand why you don't know. You're in charge of the finances. You're involved with the whole thing. I can't believe that you don't know, that it is a shock. I don't know why you are coming to me with it, because I don't have anything to do with that end of the business."

Bernstein responded that the company's overhead was inflated by too many people on the payroll who weren't earning their keep, people Ralph had insisted on hiring.

This was not what Ralph wanted to hear. If Michael Bernstein didn't know whether the company was making or losing money, why was Ralph paying him to be the company's financial officer?

Altogether, Polo's total exposure (unsecured debt) to J. P. Maguire amounted to $697,000. That was a lot of money for a company Polo's size, and it raised questions. What about the sales projections Michael Bernstein had prepared prior to the Norman Hilton buyout? The way it looked now, Ralph Lauren had paid $633,000 for a company that was nearly bankrupt.

"When I bought out Hilton, Michael Bernstein laid out the figures," says Ralph. "He said, 'Ralph, we're okay, here's our projections, and based on our figures, after we pay off Norman we'll be in good shape.' I went to the lawyer and he asked the same questions. Michael was the guy with the numbers. I wasn't sitting in on the projections. I could say, 'I know this is great, this will be strong, I know how to design it,' but I can't sit and work on everything."

The pro forma statement prepared by Dave Goldberg cost Bernstein his job. Ralph had already asked his oldest brother, Lenny Lauren, to join Polo as vice-president and manager in March 1973. (Jerry Lauren, a men's wear designer, would join Polo later; today he is senior vice-president of men's design.) Lenny Lauren didn't have any background in the apparel industry. He was an experienced jewelry box and display manufacturer. Ralph, though, needed somebody nearby he could trust, and he reached out to Lenny.

"Ralph told me, 'Come in and find your own level.' I couldn't. I was too busy putting out fires," says Lenny.

In early June Ralph walked into Michael Bernstein's office

and talked to him for about forty-five minutes. Bernstein should have known the company was in this much trouble, Ralph said. Now Polo was broke. Finally Ralph turned to Bernstein and told him he was fired.

Michael Bernstein didn't want to leave.

He had worked too hard for too long. Besides he had a new two-year employment contract. "You can't fire me," he replied. "You have no business without me."

The problems were Ralph's fault, not his, Bernstein continued. Ralph spent too much on piece goods; Ralph refused to finish the collections so they could be delivered on time; Ralph added a big staff, inflating the overhead. Ralph Lauren was the president of the company, owned 90 percent of the business, and had been told for the last six months that Polo was having problems.

If Ralph didn't like the way he did the job, why had Ralph just given him a new two-year contract? Why had he sold him the stock?

It didn't make sense, Bernstein said. But on June 8, Michael Bernstein's name appeared on Polo's payroll for the last time.

It was more than an ordinary firing.

Since joining the company two years earlier, Michael Bernstein had become one of Ralph's closest friends. They socialized together, their wives were friendly, their extended families knew and approved of each other. They were partners.

Firing Michael Bernstein involved more than business.

It was personal.

The first two weeks of June 1973 were anxiety producing for everybody at Polo Fashions, everybody, that is, except for Sidney Horowitz, the production manager Michael Bernstein had wanted to replace two years earlier.

Horowitz was so pleased Bernstein had been fired that he put a copy of Bernstein's termination notice in his safe deposit box.

It was still there, next to his most private and intimate papers, when Sidney Horowitz died almost thirteen years later.

Ralph was under terrific pressure, then, throughout 1973. Yet not only did he work well, but his reviews that year were among the best he has ever received. Further, in June Ralph won his second Coty Award for men's wear. "They always used to announce the winners at the end of the day on a Thursday," says designer Jeffrey Banks. "Ralph was delirious, really happy and excited. He was really determined it would be a fabulous show, too, because by then he didn't like the first Coty show he'd given back in 1971.

"As happy as he was, the next day, Friday, he couldn't meet the payroll. It was pouring outside, and Ralph came to work in jeans and a chambray shirt. Near lunchtime, he said, 'I've got to go home and change now. I'm having lunch with Marvin Traub.' [Traub was then president of Bloomingdale's; he is now chairman.]

"The reason he was having lunch with Marvin was that he'd asked Bloomingdale's to advance him money on fall merchandise. This was June, and that merchandise wouldn't be shipped until July or August. Anyway, Ralph went home in the pouring rain, and changed into a suit. I went with him.

"The interesting thing was that in the cab from his apartment to Bloomingdale's, Ralph didn't talk about Marvin or not being able to make payroll. What he did talk about was what would be great for the Coty show. Anybody else would be in hives, would be dying. And here was Ralph saying, 'I want it to be *Great Gatsby,* I want it to be fabulous . . .'

"So we discussed doing a black-and-white presentation, which is what we ended up doing. We used projections of Robert Montgomery and Cary Grant and we had models walking out in black cashmere turtlenecks, white jodhpurs, and carrying polo mallets. We even had white flannel pants with a white cashmere polo coat. We had shoes made in England and Cartier ivory cigarette holders and it cost a fortune.

"What was really amazing was that Ralph was that confident. He knew he would get over that hump. And at lunch, Marvin said he would make an exception and advance Ralph the money he needed. Ralph made his payroll with the check Bloomingdale's gave him."

Not all the problems would be fixed that quickly. In August, Michael Bernstein filed suit against Polo Fashions, Ralph

Lauren, and Ezra Levin, one of Polo's attorneys, in the Supreme Court of the state of New York.

Among his charges:

• Ralph Lauren and Polo Fashions, without just cause, had fired him only a few months after he signed a new two-year contract, thereby causing him to suffer damages valued at $108,000 plus the loss of fringe benefits.

• Ralph Lauren had taken excessive compensation and reimbursement for expenses; failed to adequately supervise the production of Polo's line; hired incompetent employees; failed to do adequate research before bringing out new products, and sold merchandise to favored customers who were bad credit risks. These mistakes, Bernstein continued, so damaged the company that the value of his stock had depreciated to virtually zero.

• That as an officer of the company, Michael Bernstein had personally guaranteed certain loans and advances made by J. P. Maguire. Because of Ralph Lauren's incompetence, Bernstein now faced the possibility of having to make payments on those guarantees.

• Ralph Lauren and Ezra Levin had conspired to deprive him of his stock by encouraging him to sign a stock purchase agreement that did not adequately protect his rights.

Michael Bernstein and Ralph Lauren had been friends as kids and grown even closer as partners. Now that was over. Bernstein demanded Polo Fashions pay him $108,000 in lost salary plus the value of his fringe benefits; he sought the same amount from Ralph Lauren. More, he wanted Polo to return the $8,000 he had paid for his stock, as well as payments made on the $32,000 promissory note he had given Polo. He also requested indemnification against any payments he might have to make to J. P. Maguire & Co. because of personal guarantees he had signed while working at Polo.

There was more. The way Michael Bernstein looked at it, his Polo stock would have been worth $1.2 million in 1975. So he asked for that, too. (Where did the $1.2 million figure come from? Hard to say. Polo stock was worthless in August 1973.)

Later Bernstein filed a separate, amended complaint. It

read like a filing in a divorce case. Not only did it portray Ralph Lauren as an incompetent, but it also questioned his integrity.

Ralph Lauren had used company funds to pay for the decoration of his home and to put his father and his personal maid on the corporate books — even though they performed no services for Polo, Bernstein alleged. Ralph also used company money to buy personal gifts, pay for a pleasure trip to Barbados, and buy his wife a fur coat, Bernstein contended.

Then, in his sworn 473-page deposition, Michael Bernstein gave his version of what had happened to Polo and who was to blame.

The way Michael Bernstein saw it, it was all Ralph Lauren's fault.

Ralph Lauren took excessive compensation at a time when the company couldn't pay its payroll taxes on time, Bernstein said. Ralph Lauren put in for business expenses over and above the norm. Worse still, Ralph Lauren didn't know anything about merchandising or marketing clothes, and he made bad deals with retailers on the basis of general feelings and whims. This resulted in overproduction of inventory. Ralph also hired the wrong people, people who didn't have the necessary technical competence to make the clothes.

Why didn't Michael Bernstein point this out when he worked at Polo? He did, Bernstein said, but Ralph refused to hire adequate executive help in the areas of accounting, production, sales, or in any other facet of the company that was recommended to him. Ralph also insisted on selling merchandise to customers who were technically bankrupt, Bernstein continued, which meant the company sustained thousands of dollars in bad debts.

Not only was Ralph an incompetent businessman, Bernstein added, but he didn't know much about introducing new products either. Ralph had pushed Polo into women's wear, imports, and sportswear without knowing how big the markets would be for those clothes, without knowing which contractors could make them for him at a profit, and without knowing if the stores would buy them. Market research? Ralph never did any, Bernstein complained.

"The facts prove, and the financial statements prove, and the losses prove, that in every category that Mr. Lauren controlled he did not know what he was doing as far as owning and running this business," Bernstein concluded.

Anybody reading Bernstein's suit, his amended complaint, and his deposition would think Ralph Lauren fortunate to own two pencils and a tin cup.

Ralph's lawyers then filed their own charges. Michael Bernstein, they alleged, had improperly authorized a payment of $2,900 toward the purchase by Polo of a 1973 Chevrolet Impala. Although the car was registered in the name of Polo Fashions, it was basically Michael's car. The lawyers also alleged that Michael Bernstein had improperly authorized the payment of $2,900 for two life insurance policies that would have benefited Bernstein's wife.

(Considering the seriousness of Bernstein's suit, these counterclaims didn't amount to much. At Polo, Bernstein was managing a business doing nearly $8 million a year in sales. If he wanted to steal, he certainly had access to more than $6,000. Michael Bernstein was not a thief.)

The case dragged on. Arguments were made. Appeals were filed. Judgments were handed down.

In 1978 Ralph changed law firms, dismissing Marshall, Bratter, Greene, Allison & Tucker, and hiring Skadden, Arps, Slate, Meagher & Flom, a law firm that would later become famous specialists in corporate takeovers. Among its partners was Ralph's friend Mark Kaplan, the former head of Drexel Burnham Lambert.

Two years later, in July 1980, the case was finally settled. After nearly seven years of litigation, Polo agreed to pay Michael Bernstein $175,000. .

Who won?

The lawyers, mostly. Ralph's legal fees were considerably higher than the settlement figure. This may well have been true for Michael Bernstein; he's not talking. One way of looking at the settlement is to say that Bernstein received the full amount of his two-year contract plus interest. He received nothing for the value of his stock, but when Bernstein was fired, Polo's stock was worthless.

When Michael Bernstein speaks about Ralph Lauren these

days he sounds wistful. (On several occasions Bernstein came to the phone to chat with this writer, but he would never grant a regular interview.) Part of that disappointment derives perhaps from knowing he was once a partner in what later became a major business. Part also reflects the fact that he was asked to do too much. The accounting challenges alone were daunting; then he became involved in sales, shipping, production. Later, when the problems intensified, he had no management team to help him. The memos he sent Ralph Lauren may have been calls for help as much as anything else. Indeed, the eventual turnaround at Polo resulted from a team effort.

Finally, some of Bernstein's regret may reflect the fact that Ralph was a part of his childhood, a part that made their adult relationship special. Bernstein's firing and the lawsuit that followed reduced all to a dreary accounting of money made and lost. It was not supposed to end this way for two guys from the Bronx who had once played basketball together.

Nineteen seventy-three was also the year Hollywood beckoned.

From the moment Broadway producer David Merrick announced in 1972 that he intended to remake *The Great Gatsby* for Paramount Pictures, Hollywood started buzzing. Much of the excitement had to do with the casting: Robert Redford as Jay Gatsby, Mia Farrow as Daisy Buchanan, Bruce Dern as Tom Buchanan, and Sam Waterston as Nick Carraway. Part of the excitement came, too, from the knowledge that this movie would influence the way people dressed and how they spent their money. One manufacturer, the Robert Bruce company of Philadelphia, even licensed the "Gatsby" name and created a sportswear line called Gatsby.

In March 1973 Paramount asked Theoni Aldredge to design all the costumes. This meant overseeing the making and selection of hundreds of outfits; Mia Farrow alone required thirty changes. Aldredge, closely associated with Joe Papp, had already worked on eleven films, and she knew immediately that she needed help with the men's clothes.

To her everlasting regret, she turned to Ralph Lauren. Today she describes him simply as "a worm."

Aldredge chose Ralph because his clothes best reflected

the 1920s and Jay Gatsby's style. One of the first suits Ralph ever designed was made from white linen and cut with a belted back and pleated trousers — much like the famous pink linen suit Robert Redford would wear in the movie. Not only did Ralph understand the clothes F. Scott Fitzgerald so precisely described in his novel, he understood the life-style Gatsby tried to imitate. Remember, as a salesman Ralph didn't drive any car, he drove a Morgan. He didn't sell any tie, he sold the widest, most expensive ties in the country. (Ralph's alter ego was not Jay Gatsby, a gangster who drifted through life deceiving people.)

Luck, too, played a part. Sal Cesarani, one of Ralph's design assistants, had earlier sold two Ralph Lauren Shaker-knit sweaters to Theoni Aldredge for use in a Broadway show. When Cesarani heard that Aldredge would be designing the clothes for *Gatsby*, he called and asked her to come to the Polo showroom at 40 West 55th Street and see Ralph's men's collection.

Aldredge arrived, and after she had looked through Ralph's workroom she was impressed. Hanging by the dozen were the wide-lapeled, luxuriously cut suits she had envisioned. Ralph understood the look, the sleeveless sweaters, the white flannels with blue pinstripes, pin- and round-collared shirts, the two-toned shoes. She talked to Ralph and Sal Cesarani and Buffy Birrittella, and she then offered Ralph the opportunity to make the men's clothes for the movie.

"I discovered Ralph was already so into the period," Theoni Aldredge told one interviewer that year. "I fell in love with everything I saw. We've only had to make minor adjustments. We've closed the side vents, for example. And the toes of the two-tone, wing tip oxfords were more pointed in the Gatsby era. What we show has got to be good to the 1973 eye."

Her offer to Ralph to work on the movie seemed too good to be true. Everybody associated *Gatsby* with finely tailored men's clothes, and already the big department stores were running *Gatsby* promotions. Not only was there Gatsby's famous pink suit, but there was a terrific Fitzgerald scene in which Gatsby, while showing Daisy Buchanan and Nick Carraway his wardrobe, flings dozens of linen shirts into the air, shirts so beautiful that Daisy bursts into tears. Mort Gordon, writing in an issue of *Men's Wear* devoted entirely to *Gatsby*, reported that

manufacturers were already using "Gatsby" to "describe merchandise geared for the New Establishment, or the twenty-five-
to forty-year-old who doesn't want to look like his father or
his kid brother." It was romantic and it was carefree. It was
also expensive and therefore respectable.

Nobody better understood the New Establishment than
Ralph Lauren, who repeatedly described his clothes as "the
old money look." Polo Fashions was built on redefining the
Old Establishment, the establishment whose tastes had been
shaped in the 1920s and 1930s.

"The day Ralph got the movie he was the most emotional
I've ever seen him," says Jeffrey Banks, then one of Ralph's design assistants. "He hugged Sal. I don't think Theoni realized
Ralph was a force to be reckoned with. She thought he would
be this tailor and make what she directed. But he had his
opinions and his taste level and he knew what he wanted to do."

Working on a project as big as *The Great Gatsby* meant
dressing not only the leading actors but dozens of extras as
well. For Ralph Lauren this meant producing scores of shirts,
pants, and suits on command. He even sent Sal Cesarani to
the Paramount Studio in Los Angeles, where Cesarani first
studied the costume books in Paramount's library. Then, in
Edith Head's studio, Cesarani and Theoni Aldredge took Robert Redford's and Bruce Dern's measurements: waist, arms,
inseam, chest . . . Cesarani and Aldredge also worked their
way through the script together, with Aldredge specifying the
styles and the colors she wanted in each scene. Most of the
actual fittings were done at Polo.

Aldredge would always have the final say. If she decided
she didn't like a yellow tie, the color was changed. Those choices
were hers, and Ralph was there to execute her needs. Yet the
label in every jacket was Polo; the clothes themselves looked as
though they came straight from Polo's latest collection. Indeed, within months Bloomingdale's was selling Polo's pale
cream and off-white suits, light-colored silk jackets, and white
flannel pants. Done right, *Gatsby* would mean big sales at retail.

"The trick is not to look like Polo but the period," Ralph
told *GQ* reporter Bill Gale in March 1974. "In 1925, shirts
were cut fuller and collars were shorter and not spread so wide,

and they took a smaller, knotted, unlined tie. Suit jackets had narrower lapels, no vents, and were slightly shorter. Compare a suit of that period with one of mine today, and you see the difference. Still, you'd need a trained eye to see the difference." Not everybody needed a trained eye, however. One New York actor wrote Ralph a scathing letter complaining about what he considered to be the lack of authentic detail. Paramount, he complained, hadn't insisted that the actors have period haircuts. The actors should have worn pocket watches, not wristwatches. And they should have had celluloid collars, not starched collars. He was on the set in Rhode Island, working, he continued, and he didn't understand why these things hadn't been done right.

He would be the exception, not the rule. For most viewers, the clothes Ralph created mirrored the clothes they expected to see on the screen. Professionally, Theoni Aldredge had good reason to be satisfied with Ralph Lauren's contribution.

On a personal level she was furious because she felt Ralph Lauren was claiming credit for her work. Every time she picked up a newspaper or a magazine she read that Ralph was designing, not making, the clothes for *The Great Gatsby*.

Typical was an item which ran in *Daily News Record* on May 25, accompanied by a picture of Robert Redford. The trade paper reported that actors Redford, Bruce Dern, and Sam Waterston had reported for their first fittings at Polo's New York offices in preparation for their roles in *The Great Gatsby*. Ralph had a white flannel suit waiting for Redford, *DNR* said, one of fifteen different outfits Redford would be wearing in the picture. Quoting a company spokesman, *DNR* then added, "Lauren will design hundreds of costumes for *GG* actors."

Aldredge blamed Ralph for this article.

For despite her efforts, Aldredge could not make anybody understand that she was the men's wear designer and Ralph Lauren was only the manufacturer. Aldredge had even stipulated in Ralph Lauren's contract that he would not receive a designer credit for his contribution. And indeed, the credits inside a twenty-four-page, color *Great Gatsby* souvenir book read as follows: "Costumes by Theoni V. Aldredge; women's wardrobe executed by Barbara Matera Ltd.; men's wardrobe by

Ralph Lauren." Polo Fashions was paid for the clothes it made for *Gatsby,* but Ralph Lauren did not earn a design fee.

"Theoni said, 'I'm the designer of the movie. I came to you because your clothes have that sense of what I need and I naturally have to change them to make them work for the movie,'" says Sal Cesarani, "Yet *Daily News Record* and the rest of the press gave Ralph the design credit for the men's wardrobe. This wasn't the most important thing in Ralph's life, but at the same time, it was. He was getting recognition as the guy who launched the Great Gatsby look. It made him whole. His clothes exemplified *Gatsby,* it was all the things he believed in, and it rounded him out."

It also did wonders for his career. For despite the Coty Awards, the store on Rodeo Drive, and the support from Bloomingdale's, the name Ralph Lauren was little known to the general public. Now he was getting national exposure.

"I was doing Gatsby long before *The Great Gatsby* came out," says Ralph Lauren. "That's what I did. It was glamorous. When people couldn't understand what my clothes were about I talked about Gatsby — it was the era of the jackets with belted backs, of flannel suits. It wasn't the story as much as it was a look. Before Theoni ever came here I was doing flannels and things like that. When she came to my office she could see it. That's the reason she picked me: she saw the white flannels and the stripes I was doing. It was a natural. And she loved what she saw.

"I asked her, 'Am I eligible to be part of this, can I get an Academy Award? Can I be part of the union?' She refused. I spoke to her. She saw me as someone breathing down her neck . . . I don't know why. The movie got a lot of publicity, and what I was doing was getting more recognition.

"The men's fashions were the key . . . it was his shirts laid out . . . his suit . . . his look. The girls were flappers.

"Theoni always thought . . . I don't know . . . because she was in the theater and loving the theater . . . that I was a man of business . . . I was in a different world than she was and I was a promoter."

Theoni Aldredge raged, first quietly, later openly to the press. She also had the final say.

In 1974 *The Great Gatsby* was nominated for an Academy Award for its costume design.

The 47th Academy Awards were held on April 18, 1975, in Los Angeles. Competing for the best costume category were four movies: *Chinatown, Daisy Miller, The Godfather: II,* and *The Great Gatsby.* The presenter was Lauren Bacall, stunning in a black halter dress.

"Movies are influencing fashion again," said Bacall. "There was a time when every woman wanted to dress like Garbo or Lombard; Clark Gable took his shirt off, that happened in *It Happened One Night,* and it took eighteen years and Brando to bring the tee shirt back. Most of the designs nominated this year are based on yesterday. And once again they are influencing the fashion of today. I like that. It means romance is on its way. Are you ready for it? I am."

The audience applauded that it, too, was ready.

After four short song-and-dance numbers in which performers wore clothes from each film, Bacall opened the envelope and announced that her good friend Theoni V. Aldredge was the winner.

As millions of television viewers watched, Aldredge marched up to the stage in a black, bell-bottomed tuxedo with a white, high-necked ruffled shirt, which she wore out and belted on the hips.

She kept her acceptance speech short and to the point. Which was the point.

"I would like to thank the members of the Academy, Paramount, Hank Moonjean [associate producer] and my director, Jack Clayton. I love you, Jack, and I'm very proud to have been a part of your film. Thank you, ladies and gentlemen."

She then stepped down.

If Ralph Lauren had contributed anything to the picture, and Theoni Aldredge's Academy Award, nobody knew it that night.

Now that Michael Bernstein was gone, Ralph Lauren was running the business with the help of his oldest brother, Lenny. Lenny Lauren had worked for his father-in-law, making and selling boxes to jewelry manufacturers. He liked people, they liked him, and he was by nature serious and hardworking. What he knew how to do was work with reasonable people. This did not help him in the garment center, because many there did not understand the nuances associated with being reasonable.

Lenny needed help, and at Dave Goldberg's urging, Ralph hired Harvey Hellman in September 1973 to work on untangling the bookkeeping and production snarls. Hellman was a serious, plain-spoken accountant with steady brown eyes and a self-confident manner. If you were having payroll and production problems, you wanted Harvey Hellman sitting in the chair next to you. Hellman had worked for Bobbie Brooks, Inc., the sportswear company, as well as Big Yank, a blue jeans maker. He knew how to structure a payback schedule, and he understood the importance of meeting deadlines. His official title was vice-president/finance and administration. Unofficially, he was Polo's hand-holder.

The company needed a hand-holder for the creditors because its books were a mess. "There were no systems and no sophistication in terms of accounting procedures, credit procedures, returns, and even administration, such as fringe benefits, holidays, salary reviews, sick days," says Hellman. "The first day I walked into the administrative offices on West 26th Street, there was a lawsuit on my desk from Burlington Industries, a major piece goods supplier. They wanted money."

After Harvey Hellman came Arnold Cohen, a partner in Mahoney & Cohen, a small accounting firm. Cohen would later become Polo's chief financial adviser, and he would use his relationship with Ralph Lauren to build one of the largest accounting firms in New York. "It was an administrative nightmare in the beginning," says Cohen. "Ralph didn't have the net worth necessary to do the volume he was doing. If you come along today and say, 'Arnold, I have a million dollars in orders from Bloomingdale's,' it doesn't mean anything unless you have a certain amount of equity. People in this business don't sell piece goods based on sales to come. And no contractor will cut goods either on that basis. They want to be paid first. Ralph couldn't afford the constant turning of the inventory. He didn't have enough equity, and the piece goods houses wouldn't give him credit.

"Also, buying Norman Hilton's stock was a catastrophe, because it wiped out Polo's net worth."

Those were the financial realities of running a business that was nearly bankrupt.

The daily personal embarrassments were worse.

People stopped Ralph on the street, in showrooms, at lunch. What's wrong with your business, they'd ask. How many people have you laid off? Then they'd shake their heads, shrug their shoulders to show they too had been in tough spots, and turn away. This was not sympathy. Polo Fashions had been so hot, so successful, and Ralph Lauren had been so cocky, so full of himself. Now, before his business hit bottom and he slunk back to the Bronx, everybody wanted a last look, a final word. Fat ties, wide lapels, suits for women, cowboys . . . finally, Ralph Lauren was getting his.

There was fear in the showroom, fear in the factories, fear in the design studio. Many of those closest to Ralph quit for better jobs. Knit shirt designer Gil Truedsson left. Paul Wasserman, who worked for Truedsson in the import division, left. Sal Cesarani left to join Country Britches, a women's wear maker, and soon after, George Saffo, the Chaps salesman, left to join him. Everybody had a reason: Cesarani always dreamed of designing his own line. Saffo? He was so certain Polo was about to go bankrupt that he decided he had to leave to protect his co-op. "I didn't know if I'd have a job," says Saffo. "I thought, 'My God, I just bought the apartment. . . .'"

To Ralph, each resignation was a personal rebuke.

It was Sal Cesarani's departure, though, that hurt most of all. Sal Cesarani treated Ralph Lauren as though he were a god. An icon. Nobody believed in Ralph Lauren the way Sal Cesarani believed. Then, one morning, he told Ralph he needed to quit. His wife, Nancy, wanted him to put his family first, Cesarani told him. He also had an offer to design his own line. "I lived morning, noon, and night at Polo," says Cesarani. "I didn't have the time to breathe. I had to get away."

Didn't Cesarani flee because he thought Polo was going bankrupt?

"The Lord is my witness and by everything holy, I never knew the internal struggles," says Cesarani. "I didn't know about the money. Ralph said, 'I'll give you name credit.' I said, 'I don't want name credit. I'm going to be designing something called Country Britches. It doesn't have my name on it.' But I wanted people to know I was a designer, that I selected fabrics, that I had a taste level."

Sal Cesarani won a Coty Award in 1974 for his first Country Britches collection. It didn't hurt that the clothes looked as if they had walked out of the Ralph Lauren design studio.

"Sal left me when I was choking and opened his own showroom," says Ralph Lauren. "Then, a year later, Sal called my interior decorator, Tom O'Toole, and hired him. That killed me. I always liked Sal. He's a loving guy. But he would always say, 'Can I carry your bag, Ralph? I'll carry your bag.'

"I'd say, 'You're not my slave, Sal. Don't do that.' Then, after all that, he pulled out and left me. He didn't believe in me. He'd carry my bag, but then he screwed me. I needed somebody to help me, somebody to stay. It was a very frightening moment."

It was business, but it was a personal business.

Ralph Lauren would walk into a piece goods showroom, look over the line, and then write his orders for the English flannels and tweeds he loved.

Then, before he could leave, a salesman would quietly but firmly explain that his credit wasn't good. Ralph Lauren was a Coty winner but he had to pay cash. "He'd go into a showroom and be embarrassed, and then he'd call me on the phone because he didn't understand it," says Harvey Hellman. "I'd then hurry over and see if we could work out some sort of payout schedule."

This is how Ralph learned Polo Fashions was two companies. There was the design business, the business that depended on his eye, his taste, his feelings. Then there was the business side, where nobody cared about his eye, his taste, or his feelings. Only money counted, not dreams. And Ralph Lauren didn't have any money. For the first time since he'd persuaded Ned Brower at Beau Brummell to open Polo Fashions, Ralph Lauren understood how easily he could lose everything. And it terrified him. Not only because he had once been poor and understood better than most what it meant not to have any money, but because he also saw that nobody paid attention to the losers.

And Ralph Lauren liked being in the limelight. He liked seeing his name in print. He liked the attention the stores gave him. He liked seeing his clothes sketched in *Women's Wear Daily* and *Daily News Record*. Ralph wanted to be recognized when he walked into a room.

Dave Goldberg insisted Polo Fashions had to do four things to survive. Licensing the women's wear business, a cash drain, was first. Then Ralph had to invest more capital in the business. Third, Polo needed to work out a deferral program on the $500,000 it owed L. Greif & Bros., the big men's clothing company then making Polo's suits. Finally, Polo also needed to renegotiate the repayment terms of the $480,000 it owed Norman Hilton.

Ralph did these things.

He started in October by signing a ten-year licensing deal for his women's wear. In exchange for $250,000 plus the standard royalty payments of 5 to 7 percent of sales, he gave the rights to make Polo's women's wear to Stuart Kreisler. This accomplished two of Goldberg's requirements: it licensed out a money-loser, and it added capital to the company coffers.

Kreisler was then only twenty-seven years old and as engaging and personable as he was young and ambitious. Kreisler had grown up in Brooklyn with one dream: he wanted to work in the garment industry, just like his dad. Stuart wore an I.D. bracelet and gold cuff links and a pinkie ring, and at lunchtime he was just as likely to have his limo drive him to Coney Island for hot dogs as the fancy places like Orsini's or La Grenouille. Everybody knew Stuart Kreisler, and when his first company went bust few thought less of him for it. Kreisler was smart, he had good instincts, and he loved the business. He was also one of the first people on Seventh Avenue to see that in the 1970s American fashion designers would remake the industry. He opened the Kreisler Group in 1972 to make designer clothes, and soon he had under contract such names as Jonathan Hitchcock and Clovis Ruffin and John Kloss. Along the way he met and formed a friendship with Ralph Lauren, and when Ralph needed money, Kreisler was able to raise the cash necessary to keep Polo solvent.

He did this by putting up personal guarantees.

(Later, when the Kreisler Group went into Chapter 11 [voluntary bankruptcy] in 1979, Ralph Lauren made sure that the new women's wear licensee, Bidermann Industries, kept Stuart Kreisler in place. Kreisler is president of Ralph Lauren Womenswear today.)

"His women's wear wasn't losing money because it was badly styled, it was losing money because of the way the business was managed," says Kreisler. "He always wanted his product to have integrity, and this caused problems with production time-tables. He wasn't ready to do five seasons a year. What did come through was his terrific sense of fabrics, his style, and a look that was very feminine."

Licensing the women's wear meant Ralph Lauren was responsible only for designing the collection, not manufacturing it. He no longer had to buy the piece goods or hire the contractors or ship the finished product. It also meant he could concentrate on making the men's wear, which is what his company did best. Not that the relationship between Stuart Kreisler and Ralph Lauren was trouble-free. Kreisler wanted to move product, and he hired aggressive salespeople who understood this.

"The name of this industry is the garment industry. We've got to sell garments," explained the late Frank Young, vice-president of marketing at Kreisler's Ralph Lauren division. (Young passed away in 1987.)

"There are lots of guys with impeccable taste, guys who want to buy sixty-dollar fabrics," he continued. "Then those guys end up on the wrong side of the street. We had some high-priced piece goods, mostly from men's wear. Ralph had expensive taste even in those days. He liked cashmere sweaters, for example. I went over to Italy to price them out and I saw the prices were a hundred, two hundred dollars. It was unbelievable."

Young called Kreisler and told him not to buy the sweaters. How many $200 sweaters would they sell in a season, maybe two, maybe three? It was ridiculous. The same with the vicuña coats Ralph wanted. Frank Young didn't want to invest $300 in fabric for a single coat.

Ralph Lauren's attitude was: "I want it."

Stuart Kreisler gave it to him.

"You make money in this business because you've got good markups," says Young. "We understood the cost of goods and markups better than Ralph did. Our mentality on Seventh Avenue is . . . who are we going to sell, how many are we going to sell, what's the markup, and what's the profitability?"

What Frank Young didn't understand was Ralph's insistence on making the biggest collection in New York. Young thought 200 different styles was enough. Ralph Lauren wanted 500, 600, 700 in a fall line. This meant sweaters and pants and jackets in dozens of different shapes and patterns.

The most amazing thing, Young thought, was that Ralph seemed able to remember all of them. Especially the ones Young cut out of the collections because he didn't think they'd sell.

"Ralph would look at the girls modeling the clothes, and then he'd say, 'Hey, where are the pants that go with those jackets?' Then the girls would tell him that I took them off the line and he'd get furious. He'd shout, 'You can't do that,' and we'd fight. It was the only thing we fought over. He didn't care that I couldn't sell those pants. He wanted them on the line because it was part of his concept, part of his package.

"We had to treat Ralph like the leader he was," added Young. "You don't upset a fine piece of Steuben, because it will crack. I was brought up in this business to think of the customer first . . . Then I got to understand Ralph, so we bought the cashmere sweaters and the vicuña coats."

It was not easy going. Before the end of 1973, *Women's Wear Daily* asked Kreisler if the Ralph Lauren women's business was in trouble. "Ralph opened late with the line," he replied. "But we still showed it to all the accounts, since he has a specialized distribution." In May 1974 Ralph showed his first full collection for the Kreisler Group, and the reviews were mixed at best.

Part of the problem was that the collection was unusually diverse. It included clothes worn by Scottish gamekeepers, cowboys, and firemen.

Stuart Kreisler, though, understood how the women's wear business worked as well as anybody on Seventh Avenue and, for the first time, the deliveries of Ralph Lauren's women's clothes were made on time and the collection began to make money.

"We were able to make adjustments to the clothes," says Kreisler. "Ralph wanted everything to be authentic. If he was making a woman's shirt, he wanted the button placement on the placket to be like the men's placing. But if you do that, the shirt gaps across the bustline. We brought in people who knew how to achieve what Ralph wanted by turning the screw a quarter of an inch. It was making the minor adjustments, getting it out on time, supporting it with pattern making. For example, Ralph used a man's zipper in his pants. By shortening that zipper, we were able to scoop out more of the pant and give it a better fit for women.

"Other things. It took seventy-two different steps to make his jackets the way he wanted them made. Other makers would produce the same jacket in twenty-five steps. But our product was the one that stayed in the wardrobe."

"I remember the night when I got the money I needed to back his collection," Kreisler continued. "It was the evening before Yom Kippur, and I was so excited I called Ralph at home. I really believed in him, and I was sure that we were going to do the business we wanted. Ralph made me promise one thing. He said, 'Stuart, if I do something and it is new and a magazine picks it up, produce it for me. Don't stifle me.' Well, he did a bright-colored poplin jumpsuit, and a magazine picked it up. We cut it and tested it and in the fall we opened with tailored jumpsuits in beautiful flannels and stripes and plaids. We sold two thousand units. That jumpsuit retailed for three hundred and ninety dollars, but it sold."

Business at Polo Fashions also started improving. Arnold Cohen and Harvey Hellman sifted their way through the books, coddled the creditors, made new promises to new creditors, and gradually began to restore Polo's credibility in the market. Then, in January 1974, Ralph licensed his Chaps collection to L. Greif & Bros., the $100 million (sales) Genesco division based in Baltimore. (Robert Stock, who owned 20 percent of Chaps, settled with Polo and left the company.) Greif's English American Tailoring division made Polo's suits under a contracting arrangement, and Greif consequently was one of Polo's largest creditors. The Chaps deal was a sign of good faith that Ralph intended to repay that debt. It also gave Genesco an additional reason to extend Ralph's terms.

"Ralph was tight as hell on money," says Ted Decker, who was then president of Greif. "He owed Hilton, and he owed money around the marketplace for piece goods, and he owed us at least five hundred thousand. It was one hell of a lot of money, and it was past due."

Prompted by Ted Decker, Genesco decided that licensing Chaps made more sense than forcing Polo Fashions into bankruptcy.

J. P. Maguire, on the other hand, wanted out.

"Inside my company there was reluctance to continue to finance what turned out to be a massive expansion," says Dave Goldberg. "Polo's sales continued to mushroom, and it was going to require a tremendous increase in support from our end. My feeling at the time was that we'd been through the worst and Polo was now emerging as a good piece of business. Not everybody agreed."

Goldberg liked the way Hellman and Cohen were working together, and he thought the financial plan they'd developed for paying down Polo's debts was sensible. Bloomingdale's remained a strong backer, Norman Hilton had agreed to a longer payout schedule, and there was reason to think that the worst was now over. Goldberg's bosses disagreed, and as the year ended J. P. Maguire sent Polo a 60-day termination notice.

"There couldn't be anything worse," says Arnold Cohen. "If a factor doesn't support you, why should somebody in the trade? Not only does it mean you've lost your cash flow, but look at the reaction of the people doing business with you . . . 'Your bank told you to leave? Why should I give you credit?' It's a kiss of death."

Finally, the United Virginia Factoring Company stepped in and took over the account. Finding a new factor was Polo's last major financial hurdle. With its overhead reduced and its Chaps and women's wear business licensed out, Polo began to make money.

"By making our payments when we promised, we started to build credibility," says Harvey Hellman. "And for the fiscal year ending March 31, 1974, we showed a profit." That year Polo earned more than $200,000 against a loss of $10,000, on sales of about $5 million. (Sales were down because the company no longer included revenues from Chaps or women's wear.)

Ralph Lauren could even buy piece goods on credit again.

That summer, Ralph won his third Coty Award, this time for women's design. He was surprised, the trade was surprised, everybody was surprised. Ralph Lauren had been making women's clothes for only two years.

What he needed now, he decided, was somebody who understood how to move merchandise, understood production, and could manage the business.

What he got was Franklin Bober.

Bober was a high-powered, take-charge manufacturer whose last company had gone bankrupt. That did not faze Ralph. Bober joined Polo in the late fall of 1974 after Ralph had promised to sell him 10 percent of the company and name him president. Bober thought he knew everything about making a garment, and if Ralph Lauren would listen to him, he would teach Ralph everything he needed to know. Franklin Bober had an opinion on everything. Nobody had to ask for it twice.

"I had this attitude, you've given me responsibility, I'm going to take control," says Bober. "That didn't sit well with Ralph, and he was right."

What didn't sit well was that Bober started to tell Ralph

how to run his business. Polo still couldn't make its deliveries on time, and Bober thought Ralph's indecision was a big part of the problem.

"I lectured him," says Bober. "I said, 'Look Ralph, you're Polo. If we tell the stores gray herringbone is going to be big, then they will buy gray herringbone. Let's buy a lot of it so we can deliver on time. Let's not buy two pieces and then have to rush back and try to reorder thirty more. That way we disappoint everybody.' One of the problems I had selling was that the stores would say, 'We love Polo and we love the look, even though it's high-priced. But he doesn't deliver.' My job was very hard. I was trying to convince Ralph to get big. Let's go. Let's buy the fabric. Let's put it in production. . . ."

Bober also fought with Lenny Lauren. The way Bober saw it, Lenny Lauren didn't know anything about the garment business. What he should have done, Bober thought, was listen and learn.

"It's not easy being the brother of Ralph Lauren and working in his shadow," says Bober. "Lenny was another who became quite opinionated about the way things should be done. He didn't know anything about the business, yet he couldn't come in at a lower level. He was Ralph Lauren's brother. So he created trouble. He stuck his nose into things he didn't know anything about. Like production. Or piece goods buying. He wasn't a designer. He was brought in to try and help administer the business. He was in the jewelry business. He knew zero about the apparel business.

"You have to remember. It was family. A guy like me comes in, a young guy, pretty aggressive, a good salesman. Lenny felt a threat. And I'm sure I told Ralph I wouldn't have Lenny working for me. It takes time to learn. Lenny needed to be in a training program, but Lenny was too much of a big shot. He was the brother. What were you going to tell to Lenny Lauren? We had some arguments, he and I, because he got in my way and he didn't know what he was talking about."

Bober was right about one thing: Lenny Lauren was Ralph's brother. And Lenny Lauren had been there when Ralph needed him. The last thing Ralph Lauren wanted to hear was that Franklin Bober wanted to fire Lenny Lauren.

Ten weeks after Franklin Bober joined the company, he left. He would later jest that he was the company's shortest-term employee.

"The thing that set Ralph apart was his single-mindedness of purpose," adds Bober. "Everybody else moved from place to place, from trend to trend. He wasn't trendy. What he did might have been trendy, but he stayed with it. It's the single most important thing about him. To this day there are people walking around saying Ralph Lauren isn't that special, I could have done it. It's the weirdest thing. They couldn't be more wrong. Ralph is the most special guy in the apparel business. He had integrity. He didn't invent the Duke of Windsor. But he created an attitude. Our problem was that I wanted to run the show. With me there is only going to be one star, me, and with him there is only going to be one star, him. Stars collide."

When Franklin Bober moved out, Peter Strom moved in.

Peter Strom, remember, was Norman Hilton's top sales-man and adviser. Peter Strom had persuaded Hilton to accept a fifty-fifty partnership with Ralph Lauren and then buy the business from Beau Brummell. Later, when Norman Hilton sold his interest in Polo, he gave Peter Strom 10 percent of the sales price. "Pete earned it," Hilton says.

The job, however, also made Peter Strom a little crazy. Eventually he developed an ulcer, which led to a major oper-ation.

One morning in June 1974, he and Hilton visited a con-tractor's shop in Greenwich Village and afterwards went to a coffee shop. They paid their bill and started to walk down the block. Then Strom turned to Hilton and said, "I've got to tell you something. I've got to leave you."

"What are you talking about?" Hilton replied.

"Well, my ulcers are coming back. And the doctors say I have to get out of the business."

Norman Hilton started to cry.

But Peter Strom left. Working for Norman Hilton was no longer a job, it was a nightmare.

What he did was go into the carpet business with a friend on Long Island. No sooner had he started than Ralph Lauren began calling him at home, asking his advice about Franklin Bober.

Finally Strom said there was only so much he could do by phone. So Ralph fired Franklin Bober and hired Peter Strom.

"I brought Peter in because I knew he was somebody I could talk with every day, somebody I could trust," says Ralph. "He wasn't flashy. He worked with Norman Hilton for seventeen years. He was a salesman. He didn't run that business. He didn't make licensing deals. When I brought him in he was selling carpets. But I hired him because I liked him and thought I could work with him and build the business with him. Not everybody thought he was the right guy. Not everybody agreed. But I wanted him. I thought he was right for the company. You can see what he's done."

Peter Strom stands about six feet tall and is broad across the shoulders. He has a lined face, short gray hair, and pale blue eyes that never look away. What he values is consistency, and in his dress, which leans toward dark suits and paisley ties, he resembles a conservative banker. He is a good listener. This is important because he makes most of his decisions on the basis of common sense. There is nothing slick about him. What he knew how to do when he joined Ralph Lauren was make and sell clothes. What Peter Strom did when he joined the business was wait. Wait and watch. There were only three salesmen left at Polo: Alton Siebuhr, Ron Cummings, and Bruce Stelzer. All were low-key, good dressers who understood the business. All knew Polo was in trouble; less than half of what they were selling ever got delivered. They reported to Lenny Lauren, but they also knew Polo needed somebody who could get the clothes made and delivered on time.

There were no secrets. When Ralph Lauren came to work wearing a pin-striped suit, everybody knew he was going to talk to the creditors. It was as much a collegial atmosphere as it was a business. Everybody sacrificed, everybody felt close.

Peter Strom saw the closeness. But he saw something else he didn't like, something he described as an attitude. "It was like 'We're Polo, we're great, and take it or leave it,' " says Strom. "A lot of people left it and I didn't blame them.

"The truth of the matter is that the only great thing about Polo was Ralph; everything else was terrible. The deliveries to the stores were absolutely horrendous, and the relationships between the company and the stores were nonexistent. Polo wasn't shipping eighty percent of what it sold, and what it did ship it shipped late. Our volume was about five million and I think we had over five hundred accounts on the books. This meant we were selling a little bit to a lot of people, and that we didn't mean anything to anybody. It also meant nobody meant much to us. I wanted to change that.

"Also, because the company was in dire financial straits, Polo was being frugal when it came to expenses. And in its attempts at frugality, it asked its sales force not to travel, or to travel minimally, and to avoid entertaining at lunch or dinner.

"I knew that was wrong. You can't sell people and not visit their stores, especially the small stores that couldn't afford to make the trips to New York. We had to reach them. And when it came to entertaining, it's just gracious to invite somebody to have lunch with you at lunch hour."

After three months, Peter Strom made his moves.

First he fired Bruce Stelzer, who had joined the company a few years earlier, when he was only twenty-one. To be fired now, after having lasted out two tough years, was a shock. A month later, Strom fired Ron Cummings, who had been acting as sales manager while reporting to Lenny Lauren.

That left soft-spoken Alton Siebuhr. Siebuhr's territory included New York and New England. Siebuhr also sold the celebrities who bought their clothes direct from Ralph Lauren. This meant Bruce Dern and Robert Redford and Tony Perkins and even designer Oscar de la Renta, who used to come by at the end of every selling season, shopping bag in hand.

"I think I had the kindest firing of all three," says Siebuhr. "I was the last. Everybody said, 'You won't . . .' But I said, 'I will.'

"It was a new broom sweeps clean. First Bruce, then Ron. It was terrible. You just felt numb. Everything was changing. Two brothers were dead and gone. That was the feeling. Then I walked in one morning and I knew it was my day.

"Peter said, 'Well, I guess you know why you are here.'

"I said, 'Yeah, I know.'

"Then he said that if he could have done it any differently he wouldn't be doing this to me. I sat there, and I am sure I broke down. I'm sure I said I really cared and would do anything for the company.

"But he knew that. And that was not the point. The point was the new broom sweeps clean. You had to bring in your own people.

"The last thing Peter said to me was, 'Any clothes you want, you can come up here and buy them.' I never did. He was trying to be as kind as he could, but it became ludicrous.

"What probably had happened was that Peter said, 'Ralph, you know what I have to do. I have to reset this whole thing up, and bring in my own people.' It's not complicated to figure out. He had to bring in people he'd worked with before, people who could finish his sentences for him and dot his *i*'s, rather than having to deal with, 'Here comes the outsider.' It's not that we couldn't do it. But he saw it another way, and Ralph had to give him carte blanche."

Peter Strom did more than fire the salesmen and bring in his own people.

He had started his career working in a factory. This meant he understood production schedules, and how to talk with manufacturers. He knew what they wanted, and what their needs were. Also, Strom didn't want to ship goods during the allotted shipping window, say February 1 to April 30. What he wanted to do was ship as much as early into the cycle as possible. Making an April 30 deadline on April 30 means having missed three months of selling time.

"My sense was that if Ralph spent too much time fussing with the line, it was because nobody explained it to him properly," says Strom. "Once we started talking he understood, and it wasn't a conflict.

"I would say this. A designer has a right to change his mind about things. I think that's what makes a designer a designer as opposed to a production person. A good production person is like a Marine. A designer, though, is creative, and the creative process is stressful. You don't understand why you can't get something to come out the way you want it to look. Ralph is a perfectionist and he will frequently change his mind at the last minute. Everybody then has to scramble . . . I wouldn't say it didn't bother me, but I understood it and I wanted that for him because I knew it was one of the things which distinguished him from others. There is always that struggle between production and the creative process and it will always exist. It's healthy."

This was 1975. The bill paying improved. The deliveries improved. And soon other parts of Ralph's business improved also. Hishiya Co., Ltd., became Polo's first Japanese licensee, acquiring the rights to make and distribute Polo ties in that country. Saks Fifth Avenue agreed to become the second major retailer in New York to sell the Polo line with the Polo label; prior to this, Saks had sold Polo's suits with Saks's label inside. The Menswear Retailers of America estimated that designer clothes would amount to 5 percent of the $25 billion men's retail market; this ended the debate over whether men's wear designers were simply a fad. Ralph's own fall men's wear collection was shown in the Explorers Club, where it was favorably reviewed.

Peter Strom had joined Polo because Ralph Lauren had promised to sell him 10 percent of Polo's stock at a future date. Once the Michael Bernstein problem was resolved, Ralph said, Peter would get his stock. Peter, however, wasn't the only one who expected to get stock in the business. Harvey Hellman did, also.

"In early 1975 I was running the warehouse on West Twenty-sixth Street," says Hellman. "That meant I was responsible for shipping, credit, accounting. I was on the phone daily restoring credibility, reacting with people, performing the right way to restore credibility. Then the numbers started to look good and that gave us credibility. So shortly after Peter joined the company, I told Ralph I wanted some stock. By then we had one point five million in financing available to us, we had great relationships again with trade, and we were paying the bills. The banks were happy, the factor was happy, Ralph was happy. The first year I took over we made a profit. So I said to Ralph, 'Don't you think I can get some stock? Even just two percent?'

"And Ralph said, 'If you can get me the money for the apartment, I'll get you the stock.' "

Ralph had seen a duplex on upper Fifth Avenue he wanted to buy. He didn't have much in the way of savings, and he thought maybe Polo's factors could lend it to him against Polo's future earnings.

Hellman says he arranged this for Ralph, which is how Ralph was able to buy his apartment.

Soon afterwards, Ralph and Harvey Hellman had lunch together at the Italian Pavillion.

Hellman brought up the subject of the stock he wanted to buy. Ralph shook his head. "I really don't want to give you stock," he said. "I will take care of you, you're part of my family, I consider you like a brother, you've done a fabulous job. But I didn't give Jerry stock and I just can't give you stock."

That was it. No deal. Hellman was angry, but he saw that Jerry Lauren didn't have stock and that Lenny Lauren didn't have stock. So he stayed. "I don't have any memory of that lunch meeting," says Ralph. "There was never any talk of Harvey Hellman buying into the company. I respected him, but the only person I spoke to about buying into the company was Peter Strom."

Harvey Hellman and Peter Strom were able to work together. Peter Strom and Lenny Lauren were not. With Peter in charge of sales, there really wasn't a place for Lenny.

Ralph and Peter decided Lenny would learn the production side of the business. This meant he gave up his office on West 55th Street and moved to the company's new 75,000-square-foot warehouse in North Bergen, New Jersey.

"The attitude was, 'Let's get Lenny involved in production,'" says Hellman. "But in a very short time it was clear it wouldn't work. Lenny didn't like the job, and he had a poor relationship with Peter. Lenny saw it, but he was the brother. He was the guy who was there with Bernstein. He was the guy called in to help Ralph out of a bind. Then Peter comes in and Lenny is thrown out of New York and the sales area where he felt comfortable. Lenny is a salesman. How can you stick him in production? It was terrible.

"The whole thing was done badly. Before I moved out to North Bergen, Lenny went out as the pioneer. I'll never forget this: he picked the biggest office as his office. That meant I was going to have the smaller, dinkier office. I mentioned this to Peter and Ralph and they said, 'Get Lenny out of that office. Give him the smaller office. You have the big office.'

"Peter called him up and said, 'That's not your office. You are in the office next to his.' It was terrible. Right after that Lenny was gone. He lasted maybe a month in production, and then he went back to New York, where there wasn't a job for him."

Everybody knew Lenny Lauren was going to have to leave the company.

Nobody knew how to tell him, especially Ralph.

Finally, Peter Strom and Lenny sat down and talked about Lenny's future with the company, and at the end of that talk Lenny agreed to leave.

"I felt bad that Ralph didn't have the sensitivity to talk to me himself, and that he would do this without hearing my side," says Lenny. "We have never really talked about it."

Lenny was his brother. Ralph loved him. But this was business.

And Ralph had learned that he had to run his business like a business.

Ralph was now on a roll. By fall of 1976 Polo's licensees included Tiffany & Company; a fur maker; a shoemaker; a lingerie maker; Seibu & Co., Ltd., a Japanese men's clothing maker; a scarf maker; L. Greif & Bros; the Kreisler Group; and an eyeglass frame maker. Altogether, Polo's volume, including sales from licensed products, was about $18 million. Ralph even won Coty Awards for his men's and women's collections.

Ralph, though, was still not nearly as well known as the famous designers like Bill Blass and Pierre Cardin. But the business was growing. And he was already learning what would be the most important lesson in the fashion business: it almost didn't matter how much money a designer made or lost producing his own collections, as long as he signed enough lucrative licensing deals. And then controlled the quality of the products made bearing his name or logo. Bill Blass's licensing business, for example, was expected to top $100 million in retail sales in 1976. The collections Blass made himself were expected to do no more than $25 million at retail.

Licensing would explain how the designers amassed such large fortunes so quickly. Licensing didn't require inventory or investment or manufacturing know-how.

All it demanded was an understanding of what the customers wanted.

And the right image.

Ralph Lauren, lover of old movies, knew all about images. He knew an image was more powerful than an idea, more satisfying than a new dress or a new suit. An image meant identity; buying somebody else's image meant sharing that identity. That's why the customers became such eager brand consumers.

Ralph would show exactly how well he understood this when he signed, in October 1976, what would be one of the most lucrative licensing deals on Seventh Avenue, a deal that a decade later was still producing royalties of more than $5 million a year.

Ralph Lauren, designer, would become Ralph Lauren, perfume seller. It didn't matter that he didn't know anything about ylang-ylang flowers from Madagascar, or castoreum from the beaver, or natural oils from jasmine or orange flowers.

He wasn't selling a scent; he was selling an image of how that scent would make its wearer feel. And as his perfumes would show, he understood this far better than anybody else had before him.

There was a time in New York when a company that wanted to give the impression of generosity when it came to hors d'oeuvres and drinks and knowing how to throw a good party automatically went to the "21" Club. The "21" Club's history as New York's most famous bar during Prohibition gave it a slightly raffish air, and after 5 P.M. people who worked at such nearby media companies as Time Inc. and CBS would drop by the bar before taking the train home. The "21" Club was expensive and sophisticated, and it was here on October 7, 1976, that Warner Communications gave a big press party to introduce Warner/Lauren Ltd.

Why the "21" Club? Because the fragrance and cosmetics business was built on glamour and romance, and those who were deemed dispensers of glamour and romance were expected to spend money. This was a business where investing millions to build the right product image was deemed as important as investments in new factories. Extravagance was acceptable because the product itself was extravagant. Nobody needed to wear perfume. They wore it because it made them feel more desirable and therefore better about themselves.

Fragrance was about identity and self-image.

Here was a business that prospered by creating an atmosphere heavy with sensuality. There were the famous ingredients, like sandalwood from India and ambergris from the sperm whale and civet from the civet cat in Ethiopia and jasmine from flowered fields in the south of France. There were the famous legends, too. How Napoleon's mistress Josephine was so partial to musk that her bedroom still smelled of it sixty years after her death. Or how the barge on which Cleopatra sailed to meet Mark Antony was so laden with fragrances that, as Shakespeare wrote, "The winds were love-sick." Even the advertising was different. When it came to selling perfumes, there were few objections when manufacturers showed bared breasts or total nudity. In a thick "official jubilee edition" of a publication celebrating the *City of New York, Golden Anniversary of Fashion, 1898–1948,* Nettie Rosenstein promoted her Odalisque perfume with a grainy photograph of a woman lying on her side, her head supported by her right arm, her left arm draped across her forehead as though she were exhausted. She is wearing only a few bracelets. Acceptable? Yes, because everybody knew perfume was bought and sold on the basis that it accented the mystery of feminine sexuality.

This was an industry, too, built on advertising and promotion and marketing. Unlike Detroit, which marketed its cars on the basis of more miles per gallon or better handling or a smoother ride, the fragrance industry was never product driven. Perfume makers sold romance and the promise of sexual fulfillment. Sure, the scent had to be attractive; otherwise the customers didn't come back. But just as important was how that scent was packaged and priced and where it was promoted and distributed. This was done with in-store promotions (free gifts, or gifts with purchases), and major ad campaigns in women's fashion magazines such as *Vogue* or *Harper's Bazaar.* Not only did the fragrance makers spend money on fabulous parties and the like when they introduced new perfumes, but they also had to spend money year-round to keep the customers interested.

It is a business of predictable cycles. With the exception of Christmas, shoppers don't ordinarily go into the department stores intending to buy fragrances. Cosmetics, in contrast, sell twelve months a year. Most women already own a dozen lipsticks. But when they walk into a store and see a beautiful bag and people in the aisles spray perfumes on them, they buy. Although packaging and advertising count, the most cost-efficient way of selling fragrances at the department stores is through in-store promotion. Not only do such promotions build fragrance sales, but they also increase the sales of other designer products.

That is why the great European designers were so eager to have their own fragrances. First Chanel put her name on Chanel No. 5 in the early 1920s. Jeanne Lanvin introduced My Sin in 1925, Jean Patou launched Joy in 1930; and Christian Dior presented Miss Dior in 1947. Twenty-one years later, in 1968, Revlon introduced Norell, the first perfume named for an American designer. (Norman Norell was born Norman Levinson in Noblesville, Indiana, in 1900 and died in 1972. He was best known for his sequin-covered sheath dresses.) Norell, with its rich floral scent, was so successful that many major perfume makers here began to contemplate designer scents. Like movie sequels, such scents start with built-in name recognition and loyal customers, a valuable advantage in a marketplace crammed with dozens of fragrances. Also, the fashion designer business has always been about seduction. Few products were more intimately linked to seduction than perfume. (No wonder designers would later be so successful with their collections of bed sheets and linens.)

It didn't hurt that fragrances also could generate profit margins in excess of 25 percent.

That explains why Ralph Lauren was steadily wooed by Lanvin-Charles of the Ritz and Estée Lauder to create his own fragrance in the early 1970s. Ralph would listen, he would negotiate, he would listen some more. It was a new business and he didn't want to rush, or be rushed. His biggest concern was that his would be one of many fragrances the company made and sold, and that as time passed and new fragrances were introduced, his would be forgotten. Nobody understood this better than George Friedman, the intense Estée Lauder executive who had helped build Aramis into one of the top men's fragrances in the world.

In Ralph's obstinacy he sensed an opportunity.

"I used to see George all the time in the street," says Ralph. "He loved Polo, and he knew I was making deals. People would ask me about fragrances, I'd show him the deal, and say, 'George, what do you think?'

"He'd say, 'Yeah, it's good Ralph, but why don't you wait and we'll do it together?'

"I didn't want to be with a stable of people. I wanted to build as the basis of the company, the way Estée Lauder was built as the basis of that company. I didn't want to be one of many but the only one. Then George went to Estée Lauder and said, 'I want to do Ralph Lauren. I think it would be fabulous.' But they finally said they didn't want any names other than their own. So I waited."

Some of that hesitation reflected how little Ralph knew

about how the fragrance business worked. Polo itself was still small, its staff young and inexperienced. Licensing was very much a new concept. The money sounded impressive, but what did it mean? How did you protect yourself against makers who would put your name on cheap products and ruin your company's reputation? Ralph didn't know. Anybody could promise to make him rich. Or flat-out lie to him. What licensing really meant was . . . losing control. Better to wait until he met somebody he could trust. Ralph didn't put his faith in contracts. What mattered was the degree of personal commitment. Ralph, too, wanted to be seduced. Not with promises of money, because everybody talked about giving him money, but with visions of where he and Polo would be in five years.

As it turned out, David Horowitz understood this perfectly.

Horowitz was an executive vice-president with Warner Communications, Inc., the fast-growing entertainment conglomerate which in the early 1970s made big movies like *The Exorcist* and *Blazing Saddles* and television shows like "Harry O." In the summer of 1976 Horowitz and his family rented the East Hampton house next to the one Ralph was renting, and the two men became friendly. Horowitz prided himself not only on mastering the business side of the entertainment industry, but on nurturing friendships with people whose creativity often made them high-strung. Ever-serious, Horowitz was so cool, so controlled, that he practically whispered when he spoke. The only personal note that hinted at a sense of whimsy was a thick mustache. If anything, David Horowitz talked in an even quieter, less threatening voice than Ralph Lauren. And little impressed Ralph more than somebody with access to money and power who conducted himself with modesty and restraint.

"We became friends because we started as good neighbors," says Horowitz. "We're both very private people, and we like our privacy respected. We both knew the other would not be bouncing over all the time. I was struck by how young he and Ricky were. They not only looked young, they were young, yet Ralph was an important fashion designer. Gradually we began to talk about each other's business. He was curious about what I did, and I was interested in what he did."

Horowitz was then managing Warner's famous record business, which included the Atlantic, Elektra, and Warner labels. He also oversaw its growing holdings in cable television, helping to launch the Warner Amex Satellite Entertainment Company, a programming business which became MTV Networks. (When MTV went public in 1984, Horowitz was named president.) Ralph Lauren was fascinated by the opulent scale on which Warner operated, by Warner's moviemaking, and by Steve Ross, Warner's blunt, savvy chief executive. Ross had started with his father-in-law's funeral business and then branched into parking lots and cleaning companies, all under the mantle of Kinney Services, Inc. Ross took his biggest gamble in 1969, when he bought Warner Bros.-Seven Arts, Ltd., in a stock swap valued at $400 million. Included were Warner Bros. Pictures, Warner Bros. Television, Warner Bros. Records, Atlantic Records, and Warner Bros. Music. Two years later, these properties were restructured under the rubric of Warner Communications, Inc.

WCI would be a roller coaster of a company, its stock rising to $50 in 1972, and then dropping back to $8 two years later. Stock analysts found Warner alluring because of its steady stream of top-rated movies and records. Those same analysts gradually became less enchanted, however, by the unconnected businesses Ross had accumulated. In the late 1960s Wall Street praised conglomerates for their diversity; by the mid-1970s, conglomerates had fallen out of favor for the same reason.

None of this troubled Ralph. He liked the people he met through David Horowitz. They were attentive, bright, and obviously lived well. Their confidence in who they were and where they were going was attractive, and Ralph decided he wanted to do business with them. Ralph knew Warner was a big business. What mattered was how much attention and care it would give him. He and David Horowitz began to talk about fragrances, and one afternoon Ralph said he wanted Horowitz to meet his friend George Friedman. The talk was no longer casual conversation.

"Ralph knew that there were only so many people who could afford to buy his clothing," says David Horowitz. "Fragrances open a much wider world because they're low-cost items. Everybody could afford to own a piece of Ralph Lauren, to share in the aura. And because it would be a licensed business, Ralph would have none of the problems of manufacturing, distribution, or sales. You simply get a percentage of the gross.

"Ralph also knew that this was a business with the potential to be his largest income producer, and a business that would be impossible to revive later if the initial launch was a failure. So he wanted it done right. What he liked was that this would be Warner's only fragrance venture. The negatives were along the lines of 'what did we know about the business?' But when you got down deep, it wasn't such a crazy idea. Warner was in the movie and record businesses and very good at marketing dreams. To make the cheese more binding, I introduced Ralph to Steve Ross. The chemistry was very good. Ralph felt there were people at this company he could trust, who would be responsive if he had problems along the way, and who would do everything necessary to make it work."

Soon after Friedman and Horowitz met, Friedman's friend Bob Ruttenberg drove to Friedman's home in Bridgehampton one Saturday afternoon to pick up his son. The two men were close. Both wanted their own businesses, both were strong-willed, both were successful fragrance executives. Ruttenberg and Friedman had first met in 1964 when Ruttenberg was at the advertising agency Foote, Cone & Belding and George Friedman represented Clairol. After Friedman moved to Estée Lauder, he hired Ruttenberg to work with him. Ruttenberg eventually moved on to Revlon, but the two remained good friends, and Friedman was well aware that Ruttenberg had helped make Charlie, Revlon's women's fragrance, one of the top performers in the business. Friedman also knew that Ruttenberg was emotional, edgy, and driven.

When Ruttenberg walked into Friedman's house that day he was startled to see Friedman sitting at his kitchen table, working. After a little initial hesitation, Friedman explained he was putting together a fragrance proposal involving Ralph Lauren. Ruttenberg and Friedman talked for hours, and when the afternoon drew to a close, they both understood that there wouldn't be room for Ruttenberg in the new company. Polo would be a men's fragrance, and it couldn't support two executive salaries.

Later that evening Ruttenberg had an idea. What if there were two Ralph Lauren fragrances, a men's scent and a women's scent? It would mean twice as much real estate in the department stores, which would mean bigger revenues. Launching two fragrances back-to-back would also mean that the stores would promote Ralph Lauren's name for four weeks in a row. (Fragrance launches last two weeks.) Nobody had ever introduced two fragrances like this before, and it would certainly generate tremendous publicity. It would also mean a job for Bob Ruttenberg.

"George loved the idea," says Ruttenberg. "It was new, and it had never been done before. But Ralph said, 'No, I'm strong in men's, not in women's, and you'll dilute one by doing both. I really care about the men's. No way.' "

George Friedman argued otherwise. Launching two perfumes would give him the chance to quickly establish Ralph Lauren's importance to the department stores. More than half the battle involved in launching any new fragrance company is gaining shelf space; a company that introduced men's and women's fragrance lines at the same time would obviously acquire more space than one with a traditional single launch. Friedman also wanted a friend in the company, somebody with whom he could talk and plan the business.

So Bob Ruttenberg started to attend the meetings with Warner, too. And when his two-year contract expired with Revlon in July 1976, Steve Ross signed him to a Warner contract despite the fact that Warner did not yet own the Ralph Lauren license. This showed everybody Ross was taking the proposed fragrance deal seriously. Later, when Ruttenberg reported to work his first day, Warner gave him a check representing his first month's salary. Ruttenberg was especially appreciative because he knew Warner had just spent $28 million to acquire a little maker of computer games called Atari.

A major problem then developed. George Friedman had a valid employment contract with Estée Lauder. He was concerned that Lauder might not let him go. The timing was particularly touchy because Lauder intended to introduce another men's fragrance, Devin, in addition to Aramis. At the same time, Warner, too, didn't want to appear to be encouraging other companies' executives to break their contracts.

The result? When Friedman, Ruttenberg, Ralph Lauren, and Warner Communications signed their contracts on November 22, 1976, they did so with the understanding that they wouldn't launch any products for another sixteen months. This meant they had enough time to put together their management team and establish relationships with the major retailers.

Certainly their contract with Warner had incentive for everybody. Ralph Lauren and Bob Ruttenberg each got 5 percent of the new company; George Friedman received about 15 percent, and Warner took the rest in exchange for providing start-up capital of $300,000. (Warner would invest about $6 million the first year, but that investment represented a loan to Warner/Lauren Ltd., funds that were to be paid back.) Ralph Lauren's contract also specified that he would receive 5 percent of all sales.

In return, Ralph signed what amounted to an agreement in perpetuity. That meant Warner/Lauren Ltd. would always own the rights to the Polo and Lauren fragrance names, and that Ralph Lauren or his heirs would receive royalties for as long as those products were sold.

"One of our philosophies is we like people to have equity, direct or with stock options," says Steve Ross, chairman of Warner Communications. "That was very important to us, and it was important to them. You can sleep very easily at night, knowing that when they are spending a dollar it's their dollar. So we formed a corporation and we were off to the races."

(Consider this: in 1987, worldwide sales of all Ralph Lauren fragrances amounted to $125 million — $85 million for Polo; $40 million for Lauren. That means Ralph's royalties that year were $6.25 million, despite the fact that Ralph never invested a cent of his own money in the fragrance business. This is how powerful and profitable an image can be.)

Warner/Lauren Ltd. started with two employees, George Friedman and Bob Ruttenberg. Then came Jill Resnick, who would later become known in the industry as "The Nose" for her ability to pick winning fragrances, and Oriel Raphael, an engineer by training, who was also a highly skilled package designer. Warner/Lauren had its offices at Warner Communications, near those of actor Robert Redford, complete with a first-rate view of Central Park. Sometimes Ruttenberg and Friedman would meet Redford in the halls, and they would all chat about business and the projects they were working on.

It was an atmosphere that bred confidence, arrogance, and great expectations. For instead of insisting that the company suffer the normal budget restraints that accompany most start-ups, Steve Ross allowed his new team to lead a life of perks and privileges. The message he was sending was a simple one: I expect you to be successes; therefore, you will be treated as though you already are.

"Working there was wonderful and awful," says Jill Resnick. "I cried a lot. They used to beat up on me. They were crazy. They were so emotional, and they'd make you feel like a real idiot. You'd sit in a meeting and say something and they'd look at you as if to say, you jerk. There was lots of emotion and there was no protocol, no business formalities. There were just four of us. You'd go in and Ralph would be sitting there and everybody would offer an opinion. Still, Ralph was a little uncomfortable with me. I'm tall, for starters. And he really didn't understand how I did what I did. He felt much more comfortable with George and Bob, because I think he could express himself more easily with the boys."

Resnick learned this the hard way. One afternoon she saw Ralph leaving George Friedman's office. She walked past and Friedman turned to her and quietly said, "Ralph doesn't like this scent."

Resnick couldn't help herself. This was a smell she'd worked on for months, and the last thing she wanted to do was start all over again.

"Dammit," she said. She said it loud enough for Ralph Lauren to hear.

This, as she learned, was a big mistake.

Ralph became so upset that Friedman and Ruttenberg had to hide Resnick in another room when Ralph came by over the next few months.

"He thought I had said something disparaging about him, as in he's full of it," says Resnick. "But I was simply frustrated. I wanted him to like it so we could get on with the job."

Ralph Lauren didn't know how perfumes were made, or what women wanted in a scent, or why they wore them when they wore them, and he didn't pretend to know what he didn't know. But when it came to marketing a product, and promoting an image, Ralph Lauren understood exactly what he wanted: only the best. As soon as Friedman and Ruttenberg understood that, there wouldn't be any problems.

Some lessons were easier than others.

First came the design for the bottles. Ralph insisted his Polo fragrance be packaged in a shape that resembled a drinking flask. He also wanted the Lauren bottles to be modeled after his collection of Victorian glass inkwells. Then he asked that the two fragrances somehow be tied together. Putting a polo player motif on the front wouldn't do, he added. The solution? Both bottles are capped with the same gold doorknob top.

Then there were the debates over the cardboard packaging. Ralph Lauren studied cardboard like nobody studied cardboard. Most fragrance packaging is printed on white stock, with color applied later. Anybody who stares as carefully and diligently as Ralph Lauren, however, eventually notices that the edges always remain white. Now, most people don't see the white edges because they don't care. They're going to go home, take the bottle out, and throw the box away. End of story.

Ralph Lauren didn't want anybody to see those white edges.

This, too, created headaches until somebody found a source for burgundy-colored cardboard. Fresh burgundy ink was then added, and the letters spelling *Polo* were printed in dark green.

No white shows.

Ben Kotyuk worked with Ralph Lauren on designing the packaging; Oriel Raphael was in charge of production. Kotyuk and Raphael were both unusually patient people. That was a blessing, because even Ralph's simplest requests were difficult to execute.

Take the red-colored Lauren bottles. The concept was to create a crystal container that would hold a droplet of fragrance. Not hard . . . except Ralph insisted his bottles have the same sharp corners he so admired on his collection of Victorian inkwells. Not easy. Liquid glass doesn't flow to sharp corners in a mold as readily as it does to a round configuration. Besides, sharp corners weaken the overall bottle. This makes it harder to ship because the bottles break more readily.

What to do? American glassmakers said they couldn't do the job. Finally Oriel Raphael went to Spain, where he found an obliging factory owner. Of course making the bottles overseas raised the price of making the bottles, which meant the retail price was higher, but Ralph got distinctive bottles with sharp edges.

An important point?

Ralph thought so.

Finally there were the labels themselves.

Ralph wanted a very simple design. For Polo, this meant silk-screening a gold polo player onto green glass. That was easy. However, by law each bottle also had to be identified by batch number. Putting that number on the label, Ralph thought, gave the bottles a cluttered look. Put it on the bottom of the bottle, suggested Warner's Steve Ross. Which is where it went.

Keeping it simple meant that the word *Polo* never appears on the men's fragrance bottle: only a polo player identifies the fragrance. The women's fragrance bottle reads "Lauren by Ralph Lauren."

There is more to selling fragrances than attractive and innovative packaging. Department store customers expect to be wooed with purchase-with-purchase items, such as umbrellas or pocketbooks or makeup containers, which are sold only during the promotion. One such purchase-with-purchase for Lauren was a purse spray. Ralph saw the finished version, didn't like it, and demanded that a new mold be made. He got his way — but it cost Warner/Lauren $85,000. "It was a wonderful nineteenth-century flacon that Jill Resnick had found," says George Friedman. "It's expensive to do metal packaging, and Ralph didn't like the mold. We did it over again."

Nobody said it was going to be easy.

Finally there was the matter of price. Ralph wanted all twenty-five of his fragrances, colognes, after-shaves, talcum powders, and body lotions to cost more than any other products on the market. The higher the price, the more exclusive the customer, the better the image.

Wrong, argued Friedman and Ruttenberg. Nobody was going to buy a $10 deodorant. Be competitive. We're selling packaged goods, not clothes. The average bill here is $15, not $100. Let's turn the stock four times a year, because the goal is $50 million, not $5 million.

Eventually, it was decided to price Lauren perfume at $87.50 an ounce; an ounce of Polo cologne cost $13.50. The pricing was competitive, not extravagant.

Then there were the scents.

Choosing Polo was simple. George Friedman knew he wanted a strong, clean scent which would appeal to the same customers who bought Aramis.

Picking the Lauren scent was a nightmare.

The Lauren perfume had a fruity smell, and it was new to the market. It wasn't easy to like the first time. But it was interesting, interesting enough, Jill Resnick insisted, that women would come back a second time.

Of all those who would work at Warner/Lauren, Resnick's job was perhaps the most difficult to define. A "nose" translates what a designer is feeling into a smell. It's a job that gives the word "vague" new definition. After all, how does anybody describe a scent to a working chemist? Resnick starts with a special language, a code. Like "top notes," the first "notes" customers smell. Fragrance should sparkle and bounce off the skin, not sit there like paste. Fresh top notes are light notes, citrus notes. These notes are there and then disappear. Then, when the fragrance is balanced properly, the middle notes appear. There are other special words, too, words like "green." Not green the color, but the green associated with leaves, stems, twigs. Green notes smell like moss or grass or wet leaves, things that grow. The smell is too sweet, too rich? Call it cloying, which means the scent contains too much vanillin. Then there are the rubbery notes, notes which are too flavored with jasmine.

There are also the technical aspects associated with a scent. How long it lasts, how it diffuses off the skin. A fragrance can last for hours, but unless other people smell it, the wearer doesn't get compliments and she doesn't buy it a second time. The customers want to be told they smell good. Women want comments from other women, too. Resnick considers this the most critical of all tests, because a woman who asks another woman what she is wearing wants to buy some. She really likes it.

Ralph understood the Polo scent. He was less certain when it came to deciding on Lauren.

"He wanted it to be perfect but he didn't know how to make it perfect," says Resnick. "He couldn't wear it in order to tell me what was wrong. He was great about Polo. He loved it from day one. Polo *was* Ralph Lauren. But there was no position for Lauren. Lauren was Polo's wife. When we did the fragrance, the key was to develop a concept so that I knew what I was looking for. It wasn't so much a marketing strategy for a fragrance, it was more a marketing strategy for his clothing.

"Initially, people didn't understand Lauren because it was very different. It was the first floral fragrance, and the top notes sort of jolted people. They didn't know what to expect.

"Ralph didn't like it because it didn't smell like something he'd smelled before. It didn't smell like Chloé. He loved Chloé. He used to talk to me about Chloé. But I'd worked on Chloé when it was introduced, and I knew that nobody understood that scent when it first came out either."

Ralph wasn't the only one who didn't like Lauren. Neither did his wife, Ricky. Or the staffers at Warner. At one meeting a Warner executive stated that Lauren smelled like Glade, a household air freshener. He even sent his secretary out to buy a can so that the others could compare the smells.

This was not so good.

Eventually Bob Ruttenberg balked. Okay, he said, give us a list of people you respect. We'll run a test. Ruttenberg took that list, asked the fifty or sixty women on it what perfume they used regularly. Then he put Lauren into a blank bottle and the favorite into a blank bottle, and asked those women to sniff again. Choose, he said, which do you like better?

"Not one person knew the fragrance in one of the blank bottles was her favorite," says Ruttenberg. "I learned that at Revlon. Nobody knew, because they didn't see the packaging. Charles Revson taught us that. All we wanted with Lauren was parity, and when the women picked between the two bottles, half chose Lauren, half chose the other. That meant we'd achieved parity, and the Lauren scent was finally approved."

The months passed. New people were hired. Suppliers were found. The salesmen went into the stores. On March 13, 1978, Polo and Lauren were launched in New York at Bloomingdale's, and in Pittsburgh at Kaufmann's. Ralph Lauren even agreed to make an appearance — the only appearance he would ever make to promote any of his fragrances or, later, cosmetics.

"There is only one store that could introduce the Ralph Lauren fragrance . . . the store that introduced Ralph Lauren," reads the Bloomingdale's ad that appeared on Sunday, March 12 in the *New York Times*. Underneath that headline is a picture of Ralph, standing proudly in his blue jeans, denim shirt, and tweedy sport jacket with the wide lapels. The two top buttons of his shirt are undone, and he has his left hand on his hip. It's a sexy pose. The message was that he was selling a sexy fragrance.

For sixteen months George Friedman and Bob Ruttenberg had talked and promised and spent an incredible amount of money. Wrote Steve Ginsberg in *Women's Wear Daily* about this launch, "In freewheeling movieland style, the money has flowed. The production and start-up costs for this venture have to rival any in the fragrance industry."

Now Friedman and Ruttenberg had to deliver.

"I was so on edge that on opening day I hid behind pillars so I could watch people smelling," says Jill Resnick.

"Ralph's father was there. He was standing a few cases away, watching, not knowing who I was.

"Then he turned to me, and said, 'You know, darling, I'm Mr. Lifshitz, Ralph's father. I play the violin.'

"So I said, 'No, I don't know.' He just wanted somebody to talk to. He was just standing there, taking it all in, enjoying it."

There was a lot to enjoy. Polo sold briskly, Lauren as well. The launch was clearly a success.

Then, a short time later, the Polo bottles started to burst.

"One morning I was making a Lord and Taylor training tape for Polo, dressed in my special Ralph Lauren khaki-colored dress," says Resnick. "I laid down a tablecloth, put the Polo products on top, and then introduced each product while explaining its sales points. This took all day, and by five P.M. I was ready for the funny farm. Then I picked up a bottle of Polo and it exploded. The green ran all over my dress. I was a mess, the whole table was a mess, everything was a mess. So I went back to the office and I said, 'Oriel, a very strange thing happened. I was holding a bottle of Polo and it just exploded.'

"Oriel's eyes glazed over. He was the head of operations, and he immediately understood what had happened. He knew liquids expanded when they got hot, and that the lights from the training film had exploded the bottle. I thought he was going to kill himself. It was a nightmare."

Department stores across the country were displaying Polo in glass counters under hot spotlights. Soon caps began popping right and left, and as they popped, the smell of Polo cologne and after-shave slowly wafted through the air.

(Later, Oriel Raphael discovered that the factory responsible for filling the bottles left the fragrances outside in the cold until they were needed. That meant the perfumes were still cold when they were pumped inside. For aesthetic purposes, the fill point was just below the shoulder of the Polo bottle. But because the fragrance was cold, it was denser than it would have been normally. At room temperature it expanded to completely fill what the trade calls the head space. Under excessive heat, the fragrance expanded so rapidly that it popped off the tops.)

Even without excessive heat, some warehoused Polo shipping boxes showed leakage. Each box then had to be opened, and the excess fragrance removed from every bottle with a hypodermic needle.

Thousands of bottles were involved.

Regional sales managers across the country were armed with needles and sent into the stores, where in the early-morning hours they siphoned every bottle that had been shipped.

So much for the glamorous fragrance business.

The Lauren fragrance had different woes. Making the attractive red Lauren bottles was more difficult than first thought. One morning Jill Resnick opened an envelope containing what looked like red Saran Wrap and a letter threatening a lawsuit. Soon there were dozens of angry letters.

It turned out that if the red color on the Lauren bottles didn't seal perfectly, it would peel off if a little fragrance was spilled.

Eventually Oriel Raphael found a glass factory that fixed the problem.

This, however, was not what Ralph Lauren had meant so many months earlier when he explained what it meant to build a quality image.

Bob Ruttenberg lives today in a comfortable East Side town house and works as a consultant. George Friedman devotes himself to a national charity called the "I Have a Dream Foundation," which sends poor kids to college. David Horowitz is a leading entertainment consultant. Steve Ross has survived yet another takeover attempt at Warner Communications, Inc. What they have in common now is that all sound nostalgic when discussing the old days at Warner/Lauren Ltd.

They also sound relieved. Warner/Lauren ultimately proved a financial bonanza, just as promised. But getting there was a more gut-tightening, fingernail-chewing experience than even the skeptics predicted.

Look how the business grew. Fragrance revenues at the end of 1978 amounted to $7.5 million. Warner/Lauren didn't make any money, but everybody rationalized that this was a start-up operation. The returns would come after the distribution and merchandising systems were operating smoothly. The name Ralph Lauren was speedily gaining status with the affluent, the fragrances smelled good, the retailers were enthusiastic.

"The Lauren and Polo fragrances for women and men have recently been introduced by Warner/Lauren," announced Steve Ross in Warner Communications' 1977 annual report. "We are excited by the prospects for this new enterprise."

Why would Warner Communications, which in 1977 produced such hit movies as *A Star Is Born, The Enforcer,* and *Oh, God!* and such chart busters as "Rumours" by Fleetwood Mac and "Hotel California" by the Eagles, be excited by this small and all but unknown subsidiary?

The operative word was potential. Designer fragrances constituted the fastest-growing segment of a vigorous $3 billion industry in 1977. Steve Ross saw Ralph Lauren as a young, talented American designer with an impressively upscale following and a sure sense of what the customers wanted. In Friedman and Ruttenberg he had two experienced managers. Better, both had been previously associated with top scents, Friedman with Aramis and Ruttenberg with Charlie. Ross thought that together with Ralph Lauren they would make a terrific team. Maybe he was dreaming a little, but Ross liked to dream. Warner's was famous, or infamous, depending on your point of view, for letting its operations people operate. Ross admired creativity, nurtured it with money, and then stood back and waited for the good things to happen. Usually they did, and when they did, people said Ross was a genius. When things went bad, which they did occasionally, the critics complained that Ross ran a loose ship and didn't know anything about management.

In 1977 Ross looked like a genius. WCI that year passed the $1 billion mark in sales for the first time, earning a record $71 million, or nearly $5 a share. Both the music and the film divisions were chugging along nicely, which meant Warner was in a position to gamble on a perfume business. Besides, Warner was a big player in glamorous industries. Adding Ralph Lauren to its roster of names seemed a shrewd move both financially and psychologically. Not only would it increase Warner's visibility to consumers, but it would do so in a business that was hit-driven, something Ross knew about from the record and film industries. Ross wasn't interested in 10- or 20-percent returns on his investments. Rather, he wanted to put up $10 to make $100. And he thought the fragrance business could produce those numbers.

Warner/Lauren was presented to shareholders in a category titled "all other operations" in the annual report. In order of importance, it ranked last, behind even the Cosmos, a soccer team. Although Jungle Habitat, a zoo that Warner then owned, was not listed in the annual report that year, Ruttenberg liked to joke that he and Friedman were now one step lower than the monkeys.

Expenses were high, but nobody panicked. It would be easy enough, in 1978, to make money. All Warner/Lauren had to do was cut costs by reducing its advertising and promotional dollars.

But anybody could make money.

The challenge was making big money. Friedman and Ruttenberg, sometimes referred to inside the company as "Batman and Robin," wanted to be rich. And they positively sparkled in the glow of Warner's home run mind-set. They'd learned from the best teachers, Estée Lauder and Charles Revson, and now they had a backer who not only believed in them but also opened the company's coffers. After years of haggling for every marketing dollar, the change was almost overwhelming. It also created an emotional, energy-charged atmosphere. Intensely competitive before they ever set foot inside Warner Communications, Friedman and Ruttenberg became even more determined to prove not only that they knew how to run a business, but that they knew how to build a business.

That meant taking big risks.

Each time Warner/Lauren edged toward the black, Friedman and Ruttenberg introduced yet another new brand or product. And because this was the fragrance industry, each new launch had to be accompanied by hoopla. Otherwise, nobody would take it seriously.

Which is why year in, year out, Warner/Lauren never reported any profits.

Not in 1978, when retail fragrance sales nearly doubled to $14 million. And not in 1979, when sales doubled to $28 million.

This is where the money went. In mid-1979, Warner/Lauren launched Tuxedo, a second perfume for women. Why? Because there were still some critics inside the company who doubted Lauren's ability to attract and hold the customers. Tuxedo, they said, would broaden Warner/Lauren's base, and it would do so without hurting the Lauren business. Lauren was marketed to the woman who identified with the Ralph Lauren name. Tuxedo was aimed at a more sophisticated customer, a woman who preferred Ralph's elegant evening clothes to his tweedy daytime looks. To ensure that women understood that Tuxedo was a chicer fragrance, it was packaged in black.

Tuxedo didn't work. Although the scent was pleasing, the customers couldn't decipher whether Tuxedo was intended for men or women. The name and the packaging were confusing,

and Warner/Lauren didn't invest enough advertising and promotional dollars to overcome the misconceptions.

"It was a terrible concept," says Bob Ruttenberg. "Ralph
was thinking of evening wear then, and we thought Tuxedo
fit in with that approach. The name was wrong. People thought
it was a men's fragrance. You can see that now, but it's hind-
sight."

Despite this failure, Friedman and Ruttenberg still wanted
a name they could peddle to the drugstore chains like Genesco
and Walgreens and major mass merchandisers like Sears, Roebuck and K mart. Doing business with Bloomingdale's and Saks
Fifth Avenue was good for the ego but not so good for the
bottom line. The women with the spritzers, the samples, the
free gifts, discount umbrellas, the TV and magazine advertising, all had to be paid for.

The chain drugstore business, in contrast, was a no-frills
business. The customers didn't care about chrome display cases
or beveled mirrors. What they wanted was good, cheap stuff.
The trucks drove up, the merchandise was stacked to the ceil-
ing, and the customers were lured by cheaply printed mailers
or Sunday newspaper stuffers. Chain drugstores were the new
frontier of retailing in the 1970s.

Friedman and Ruttenberg decided they needed a men's
fragrance they could market at price points just a bit higher
than Old Spice, Brut, and Aqua Velva. They already owned
the Chaps name, having acquired it as part of their original
deal with Ralph Lauren.

Now they knew how they were going to use it.

"We were trying to convince Ralph to do a men's fragrance we could sell at the level of a K mart or Sears, Roebuck," says Ruttenberg. "He finally agreed, saying, 'I don't mind
being sold in Sears if it is the best fragrance in Sears.' "

In the fall of 1979, Friedman and Ruttenberg launched
Chaps in six test markets. Chaps would be a men's fragrance
aimed at the mass-market, chain drugstore business. It would
be the poor man's Polo, and it benefited from a certain amount
of built-in name recognition from the Chaps clothing line. The
fragrance was rolled out nationally in 1980 to 20,000 retail
stores.

"There was a critical mass in our business," says George Friedman. "Stores want to do business with the three or four people who control the business. It's important that they have the perception of your company as a major player."

There were good financial reasons, too. It doesn't cost more to promote a $25 million business than a $15 million business. At a certain critical point half of incremental sales start to drop right to the bottom line. In other words, expenses remain the same, so a larger percentage of revenues are transformed into profits. If Friedman and Ruttenberg could build more sales, they would finally make some money.

Or, as Steve Ross puts it, "The best analogy is a car going uphill. The first time you put it in neutral, look out, because it slides right down the hill. You've got to put your foot on the gas and go for it. Or don't go for it, and get out."

Hence, Chaps. Friedman and Ruttenberg had always dreamed of owning a $100 million business in seven years. To do so, they would have to compete in the mass market. They hired lanky John Horvitz, an articulate former Estée Lauder executive whose earlier jobs included eight years marketing packaged goods for the Bristol-Myers Company, to manage it for them.

"The Chaps clothing line was positioned as a younger, less expensive, western version of Polo," says Horvitz. "Chaps, as it evolved in the fragrance area, was marketed around the West, the outdoors. Almost Marlboro-like. The American hero was a cowboy, something Ralph felt very close to. So it became a logical direction to go in. But we wanted much broader distribution than Ralph's clothing had achieved."

Chaps was an immediate hit. The fragrance was strong and masculine, and its packaging was distinctly western in feel. Each Chaps box was emblazoned with a set of steer horns. Also, to accentuate its western heritage, each box was festooned with a silver buckle attached to two leather straps. (The buckles tended to fall off, which drove retailers nuts, and eventually the buckles were discontinued.) Sales in 1980 hit $14 million.

It was a terrific business, and almost anybody would have been satisfied.

Not Friedman, Ruttenberg, and Horvitz. Big was good, bigger was better. If Chaps did this well with a $3 million TV ad budget, they told Steve Ross, imagine what it would do with $6 million.

Ross liked what he heard. In 1980 Warner/Lauren's retail sales amounted to $75 million and the company employed more than 500. Polo was second in department stores sales to Aramis, while Lauren had climbed to the number four spot in women's fragrances. There were also growing sales in the United Kingdom, Puerto Rico, Canada, Switzerland, and Holland.

Warner/Lauren was still losing money, but on the positive side, the losses were declining year to year. If Friedman, Ruttenberg, and Horvitz wanted to gamble on an aggressive TV advertising campaign for Chaps, Steve Ross wouldn't deny it to them.

Do it, he said.

They did it, but it didn't work.

"We thought we could get to $24 million from $14 million," says Ruttenberg. "The stores didn't replace their inventory as fast as we expected, and while we increased our sales, we didn't deliver the $24 million. It hurt us. And it led to the only bad board meeting we ever had at Warner."

Warner might have been more understanding if Friedman and Ruttenberg hadn't launched Ralph Lauren cosmetics in February 1981, virtually the same time they were doubling the Chaps advertising budget.

Why cosmetics? Because it meant more space in the department stores. And as any manufacturer knows, more space equals more sales, which means bigger profits.

Ralph Lauren liked the idea of a cosmetics line. He had a great eye for color, and strong opinions. The more he thought about it, however, the more sure he became that his customer needed three lines, not one. There would be the cosmetics she wore during the day at the office, a second line to wear while jogging in the mornings or on the weekends, and a third, night line for after-hours. Alexandra Penney, a beauty reporter for the *New York Times,* was brought in part-time to help him develop his concept.

"Everything in Ralph's lexicon works from his woman," says Penney, who later gained fame as the author of *How to Make Love to a Man*. "It all starts with a fantasy woman of his who is very much like Ricky and who is very real for him. Ralph's fantasy life is really what makes him tick. If he puts on a pin-stripe suit, he's a businessman. If he puts on his jeans he's a Colorado cowboy. If he puts on his tuxedo with his jeans he's the easy-going, nighttime guy. The cars, the homes, the properties all fit into his fantasy."

The fantasy woman created problems. Ricky Lauren didn't wear makeup and Ralph himself didn't like red lips. This meant he wanted makeup that didn't look like makeup, nail enamel that didn't look like nail enamel. Desert colors like neutral beiges, faint reds, and dusky hues were his favorites.

The customers didn't understand. What they wanted were big, brassy colors men liked. Not that Ralph created the palette himself. That was the work of Julie Moses, a colorist who had worked with Bob Ruttenberg at Revlon. Talented, creative, and free-spirited, Moses not only mixed her colors in baby-food jars, she then described the colors over the phone to the factory manufacturing them.

"Being a color expert means being on target with fashion, knowing what the new product concepts are, and having a feeling of what's ahead," says Moses. "I remember Ralph Lauren sitting in my apartment and telling me that he liked makeup that didn't look like makeup. And I was thinking, 'Oh God, I'm a person who loves makeup.' This was at a time when everybody was overdoing makeup, and here was Ralph Lauren telling me that he wanted a refined makeup."

Julie Moses had just had a baby girl, and the last thing she intended to do was leave her child at home. She sometimes took her daughter — and in one instance her mother — with her to company meetings. That made for a complicated, sometimes hectic day. Moses could cope with that. More troubling were her instructions to create three different lines of cosmetics built around faint colors. Or even no color at all.

"I remember discussing the intensity of the lip gloss, and it became a conflict because they didn't want it to show," says Moses. "They were cutting back the color. Ralph wanted the

Ralph and Ricky on the beach at East Hampton. © Les Goldberg

Ralph riding his bike. From his first catalog, Spring 1977.
© Les Goldberg

From the Spring 1977 catalog. "You associate a man in a tuxedo with a woman in an evening dress and a limousine, and at first that's what we shot," says photographer Les Goldberg. "But it didn't work. It wasn't interesting. Ralph liked Jeeps, so he said, 'Why don't you put him in a Jeep and see what happens.' So we shot it on a muddy road in California."
© Les Goldberg

From the Spring 1977 catalog. Ralph and family in a Jeep.
© Les Goldberg

Fall 1981. Clotilde, one of Ralph's top models, is wearing a handknit sweater inspired by American Indian blankets in red, sand, and turquoise on a tan grou over chambray blouse. Note the cotton petticoat under her skirt. From Ralph's "Santa Fe" collection, inspired by a summer vacation he took with his family. © Bruce Weber

Fall 1982. A crew neck Fair Isle sweater vest, a wo tweed skirt, and a crocodi belt. Her blouse is made from handkerchief linen and has lace at the cuffs and neck. © Bruce Weber

Fall 1983. "Thoroughbred" collection, from Ralph's first group of home
furnishings. The comforter, sheets, and pillowcases are in contrasting
paisley patterns. Note the silver-framed photographs and leather-bound
books on the nearby nightstand. Today dozens of top retailers
merchandise their own lines with similar details. © Dénes Petöe

Fall 1984. "Log Cabin" collection. Nordic-inspired throw blankets and pillows mixed with tartan blanket, tartan sheets and pillow shams, and ticking-stripe dust ruffle. This shot was taken at Ralph's ranch in Colorado. A saddled horse is seen through the window. © Dénes Petöe

ring 1986 ad campaign. Men are in white or black dinner jackets. Woman in
ter is wearing a floral silk full-length halter dress; woman on right is wearing
am trousers with a floral silk evening robe. The concept: join our party, wear
r clothes. © Bruce Weber

ll 1987 ad campaign. Men
e in black wool tuxedos; she is
aring a black velvet full-length
wn with straps decorated with
gle beads. © Bruce Weber

Finishing touches being put on the Rhinelander Mansion at East 72nd Street and Madison Avenue in New York before its April 1986 opening.
© Mark Jenkinson

Full exterior of the Rhinelander Mansion. Sales the first year topped $30 million. © Dennis Phelps

Ralph and Ricky Lauren, January 12, 1987. Ralph is holding "Retailer of the Year" award given to him by the Council of Fashion Designers of America at black-tie gala at Metropolitan Museum of Art. Ricky is wearing a black cashmere, one-shoulder evening gown; Ralph is wearing blue jeans and cowboy boots, an outfit some guests found objectionable. © 1987 by Ron Galella

Spring 1987 ad campaign. Ralph sitting on the kitchen countertop at a ranch in California. This is the same designer who asks his most sophisticated customers to spend $960 for an alligator notebook. © Bruce Weber

Interior view of freestanding Polo shop in Tokyo. From New York to Europe to Japan, one merchandising point of view. Courtesy of Seibu Corporation of America

Spring 1988. Ralph's first major collection after he recovered from surgery. She is wearing a two-tiered taffeta skirt and a short-sleeved cashmere sweater with organza collar and cuffs. © George Smith

customer to be beautiful, but he didn't want the makeup to show. It was a basic conflict."

Altogether, the three collections amounted to 118 individual units, which was a lot of eye shadows and fingernail polishes and lip glosses to update every season. It would prove too complicated.

The stores, though, loved it.

The first week, Bullock's in Los Angeles did $60,000 in retail sales. Business at Filene's also exceeded plan. The advertising and in-store promotions were so successful that they also boosted sales of Ralph Lauren's fragrances and his clothes.

The concept, built around Ralph's clothes for day, evening, and active wear, lent itself to crowd-pleasing extravaganzas. Warner/Lauren built runways in the cosmetics departments at the stores, presented fashion shows of Ralph's clothes, and drew huge crowds. One of the models showing Ralph's clothes at Bloomingdale's was Amy Miles, an attractive redhead. Bob Ruttenberg married her three years later.

It sounded almost perfect.

It wasn't.

What Friedman and Ruttenberg didn't know was that a company that builds a successful cosmetics business must keep hundreds of units in stock. Maintaining and keeping track of that inventory is tough, especially for beginners. Purchasing and planning also proved to be an administrative nightmare. Getting into this business had been easy; making money was not.

"We didn't have the expertise," says Ruttenberg. "We had high out-of-stocks, and we didn't have the right forecasting procedure. We invested more than two point five million into that first year. More than the money, though, it was draining our people. Stores wrote an order for Lauren perfume and it took six minutes to fill. An order for cosmetics took six months. Sales got up to eight million, nine million a year, but we never made profits."

There was a reason for this. Not many companies earn money manufacturing makeup and color lines. The profits actually come from skin care treatment. A little jar of facial cream that costs $1 to make may retail for $35. Skin treatment is a serious business. Fashion didn't mean anything to a woman worrying about wrinkles. And try as it did, Warner/Lauren could not build a skin care treatment business at retail. Ten items were launched in 1982. They disappeared without a trace.

The customers didn't care about wrinkle cream from Ralph Lauren.

Fact was, they didn't care much about Ralph Lauren lipstick, either.

"In cosmetics you struggle, struggle, struggle," says Ruttenberg. "We were running fragrance promotions, Chaps promotions, cosmetics promotions. Every store was promoting a Ralph Lauren product eight months of the year. It was a Chaps gift-with-purchase, then a Lauren gift-with-purchase, then a Polo gift-with-purchase. We were spending a lot of money because that's how you build the business."

Warner Communications still had not seen any return on its investment, though, and the pressures began to build. What were Friedman and Ruttenberg doing? This was a business. Where were the profits?

"If you're successful in a business like Warner/Lauren the need for working capital only becomes greater, because you build your inventories far in advance of when the stores pay for them," explains David Horowitz, the executive most responsible for Warner Communications' stake in Warner/Lauren.

"Remember, we went into this to build a big company. Chaps gave us the opportunity to make a quantum leap, because as long as we were stuck at the department store level there were obvious limits to how much we could grow and how much money we could make. Chaps, though, was a major investment. We had to add distributors, salesmen, and related data processing needs, and we only had one product over which we could spread those costs. This meant we had to look for yet another fragrance. Then along came Vanderbilt."

In the late 1970s Gloria Vanderbilt, former debutante, became Gloria Vanderbilt, designer. Murjani International launched a line of Gloria Vanderbilt jeans, and overnight they became one of the best-selling jeans lines in the country. In one name recognition test, Gloria Vanderbilt achieved a 94 percent rating.

Vanderbilt would ultimately be distributed to the same stores that carried Chaps, after an initial launch in the department stores. What this meant was that the initial start-up costs would be relatively modest — with the exception of a multi-million-dollar advertising and promotion campaign. Done right, Friedman and Ruttenberg thought, it would be a bonanza.

Ralph Lauren complained that this was a terrible idea.

He'd made his deal with Warner Communications on the basis that he would be Warner/Lauren's only designer.

Now it was adding Gloria Vanderbilt?

Ralph was so angry that he called a board meeting. After he arrived with his attorney, he asked George Friedman and Bob Ruttenberg to step outside. Ralph's lawyer then harangued the board with complaints that Warner/Lauren's inventory was out of control and that Friedman and Ruttenberg were already doing too much. The last thing the business needed, he said, was yet another new product.

Especially a fragrance called Vanderbilt.

The board listened politely, thanked Ralph and his lawyer for their time, and then voted to launch Vanderbilt as soon as possible.

With good reason.

Warner/Lauren was paying as much as 16 percent interest to Warner Communications on the millions it had invested in Ralph Lauren fragrances and cosmetics. That year, 1982, was also the year that Atari, the home video game company, peaked and began to lose money, with bigger losses soon to follow. Steve Ross had been patient long enough; he now had good reason to want better performance from the fragrance division, and everybody knew the Vanderbilt line could mean the difference. Friedman and Ruttenberg were planning to sell it in 20,000 stores compared to the 2,000 stores that carried the Lauren fragrance. This alone would justify the hiring of a direct sales force, a move that would increase Chaps' distribution.

Launching Vanderbilt was a business decision, but Ralph took it personally. He was so angry he stopped talking to George Friedman.

Ralph couldn't walk away, though. His Warner/Lauren contract was unbreakable.

And it didn't help that Vanderbilt was a smash.

In 1982, its first year, Vanderbilt did over $50 million in retail sales, or nearly twice the original sales projections. This made it one of the biggest successes in the history of the fragrance industry.

Thanks to the Vanderbilt fragrance, Warner/Lauren reported its first operating profits in 1982 on worldwide sales of nearly $200 million at retail. Those sales increases represented more than a 75 percent gain over 1981 and nearly a threefold gain over 1980. The volume also included nearly $20 million in cosmetics revenues. (The cosmetics line would not make its first marginal profits until 1983.)

Despite his 5 percent ownership stake in the company, Ralph Lauren was angry and hurt. He also felt betrayed, especially as he'd developed a close relationship with Steve Ross. Ross was outgoing and enthusiastic. He was also generous when it came to paying his executives and his performers, and this generosity as well as his charm had won him the personal loyalty of such entertainers as Clint Eastwood, Barbra Streisand, and Frank Sinatra. His friendship with Ralph Lauren also extended well beyond business levels. When Ralph told Ross that Frank Sinatra had always been one of his idols, Ross promptly invited Ralph to a Carnegie Hall appearance Sinatra was making to benefit the Police Athletic League. Then Ross took Ralph backstage to meet Sinatra, followed by dinner where Ralph sat at Sinatra's table. Later, Ralph Lauren would share a microphone with Frank Sinatra at one of Steve Ross's parties. Those were moments Ralph Lauren would remember his entire life, and not surprisingly, his feelings for Steve Ross were very strong. Steve Ross was not only his business partner, he was his friend.

"There was tremendous faith and trust between Ralph and me . . . it was almost blind faith," says Ross. "There were many things in the original agreement that he waived because they were hurting our business. For example, he took a cut in his commissions because he knew the company was losing money. Ralph might not have liked Vanderbilt, but he understood the needs of the company. It was a beautiful marriage."

The marriage ended in early 1984.

Blame it on the video game business.

Atari, the video game maker, lost $539 million in 1983, and its performance was threatening the health of the entire company. To make matters worse, Rupert Murdoch acquired 7 percent of Warner's stock and eventually began making noises about taking it over.

Steve Ross needed to raise cash fast. This meant selling some of Warner's profitable divisions, including Warner/Lauren. "The problem wasn't Rupert Murdoch," says Ross. "It was strictly the losses at Atari."

The key question was where the company would be sold. One thing was certain. Friedman and Ruttenberg didn't want to be bought by Estée Lauder or Revlon. Then, in December, Friedman met with representatives of Cosmair, Inc., the U.S. licensee for L'Oréal, S.A., a worldwide cosmetics company based in Paris. (The majority stockholder in L'Oréal, S.A., is Nestlé, S.A., the giant Swiss food conglomerate.)

Cosmair's product line included Lancôme and L'Oréal. Now it wanted to build market share by acquiring an existing company. What it most sorely lacked was a fragrance business, and Warner/Lauren, with its famous brands and growing international sales, appeared a perfect fit. Friedman and Ruttenberg had heard only positive things about Cosmair, and when Cosmair offered $145 million on January 6, 1984, they and Steve Ross were receptive. (Warner/Lauren's sales were about $210 million at that point. Its long-term debt amounted to $65 million.) The acquisition included the Ralph Lauren fragrances and cosmetics as well as Vanderbilt.

It seemed a good deal.

Clearly, George Friedman and Bob Ruttenberg thought so. Not only would it make them rich, but the payout would be immediate. Friedman stood to walk away with $15 million. Ralph Lauren and Bob Ruttenberg would each receive about $7 million for their shares. Warner Communications would get the rest, about $116 million.

It was a lot of money for a business that hadn't turned its first profit until the last quarter of 1982.

But Ralph Lauren wasn't impressed.

First, he didn't need cash. By 1984 he was already a millionaire many times over. More important to Ralph were his personal relationships. Despite the hard feelings about Vanderbilt, Ralph still trusted Steve Ross. Cosmair, however, didn't mean anything to him. And he didn't want to do business with strangers.

Steve Ross took him to dinner and explained that he needed help. Warner had invested only $15 million since founding Warner/Lauren in 1976. Now it stood to make nearly an eightfold profit. Ralph Lauren was his friend, but Warner Communications was Steve Ross's life.

Ralph Lauren finally gave his blessing. He had once come close to losing his business. He understood what sleepless nights meant.

A few weeks later, the company was sold. George Friedman and Bob Ruttenberg stayed on. They knew things would be different, but dammit, they loved the business. They'd built it.

Two months later, they launched a new fragrance called Paloma Picasso, and in April 1985 they unveiled a new Ralph Lauren scent called Monogram, a citrus-and-spice fragrance packaged in a cobalt blue bottle complete with a silver, diamond-shaped RL monogram.

This did not mean that the relationship between Friedman, Ruttenberg, and the other Cosmair executives was an easy one. Both Friedman and Ruttenberg were accustomed to making the important decisions. Now they were part of a bigger team, an international team, and a team whose players didn't always agree with them.

In September 1985, George Friedman resigned. He said he wanted to teach at Brooklyn College, his alma mater, and perhaps work for a political candidate.

Shortly afterwards, Bob Ruttenberg announced that Warner/Lauren was dropping its Ralph Lauren cosmetics business. Shipments were never good, and the company was spending too much time chasing what amounted to marginal business. Retailers said they were shocked, but there was no reason to be. Few designers lasted in the color business; it was too competitive.

Nine months later, in June 1986, Ruttenberg quit. Work-

ing for the French just wasn't the same as working with George
Friedman and Steve Ross.

"When we sold the company, I was ecstatic," says Ruttenberg. "We got paid in a week, and I walked away with millions.
I was rich. But it wasn't my company any more. When George
and I started, we decided on two major policies. First, we
wouldn't hire relatives. Second, we'd close on Fridays at one
P.M. so we could go to the country.

"After Cosmair bought us I continued to leave at one P.M.
on Fridays. Cosmair hated it. So finally I left."

A year later, in 1987, Cosmair discontinued the Monogram fragrance. It can now be found in discount stores.

Today Ralph Lauren fragrances remain strong in a $4 bil-
lion plus market. As one industry analyst puts it, both Polo
and Lauren have become "classics." The fragrance business is
no longer the small, personal company Ralph Lauren once envisioned in 1976, but businesses must change as they get bigger.

Polo/Ralph Lauren is no longer the same, either.

On November 10, 1986, the following two-column advertisement appeared in the *New York Times:* "Tuesday, November 11, from 12:30–2:30 PM: Join us for apple cider and country music as Macy's celebrates the opening of our exclusive Polo by Ralph Lauren Dungaree Shop in the Herald Square Arcade." The invitation was followed, in small type, by a brief explanation: "It's a salute to American style . . . to the carefree and easy tradition that inspired this new collection of casual wear. It's a gathering of shirts, jeans and jackets that captures the comfortable character of well-worn utility clothing. Discover Polo Dungarees: style that becomes better and more personal with age."

An invitation is hard to resist. The $47.50 work shirt signaled certain problems, however. Only ten blocks away one could buy a new dress shirt at Brooks Brothers, stripes or tattersall, for $36. It's easy to imagine Dad, paintbrush in hand on Saturday morning, struggling with his conscience in front of his closet as he decides which shirt to sacrifice to redoing those tired porch chairs. There was Ralph's work shirt and, side by side, that dress shirt from Brooks Brothers. What price style?

The day Macy's picked to host its party was cold, gray, and rainy. The weather didn't stop the crowd pushing its way into the Herald Square Arcade, a passageway designed to attract young, trendy customers with such stores as David's Cookies, an Ocean Pacific boutique decorated with two orange-and-pink surfboards, and 34,000,000 B.C., purveyor of sweatshirts decorated with dinosaurs.

The customers had no problem finding Ralph's Dungaree Shop. Directly in front of it was a red velvet rope cordon, the type used in movie lines. To the left was a microphone and stool. At exactly 12:30, with perhaps fifty or so onlookers gathered, country western singer Larry Siegel broke into a foot-tapping rendition of "Wabash Cannonball" on his eight-string Gibson mandolin.

The boutique was now officially open. As Larry played, some went for the cider. Others browsed. Many simply gazed in wonder at Ralph's concept of a country store. Consider this. In addition to wooden planking bleached to affect a weathered appearance, the fixtures included one ship's steering wheel; a stuffed rooster; an egg-cabinet; half a wooden crate; a deer head with big antlers; strings of garlic cloves and dried peppers; tomato preserves; two sleds; a hay rake; and a massive cast-iron, pot-bellied stove.

Ralph used these props to create an image of a way of life even his most urbanized customers could recognize. They gave his work a context, a mood he considered as important to his marketing as magazine advertising.

In this case, though, the effect didn't work. Most of the crowd that had gathered left quickly after briefly looking over the clothes. Perhaps they considered Ralph's dungarees to be too costumey, a complaint he has heard before.

Two customers stayed though, sorting through the clothes with interest and enthusiasm. They were dedicated Ralph Lauren shoppers, and the comments they made would be typical.

"Dolores, come here," murmured Vivian Ricupero to her friend, as she picked up a $35.50 gray three-button cotton underwear shirt.

"I'm busy," replied Dolores Brechtlein, holding a Lord & Taylor bag and intently eyeballing the pants.

A few minutes later, Vivian Ricupero and Dolores Brechtlein approached the cash register.

"These are comfortable, classic looks that never go out of style," pronounced Vivian, who came from Bayside, Queens. "They are a comfortable look that can go anywhere. You can dress them up, you can dress them down. I have a Ralph Lauren two-piece denim dress, and there's so much you can do with it. His sweaters are sensational. And I love his skirts."

Her friend Dolores, who lives in the College Point section of Queens, held up a large denim shirt. "This is for me," she said. "Ralph Lauren is a genius."

Vivian thought this was overdoing it.

"Well, they say that he copied in the beginning from L. L. Bean, giving it that little extra oomph that Bean needed," she volunteered. "What I like is that Ralph Lauren is a hundred percent American."

Vivian bought the gray underwear shirt for her husband and she and Dolores left. A few minutes later, the boutique was empty of customers, and the two salesclerks were standing with nothing to do. It was now past 1 P.M. It isn't easy to please a New York lunchtime crowd, even when the cider is free. Larry put down his instruments and took a break.

A Macy's employee slipped a cassette into a tape player, and the silence was soon broken by an orchestrated rendition of "Bonanza." There had been little activity at the cash register this day. But that had happened before. Although no American designer is more closely associated with the American West than Ralph Lauren, his blue jeans have never fit well, and that is the reason his western wear line in the late 1970s was a failure.

So let's stop for a minute here, and look back to where it all started. If this were "Bonanza" and Macy's were the famed Ponderosa ranch, Ralph Lauren would have the role of "Little Joe," well-intentioned, boyishly good-looking, and always astonished when things go wrong.

Call him a cowboy at heart. The first feature story to mention Ralph, remember, appeared in *Daily News Record* on May 21, 1964. Although still a tie salesman, he'd attracted the paper's notice because of his idiosyncratic wardrobe, a wardrobe that included custom-made, corduroy riding pants shaped at the calf and fuller near the ankle.

Later, in the early 1970s, would come Ralph's western-styled jeans and shirts, clothes he designed for his Chaps division for men. Women's wear, too, would be influenced by Ralph's vision of the West. After introducing his first women's shirts in 1971, Ralph offered suits, jackets, and pants tailored for women. Those clothes sold so well that in the fall of 1974 he decided to show such western-inspired looks for women as pearl-buttoned pants and cowgirl outfits. "This is the best of the western breed, inspired by the best of the cowboys — Coop [Gary Cooper] in *The Plainsman*," read a company handout.

"Lauren's cavalry shirt of cotton corduroy has a button-on bib, and tall-in-the-saddle styling. Worn over the jean skirt with inserted V-panel."

The response?

Put the six-shooters away, urged *Women's Wear Daily*, which found the collection off-putting. Ralph, however, shrugged off the complaints, and a year later he showed yet more western shirts for women. Ralph Lauren was now growing more confident in his skills as a women's wear designer. He also seemed more sure of the loyalty of what he liked to call "his woman." Ralph had started in the women's business with men's shirts and suits, because those were the clothes he knew how to make. As his tastes became more sophisticated, his line broadened and became more feminine . . . but he didn't lose his interest in western wear.

The western clothes reflected Ralph's thinking that women's sportswear was dull and limited. "The only look in the early 1970s was the Anne Klein look," says Ralph. "Women's sportswear was hung on T-stands. Sportswear for women was garbage. It was crummy sweaters . . . it was all color coordinated, you know, pinks go with pinks, reds go with reds . . . it was not an industry, it was nothing. There was no sportswear. Anne Klein was the name. She made clothes for herself. But they were so dowdy Ricky couldn't wear them. They were boxy, big, not quality. Quality maybe for Anne Klein, but not in terms of men's wear. What I started to do was make women's clothes the way I made men's clothes, because I knew smart women would sometimes go to custom tailors for a jacket like their husbands'. They loved that look. I went with my Harris tweeds and my shetlands, and I made slim jackets. The first thing was shirts . . . nice skinny shirts with a polo player on the cuff with a white collar and bold stripes, and that became the hottest department at Bloomingdale's.

"Then they said, 'Okay, what can you do now?' The next season I put it together. A collection of suits and sportswear, mostly tailored jackets and pleated pants, some small Fair Isle sweaters. There was a shop for me, and the stuff started to sell. It was a total revelation for this whole industry. It became a big thing."

What about the problems with fit, the terrible deliveries, the endless production snafus?

There were problems, he agrees, but the customers bought anyway.

"Ralph Lauren became like a cult," he says oddly. "Henri Bendel bought my stuff. I brought back a look when there was no look. It was beautiful shirtings, beautiful jackets, beautiful trousers, things a woman couldn't get.

"I aimed at models, I aimed at sophisticated young women. Lean and tall. And then I started to make more sportswear: chino skirts and safari shirts and jumpsuits and tailored coats and British warmers that were shaped beautifully, Chesterfield coats, blazers, gray flannel skirts. They were cut differently, they were dashing, they were sexier, the fabrics were more beautiful. Women had never experienced quality clothes like that. They could never find a jacket cut with high armholes and slim shoulders . . . it was slim, lean, and shapely . . . it was sexy, not boxy or dowdy. I gave them a racy look. I also designed the clothes for Revlon's 'Charlie Girl' TV commercials. She was the young, modern, upcoming girl, the 1970s girl."

To Ralph Lauren, the young 1970s girl meant a customer who led an active, exciting life. She hiked, so he gave her rugged windbreakers, lumberjack plaid shirts, argyle socks, and laced hiking boots. She rode in jeeps, so he gave her cable sweaters, turtlenecks, corduroy pants, and down jackets. In 1976 he even offered her cavalry jodhpurs.

"No one did that stuff," says Ralph. "It didn't exist for women. You can say there was Eddie Bauer or L. L. Bean, but I took a mood and expanded it and romanticized it with color and texture. America was my inspiration. Activities of life, not the activities of fashion. I was making that life exciting and working with it. That's what I ignited: American sportswear. And there was always a story."

He presented what he describes as his first full women's collection in April 1977 at the old Biltmore Hotel. He showed burgundy cashmere dresses with lace collars and cuffs, Shaker-knit sweaters, evening sarong dresses made of blue satin, Norfolk coats, and crepe pants worn beneath a $25,000 golden sable he'd designed. There were also chamois pants, and light-weight tailored jackets and rawhide moccasins. Today everybody makes clothes from chamois. But when Ralph Lauren introduced it in 1977, it was so new that *New York Post* fashion reporter Eugenia Sheppard advised her readers not to confuse it with Ultrasuede. In June he was elected to Coty's Hall of Fame for women's wear designers; he'd been elected to the men's Hall of Fame a year earlier.

It would be the 1978 fall women's wear collection, however, that showed how much his confidence had grown, and how sharp his instincts were about the customers. Perhaps not surprisingly, he chose to emphasize, again, his western wear.

The setting that year was the rooftop of the St. Regis Hotel. There, as such celebrities as Diane Keaton, Candice Bergen, and Angelo Donghia watched in wonder, the show opened to the sounds of "Back in the Saddle Again." Before anybody could blink, Ralph's models marched out wearing the wildest mix of western looks east of the Rockies. They included suede fringed leather jackets over long flounced cotton prairie skirts, shearling coats, chamois blouses, satin cowboy blouses, satin suits, satin jeans, and brown lizard belts with silver cowboy buckles. The collection even featured velvet suits with silver buckles and satin cowboy shirts with pants for evening.

"Lots of New Collections, But Lauren Steals the Show," headlined the *Times.* "His look is American, and he manages to make foreign attempts to produce, say, the Western look, seem heavy-handed and awkward."

"Lauren: American Fantasies for Fall" headlined *WWD.*

"He took us through Matt Dillon, Miss Kitty, the Marlboro Man, the trucker, cowboys and Indians, through riding school and pilot school and the New York City girl to get a wonderful amalgam of all-American looks," Kal Ruttenstein of Bloomingdale's told that paper.

That collection influenced every retailer in the country. The stores were ready for something fresh, too. Women were tired of the baggy, loose-fitting clothes most designers were then making here and in Europe. The customers also were wary of the big shoulder pads that were being shown as alternatives.

Suddenly, American customers and retailers had something new to sell and hype. The collection also indicated how iconoclastic Ralph Lauren had become. If he liked something, he did it. He didn't care what Paris or Milan showed. If Ralph wanted to show cowboy clothes, he showed cowboy clothes. He was so far out . . . he was suddenly in.

A month later, Ralph translated his western look into furs for the Tepper Collection, dressing his models in cowboy boots and belts with big buckles and western blouses. Everybody got the message. By June, customers at fancy restaurants like La Caravelle were seen wearing wide-brimmed cowboy hats.

"New York has become something of a cowboy town," pondered the *Times*. "Men whose idea of a canyon is the space between two rows of skyscrapers take the air in full regalia — 10-gallon hat, yoked shirt, embroidered denim jacket, hand-tooled belt, jeans and boots. And the women beside them wreath their throats in bandannas, wear ankle-length skirts fit for a hoedown and — faced with inclement weather — don hats and ponchos worthy of the crew of a cattle drive."

This was Ralph Lauren's doing. Not only had he started the western wear look, but he seemed best positioned to take advantage of it once it caught on. In June he signed a contract with The Gap, a California-based retailer that did $205 million in sales for the fiscal year ended January 31, 1978.

Why The Gap? Because The Gap then sold low-priced Levi's jeans, work shirts, and rugged outdoor clothing in 310 stores across the country. Just as the department stores made low-cost copies of his Polo line, Ralph knew that cheap western wear knockoffs would soon be flooding the market. He'd countered the Polo knockoffs with his Chaps division. Now he would do the same through The Gap. There was an old personal relationship, too. He had met Don Fisher, The Gap's president, through Rose Wells. Wells, a Federated Department Stores executive, years earlier had pushed him to make his first women's shirts. Now she argued that by signing a deal with Fisher, Ralph would be able to attract the moderate-price customers who couldn't afford the Ralph Lauren collection, which was priced from $58 to $310.

Ralph and The Gap eventually formed a new company,

Polo Westernwear, which made and distributed western clothes to department and specialty stores in special Polo Westernwear in-store shops. The Gap provided the funding and put the production in place. In effect, The Gap became a Ralph Lauren licensee. There would be Polo Westernwear by Ralph Lauren for men, and Ralph Lauren Westernwear for women. The men's line included corduroy western coats ($125 retail), denim and corduroy jeans ($33 to $36), leather bolo ties ($35) and lizard belts ($225). The women's collection included jeans, shirts, and skirts priced from $22.50 to $130.

When the clothes were introduced in April 1979, five New York retailers bought the collections: Bloomingdale's, Henri Bendel, Lord & Taylor, Macy's, and Saks Fifth Avenue. Bloomingdale's even announced "Ralph Lauren Week," and put his cowboy clothes in every window in the store.

"I've been wearing cowboy boots and Western clothes for a long time," Ralph told the *New York Times*. "The image isn't fashion, it's rugged. It's part of American culture. It's one thing France can't claim is theirs. It's ours. My goal is to give it quality and dimension.

"When The Gap people came and asked me to do a jeans line, I said, 'I don't believe in designer jeans — I believe in a total concept.' So they agreed to set up a separate company to manufacture, sell and distribute the Westernwear I design. This way it can be affordable to everybody."

Look at the western-inspired ad that Bloomingdale's placed in the *New Yorker* in the April 9 issue. The photo is an awkward tableau with a woman, a man, and a horse, which must have been as uncomfortable to stage as it was to look at. "Ralph Lauren's Westernwear, first seen (and herd) at Bloomingdale's," read the copy. "How the west was worn via two spirited collections, hot as High Noon. Authentic shirts, jeans, vests, jackets and slickers. Lean jean skirt and prairie flouncers. Plus all the extrees. All corralled in two brand new quarters. For him in Polo Western, Men's Store. For her in Ralph Lauren Westernwear."

This was a terrific merchandising gimmick. Orders the first week amounted to $90,000 at Bloomingdale's. Despite shipping problems, and the fact that his women's jeans were too

tight to fit most of the customers, The Gap quickly revised its
initial estimate of $12 million in sales the first year to $25
million.

"Ralph Lauren's pioneer effort in the moderate-priced
sportswear market could prove a gold mine if early reaction
to his Western Wear holds up," wrote *WWD* in June. Stores
were quoted describing the business as alternately fantastic,
incredible, wonderful, or phenomenal.

Thus Ralph Lauren realized every New York kid's greatest fantasy: not only was he a cowboy, but he still slept every
night in his Fifth Avenue duplex. By day he was a handy guy
with a lariat, at night, a regular city slicker. In his ads he dressed
up as Gary Cooper, smiling, wearing his cowboy hat, his cowboy boots, his cowboy vests. Observed the *Daily News* in June,
"Lauren not only sells clothes these days, he sells himself —
his looks, attitude and tastes. The Western Wear advertising
campaign, for example, features a dramatic photograph of
Lauren himself in denims and a Stetson hat. The clothes, priced
considerably lower than his other divisions, seem like an afterthought. Instead, the message is this: If you look like Ralph
Lauren, maybe you could live like him."

This business was based on sharing the images and fantasies. The customers slipped on their prairie skirts and
they were Annie Oakley. They put on their riding boots,
and they were Buffalo Bill Cody. They put on their bandannas and they were John Wayne. Or they bought the entire
package and they were Ralph Lauren.

It was weird to think of sophisticated New Yorkers, their
wallets heavy with credit cards, strolling out to dinner on the
East Side dressed as though they were walking the streets of
Laredo. Every day was Halloween. These weren't clothes, they
were costumes. It was fun, it was fresh, it was authentically
American.

Then, perhaps because these clothes were costumes, the
customers got bored. Soon the Stetsons were put back in the
closet, and the customers went back to their three-piece suits
and their loafers. By the end of 1979 the dust had settled.

The Gap was very unhappy.

Donald Fisher reported sales the first year amounted to

only $12 million. And there were so many shipping, production, and fit problems that The Gap lost money on the clothes it managed to produce and distribute.

Fisher was smart enough to cut his mistakes early. By the end of March 1980, The Gap closed its Ralph Lauren Westernwear division, taking a one-time, after-tax charge of nearly $6 million.

"We had troubles with the fit," says Don Fisher. "There was a disagreement with Ralph Lauren as to what the fit should be. He wanted a much narrower and tighter fit than the market was looking for. I understood that there was a problem, but there was nothing I could do. He controlled it.

"I also think western wear was too narrow a category to support a big business. That may have been the biggest obstacle."

This hurt. Ralph loved western wear. In New York he was practically Mr. Cowboy.

What went wrong?

Listen to Joel Horowitz. Horowitz had worked for Ralph Lauren as a salesman in the late 1960s, and later helped to open the Jerry Magnin store in Beverly Hills. He eventually left that business, took other jobs, and returned as vice-president of Polo Westernwear.

"Put simply, it was a fiasco," says Horowitz, today the president of Murjani International. "It was a very bad marriage. The Gap wanted to make certain products, and Ralph wouldn't let them. I spent ninety percent of my time trying to keep things smooth between Don and Ralph.

"It wasn't personal, but neither of them saw the business the same way. When push came to shove, Ralph didn't want to do the kind of things the contract said."

On one hand, Ralph was eager for The Gap to build a successful western business and make him millions of dollars. On the other, Ralph didn't want The Gap rustling away the Polo customers. Remember, The Gap paid Ralph a licensing fee. But he owned Polo. The last thing he intended to do was compete with himself.

Ralph knew from the outset that this could be a problem. So he did two things. First, he put a price cap on how much

The Gap could charge the customers for the clothes it made. Second, he refused to let The Gap put his brand, his polo player, on its jeans.

For example: under terms of the contract, The Gap couldn't sell its shirts for more than $25 at retail. But by the time Ralph Lauren was done designing those shirts with his pearl buttons and his good-quality fabrics and all the details that make Ralph Lauren unique, The Gap had invested $25 in cost.

Worse still were Ralph's jeans, especially the jeans he made for women. Ralph wanted a woman's fitted jean to compete with Levi Strauss. But he wanted his jeans to be shaped and cut differently. He believed in clothes that were sexy and cut close to the body, and he cut his jeans accordingly.

Which meant that while they may have fitted a handful of fashion models, the average girl or woman couldn't wear them. The jeans were too tight at the hips, the waist, everywhere. Despite the complaints from Don Fisher, Ralph Lauren refused to make major alterations.

The men's jeans weren't a great fit, either. As a matter of fact, even Ralph continued to wear Levi's.

"He said his own jeans didn't fit right," says Joel Horowitz. "What he wanted was an updated Levi's jean. He wanted to make the leg a little trimmer, the rise a little higher. I have to believe that Ralph's major disappointment in life from a business standpoint is that he hasn't been able to design the next Levi's. He killed Izod Lacoste with his Polo knit shirt. But he's never made a good pair of jeans."

Joel Horowitz stayed with the Westernwear business until the very end. Once he saw that The Gap would not be able to sell its Westernwear division to Ralph Lauren, he met with Peter Strom to see if he could work out his own licensing deal.

"There were some people interested in backing me if I could get the license," says Horowitz. "But Peter said no. He said, 'We're too burned. We don't want to license this to anybody again. We'll do it ourselves, later.'"

Which explains why, six years later, Macy's built a Ralph Lauren Dungaree Shop and handed out free apple cider to its customers on a cold, rainy fall afternoon.

The cowboy fad was dead as far as The Gap was concerned.

But that didn't mean Ralph had lost his interest in the western look. In April 1981, he showed the customers what he had on his mind: The New West.

The New West meant clothes inspired by the Navaho blankets and Indian jewelry Ralph had seen in the summer of 1980, when he took Ricky and their kids to New Mexico for a vacation. He wasn't the only one. Calvin Klein had earlier shown a collection influenced by his travels to New Mexico, basically in the form of muted colors. Ralph's translation, true to form, was more literal. There were chamois skirts and turquoise hoop earrings and jacket-sized Navaho Fair Isle sweaters and long olive suede skirts. The Santa Fe–inspired wool handknit sweaters were among the most handsome of all his designs. Their strong patterns and mix of colors were unlike anything anybody had ever seen before, especially when worn over his white cotton blouse, a long, turquoise prairie skirt, and a white cotton petticoat.

Suddenly, the New Mexico look was in, which came as a big surprise to everybody, especially the people in New Mexico who had never worn suede skirts or cotton petticoats in their lives.

"I remember going to Santa Fe, which inspired me. But there was nothing like what I did in Santa Fe," says Ralph. "Then, two years later, I went back to Santa Fe, and I saw pictures of my clothes hung in the back rooms of shops where people were making clothes. I gave Santa Fe the ball. I saw the Indian rugs and said, 'I want to do sweaters like this.' I took the colors and made prairie skirts. I only used authentic concha belts, though. (Concha belts are belts made from different silver pieces. They were originally developed by the Navahos but were adapted by the Pueblo tribe of New Mexico.) Guys made businesses out of concha belts, but I only brought in one hundred of them. Then I sold them to the stores at no profit so they would have a quality look."

The Santa Fe look was so popular that on the Sunday the *New York Times Magazine* published its first pictures of Ralph's line, the phones at the Museum of the American Indian in New York rang nonstop. (The museum kept some concha belts in stock as gift items.) The belts cost $200 to $1,500, and the customers bought them sight-unseen. Although the museum was only open for four hours, there were but two belts left in stock at day's end. A second shipment arrived Monday, when the museum was closed to the public, and those belts were all gone by Tuesday evening.

The knockoffs appeared almost immediately.

Typical: a full-page, black-and-white ad for ZCMI Designer Sportswear, which appeared in the February 1982 issue of *Vogue*. Two models were posed side by side, each in Ralph Lauren–like prairie skirts and draped in Indian jewelry. Unlike Ralph's models, however, they wore unscuffed boots and their outfits retailed from $57 to $70.

In that same issue of *Vogue*, Ralph's western clothes were featured on various editorial pages; they cost from $330 to $900.

No wonder the knockoffs were such good sellers.

Then, when everybody started to manufacture Santa Fe–inspired clothes, Ralph Lauren changed direction. Since the customers associated him with rugged clothes and the West, he would give them Victorian-inspired blouses with high lace collars and velvet dresses.

Ralph Lauren, cowboy, transformed himself into Ralph Lauren, romantic, for fall 1982.

After crowding 1,000 retailers, friends, and such celebrities as Norman Parkinson, Betty Furness, Bruce Weber, and Jerry Zipkin into the ballroom of the Hotel Pierre, he showed one of the collections he would be most proud of, a collection which the *New York Times* described as elegant, subdued, and understated. There were patchwork skirts, pictorial sweaters, and blouses adorned with cameo or bar pins. "Mr. Lauren does the double-breasted dress in velvet as well as wool, and has other styles in velvet as well," wrote Bernadine Morris. "A tank-top dress, for example, is worn with creamy kid gloves that extend above the elbow. The clothes look exceedingly well-bred, and though they are nonassertive, they make a powerful statement. They rank among the best of the season."

"The lace was the breakthrough," says Ralph, who had shown some lace blouses in earlier collections. "That was the beginning of romantic clothes, and one of the great collections. It was a simple show with quiet music. Everybody else was blasting the music and showing lots of flash, and I did this chic quiet stuff with lace and antique suits and handknit sweaters. It was very Old World, and inspired by Old World appeal. Your grandmothers had this stuff, but when I showed it the customers couldn't find it. Maybe they could find it in the thrift shops, that was it."

So, how come Ralph Lauren is the Rodney Dangerfield of American fashion designers? Why is he always complaining he gets no respect?

Ask most fashion editors, retailers, or Ralph Lauren customers, and this is what they say about his clothes:

"He's a brilliant editor."

"He knocks off L. L. Bean."

"He takes and adapts an English look for the American market."

"He doesn't design, he edits."

"He's a stylist, not a designer."

Words like "original" or "creative" or "unique" are rarely heard.

"The things I've done are so subtle they are generic to the world today," counters Ralph. "If you look at Banana Republic's catalog you see my clothes in there. It's the bias cuts, the corduroy collars . . . I might have taken some classic things, but the classic things were never done the way I did them. Brooks Brothers never did what I did. England never had things like that. Everybody says I went to England and copied their look. But the English don't have a look. Yes, it's the inspiration from the Old World, from the quality world, but I added something that was so alive. I gave it to young people, I gave it a look for people that have taste and style and quality.

"Look at the loafer. When I started to do loafers, loafers weren't a look. Bass Weejuns had loafers, and a lot of kids wore them. But those loafers had that red, plastic look. I never wore a Bass Weejun loafer. I wanted to make a loafer I could wear. So I made a loafer in Maine, and I did it with a strip in front that wrapped from side to side. What happened? It got knocked off, and all of a sudden it is part of the culture of the shoe world. It just sits there."

In some ways, he is right. Ralph Lauren may be the most important shaper of popular taste in the consumer market today. This extends from shoes to blanket shawls to home furnishings to a men's industry which has enough fashion news to support monthly magazines like *M* and *GQ*. Today designer sportswear for men, designer suits for men, designer accessories for men, are taken for granted. They didn't exist twenty years ago. Ralph Lauren certainly wasn't the only designer with a fashion impact on the men's industry. Pierre Cardin was the first designer to gain cachet in men's wear; his success encouraged American manufacturers to back other "name" designers. In the last ten years, Giorgio Armani has introduced a new level of luxury fabrics to men's wear as well as changed the basic shape of men's suits. In comparison, Ralph's changes have been more subtle.

"When I was starting out in men's wear I wanted the natural shoulder guy to look more sophisticated. Everyone looked like IBM," says Ralph. "The clothes were sacks. Brooks Brothers' clothing was sacks. Three-button sacks. Pierre Cardin's coat was rigid, like a rock. I made the Ivy Leaguer exciting again. I brought newness to the traditional customer, to the customer who was looking elsewhere. The guy I knew on Madison Avenue was leaving Brooks and going to Pierre Cardin. I gave the preppy customers a mood they could relate to. It was a soft transition. I brought Paul Stuart the first two-button darted suit. They bought the Polo suit because they didn't have it in the store. Nobody had it. Then every young maker started to make it, and today it's generic. Can I tell someone I started the wide-lapeled suit? But I did.

"Answer me this: if I copied all this, who had it? Where did it come from? England? Even if there was influence I still had to explain my look. Absolutely. Believe me, England didn't have it when I went there. I had to dig out Fair Isle sweaters and find handknitters to make them. Then they started to use my stuff in brochures and say, 'This is ours.' If I copied everything, how did I build a business?

"The fact is, I didn't copy anybody. They all copied me. I

was inspired by the West, by things no longer here that I wanted to see again. I couldn't buy a great western shirt anywhere. Everything was polyester. I said I knew what was right, what was exciting.

"Look at my store. If I were an English company people would have flipped their lids. But when this Jewish kid opens this big beautiful store, an elite store, they say, 'Where did he come from, what right did he have to open this store?' Is that right? There was no store that existed like that in the world. Look at the crocodile belts and shoes. They weren't around. Then I put them in my line and suddenly they are everywhere. It doesn't get recognized at the moment. A year later it pops out and somebody else says, 'We're ready,' and *WWD* or *Vogue* does a big spread. I sit there, but I know I did it first.

"I was driving up Madison Avenue the other day, and I saw women's wear in the windows at Brooks Brothers and Tripler's. I want you to know that I started that. Let me give you the sense of what I mean. When I shopped at Brooks Brothers they had a shirt and a raincoat for women. That was it. Tripler and Paul Stuart never had clothes for women. Louis of Boston never had clothes for women. They might have a scarf or a blouse but that was it. I was the one who did it. That was what I did. When I went into the women's business, there was a Lady Manhattan, and Gant and Hathaway shirts for women. Also, occasionally a manufacturer made jackets for women. There was a preppy version for women in stores like Villager, but Villager went out of business. They were big and bombed. So there was no one doing it. I went in and started to do women's clothes that were tweedy. I made double-breasted suits and tweed jackets and we put them into Bloomingdale's and Britches of Georgetowne. No men's stores carried women's wear."

In December 1986 the *New York Times* ran a business story about Ralph Lauren.

The piece was called "Lauren Look Permeating City."

"It's beginning to look a lot like Christmas in New York," wrote Lisa Belkin. "And Christmas in the nation's largest marketplace is beginning to look a lot like Ralph Lauren.

"At The Limited store on Madison Avenue this week, the

windows featured feminine blouses with oversized lace collars — a very different look for the otherwise sleek, flashy store. At Scribner's on Fifth Avenue after Thanksgiving, books with such titles as *Victorian Home Design* and *The Englishman's Room* were propped on antique furniture and draped with lace.

"Yet the 'Laurenization of the city,' as one retailer calls it, is not just the tale of an individual. It is also an example of how a look spreads in the fashion world."

Ralph Lauren isn't satisfied.

"They've never given me credit," he says darkly. "Never."

Does money buy happiness? Sometimes, sure. But it doesn't buy peace of mind.

▶ ▶ ▶ 13

In casual conversation, Ralph Lauren's most constant reference points are old movies and Hollywood actors. It is not surprising, then, that when fragrance executive George Friedman said he wanted to introduce the Polo and Lauren scents with a TV campaign, Ralph was enthusiastic. His first national TV commercials were filmed in the fall of 1977, and their style and subject material say much about his consistency of concept and image.

The Polo commercial opens with a white ball bouncing down a grassy field. A moment later the first of eight polo players emerges charging after it. These riders are serious. Their faces are tight with concentration, their horses muscular and disciplined. In the background, the driving, compelling sound of Herbie Mann's "Aria." As the action quickens the scene dissolves into a close-up of a green Polo fragrance bottle. This cuts into a frozen still of a player about to drive the ball — star Bennie Gutierrez, wearing a blue Fairfield County Hunt Club jersey — and then suddenly switches back to live action. The players continue their chase down the field, when the action freezes yet again. There is a cut back to the bottle, and then a last frame of Gutierrez, his right arm raised, his body leaning into the shot, his teeth clenched.

"Polo isn't just a game," intones the narrator. "It's a tradition. A way of life . . . Polo, by Ralph Lauren."

This commercial was first broadcast in March 1978, when the Polo fragrance was launched. Although the same footage is still being used, it was recut in 1986, and new music was added. The freeze frame of Bennie Gutierrez has been reproduced thousands of times, not only in magazine and newspaper ads, but also on the cardboard packaging of such promotional items as a "Polo Sport Thermos," a one-quart green-plaid thermos made in Taiwan. (The Lauren fragrance commercial, which follows an attractive blonde on the sidelines as she watches the polo players move down the field, was not as dramatic. That commercial was later recut, and Ralph has since added three new ones.)

It didn't take a genius to promote Polo fragrances with scenes of a polo match. But look at the attention to detail with which it was made. Director Neil Tardio shot the first men's and women's fragrance commercials at the Oxridge Hunt Club in Darien, Connecticut, assembling eight top-grade polo players, a field judge, seventeen horses and their grooms, and a crew of about twenty. First Tardio drew a chalk line down the length of the polo field. After Andrzej *(Prizzi's Honor)* Bartkowiak set up his cameras, Tardio divided the players into teams of white jerseys and blue jerseys, and told them to play as hard as they would during a game. The shooting lasted two days, much of it done with long lenses and high-speed film, while models dressed in Ralph Lauren hacking jackets and tweeds watched. (They appeared in the Lauren commercial.) When Tardio was done he had 10,000 feet of film. Months later, he edited that down to forty-five feet, enough for thirty seconds of airtime.

"It works because we hired professional players and told them to play hard," says Tardio. "It wasn't a photographer saying move to the left, please."

The concept was to intimate things about Ralph Lauren's life-style by photographing a polo match, and then pray that the customer wanted to associate those things with his life as well. The players were handsome, obviously athletic, and probably rich. The setting was serene. All were images of a way of life that Ralph wanted people to identify with his brand.

"It's all incredible BS and it's all calculated," says Julian AvRutick, former president of Ammariti, Puris, AvRutick, the small New York agency which then had the Warner/Lauren account. "It's the same mentality as putting on a designer label. You think you are part of the club. The nascent Anglophiles or incipient yuppies bought it. If you look at the footage, all the accoutrements of the Polo concept are there. It's how they dressed, the cars on the sidelines, a life-style. It's also probably good advertising, because it comes directly from the idea inherent in the product. And it was smart advertising to stick with it."

Positioning Polo as part of the establishment was a key marketing strategy. Polo was good breeding, it was old money, it was tradition. There was the natural grace of men moving fast on horseback, and the beauty of a crisp fall afternoon when the leaves have started to turn. These were lasting images, reinforced by Hollywood and the fiction of such writers as F. Scott Fitzgerald and John O'Hara.

They were also images used to entice. Wear this fragrance, and you can become one of us and feel the way we feel. Fragrance advertising is based on sexual innuendo, because sensuality is an implicit part of the product. Yet the Polo commercial didn't say, "Wear this fragrance and you'll get the girls." There were no girls. Just men and sweaty horses. There was no mention of price, either, or claims about the product. The hard sell here is the peddling of a way of life. Pay attention, it says. This is an attractive way to live, and if you want to live this way tomorrow, Polo is the fragrance you should be wearing today.

(This commercial also reflects almost everything that some people dislike not only about Ralph Lauren but also about the clothes and way of life he sells. Polo is an elitist game played by the rich. The commercial itself was shot at a private club in a wealthy suburb. The players are white, they are wearing the uniforms of the wealthy, and they themselves are symbols of an aristocracy and a way of life in which people think nothing of paying tens of thousands of dollars for a horse while other families sleep at night in subway stations. It galls some that Ralph Lauren, who grew up in a tenement building in the Bronx wearing hand-me-downs, should now be glorifying a life-style which has historically excluded Jews, blacks, and other minorities.)

Because the Lauren and Polo fragrances were successfully introduced with TV commercials, Ralph agreed in 1979 to introduce his newest scent, Chaps, with a commercial of its own. Two commercials were created by the agency Kurtz & Tarlow, which by then had acquired the Warner/Lauren account. Dick Tarlow, together with Sandy Carlson, worked on the campaign.

The first commercial was called "History." It opened with sepia-toned old stills of western people, stills that dissolved into live-action shots of present-day cowboys. The music was from the sound track of the movie *Giant.* Interspersed in the footage was one still of Ralph Lauren dressed as a cowboy. He was not identified.

The second commercial resembled a famous scene from *The Magnificent Seven,* in which the gunfighters join up along the trail. In this commercial the riders are backlit against the hills as they come together. Then they reach their destination, which, when it comes into focus, is New York City.

It was an exciting commercial but Ralph didn't like it. Too gimmicky, he said. Too much like what he expected a TV commercial to be. Indeed, he was so enthusiastic about "History" that he told Tarlow and Carlson not to even bother testing "The Magnificent Seven." As a result, Chaps was launched with "History." That made Dick Tarlow very unhappy.

Tarlow would have the last laugh. He entered both commercials for Clio Awards, the equivalent of Oscars in the advertising industry. On the same day he learned he was a finalist in the category of best TV advertising for a men's product, Tarlow saw George Friedman, president of Warner/Lauren. He told Friedman that the commercial was up for an award that evening . . . but he didn't mention that it was the "Magnificent Seven" commercial and not "History."

The next morning, Tarlow bumped into Friedman again, and this time he told him that he had won first prize. Friedman grinned, Tarlow says, and then remarked, "You have me to thank because if we'd run that piece of crap you liked, you'd never have won anything."

"Advertisers have an inherent distrust of advertising," says Tarlow, who has since sold his agency and retired. "Ralph was an exception. He truly believed in advertising as a vehicle to build an image and consumer awareness. Sometimes when the budget is short and he really believes in something he'll say, 'All right, I'll make up the difference.' Be it four- or five-hundred thousand. The goal was to make him the number-one designer in the United States, and that's what we worked at."

Ralph Lauren was late using TV. By the time his first commercials broke, Calvin Klein had already gained an enormous head start in terms of mass appeal because of his sexy jeans commercials. Ralph Lauren, in contrast, had a 6 percent national awareness level when the first Chaps commercials aired. So not only did his involvement in fragrances earn him millions of dollars, it also built brand awareness among consumers.

Ralph Lauren knew he couldn't compete with much larger companies when it came to such promotion. (Remember, these TV commercials were paid for by Warner/Lauren, not Polo Fashions.) What he could do, with an annual budget under $400,000, was appear in several major magazines once or twice a year — with blocks of pages of advertising. Tarlow and Carlson didn't have to worry about how many readers they reached or what it cost on a per-thousand basis to reach them, because demographic information didn't interest Ralph. What mattered was that when his ads were run, the people he knew noticed. "The idea was, 'When we appear, we'll be a star.' It's like Frank Sinatra. If you see him once a year on TV, it's an event. If you see him every week, it's no big deal," says Tarlow.

Ralph would never feel completely comfortable with TV commercials, however, an attitude that grew stronger after the dungarees campaign he aired in September 1985 flopped. The commercials were the first Ralph had ever made to promote his clothes, and his agency, as well as director Bruce Weber, struggled to make them different. But ultimately Ralph was so disappointed with the results that he decided not to make any more.

"We've done television," he says. "TV is very fast. You've got to hit them hard, and you've got to be very fast. We're a lot more gentle than that in the way we design products and in the way we promote them."

Ralph Lauren may have loved the movies, but when it came to his own advertising, what he understood best was stills, not live action. Besides, the customers could linger over his photo spreads, talk about them, even argue about them.

TV commercials were different. Blink twice, and they were gone.

If there was one thing Ralph Lauren stood for, it was a look that lasted.

Ralph Lauren stands about 5'6" and weighs 140 pounds. He looks thin. He also has his mother's clear, fresh skin, which makes him appear younger than his age, and serious blue eyes. Ralph has always been vain about his good looks. In a front-page picture in *Women's Wear Daily* in September 1977, he appears bare-chested, wearing only a pair of dark sunglasses, jeans, boots, and a silver-tipped belt. Looking on in apparent disbelief are his design assistant and two models. Ralph has taken off his pink oxford shirt because he has decided it might look swell with one of the sack skirts he has designed for his resort collection.

An even odder photograph appeared in April 1987, as a two-page ad in *M* magazine. Here, in a picture taken at a ranch in California, Ralph is sitting on a countertop in the kitchen, between an ordinary sink and a four-burner gas stove. He is wearing a white patch-pocket tee shirt, blue jeans, and a white cowboy hat with a folded brim. His hair, worn long and over his ears, is almost as white as his tee shirt, and he is drinking a beer from the bottle. His arms, bare, are skinny. Ralph liked this picture because it reflects an old passion, Ralph Lauren, cowboy. He might be wearing the cleanest jeans, tee shirt, and hat in the West, but he's drinking beer in a bottle, he's got his feet up, and he's enjoying himself. The copy consists simply of the words "Ralph Lauren" spelled in large blue letters. This is the same designer who asks his most sophisticated customers to spend $960 for an alligator notebook. Calvin Klein would not appear in a photograph like this. There is more than an offbeat sense of humor at work here. Ralph Lauren is one of the wealthiest men in the United States. The picture makes one wonder why he is dressed like a ranch hand and sitting alone in a drab room.

Saks Fifth Avenue asked the same question in 1975, when it decided to run a full-page Ralph Lauren ad in the *New York Times*. Ralph said he thought that was a good idea, and he agreed to pose for it. Instead of wearing his tweediest suit and sharpest Polo loafers, Ralph arrived dressed in a pair of Levi Strauss jeans, a denim shirt, cowboy boots, and one of his wide-lapeled muted sport jackets. "They couldn't understand why I wouldn't wear the outfit that they wanted to sell on the fourth floor," says Ralph. "I said, 'This is what I'm like. This is what I want to wear. This is who I am.' I wanted to appear the way I was. It got a lot of response, and Saks loved it. That was the beginning."

People say Ralph Lauren is an expert marketer. What they mean is that he knows not only what his customers want, but how to package it so that they'll find it exciting. "His instincts about what will motivate the consumer to buy are unparalled," says David Horowitz, the former Warner Communications executive who helped launch Ralph Lauren fragrances and cosmetics. Look at the Saks ad. Rather than appear in yet another ordinary store promotion, Ralph called attention to himself in a way that was both daring and offbeat, as he did less effectively years later in the ranch kitchen ad. Because these pictures go against the grain of how fashion designers present themselves to us — sanitized and clever enough to be taken out in society — these ads catch our attention. They are unexpected and startling, and they help create an image of mystery about Ralph Lauren, which makes his clothes that much more desirable.

"People see them and they say, 'What is this guy . . . why doesn't he get dressed up . . . what else does he make . . . is he married?' So it builds something," says Ralph. "They get to know your name and what you are about. There is a personal communication. When I walk down the street, people come up to me and say, 'I love your clothes,' or 'why don't you make this,' or 'your buttons fell off.'

"I didn't create the designer mystique. There was always a mystique in the fashion business with names and people. But I don't think the customers ever got to know them or see them. In my ads I project a little more of a personal touch. I'm shot doing what I love to do. It has an environment, and the customers get a sense of what you're about. Then they can see the clothes and say, 'Oh, that looks like me. Yeah. I understand it.'

"I appear occasionally in my ads. Sometimes you want to say hello."

Ralph Lauren became a designer as an afterthought, not because he intended to spend the best years of his life picking swatches. Originally, the only clothes he made were the ones he wore himself. "I design for a guy like me," he told the *San Francisco Chronicle* in 1969. A year later he appeared in the *New York Times,* modeling a "battle-jacket suit," a look that reflected a long fascination with military-styled clothes. There are epaulets on the shoulders, a long, deep collar, and a zipper down the front. It looks like an outfit Buck Rogers might have worn. Ralph showed a similar jumpsuit that year, made from authentic parachute cloth, in an informal after-hours fashion show to a group of select retailers. Ralph stopped directly in front of buyer Joe Campo from Jordan Marsh Florida and said, "Joe, what do you think?"

Campo felt the material. It was very heavy. "Ralph, in Florida, no way." Dead silence. Then Ralph quietly said, "Joe, I thought you'd understand," and strode out of the room. That was it. Campo went back to his hotel room, crushed.

"I've seen Ralph many times since then, and we've never discussed it," says Campo, who first met Ralph Lauren when they worked together one Christmas at Brooks Brothers. "He was still struggling to make a name for himself and I thought it was an egotistical, ungentlemanly thing to do. But that's what probably made him what he is today. He so believed in whatever he was doing that even if it was out of left field, he lived and died by it. Maybe he felt I shouldn't have worried about the weather. Somehow he expected me to make it fly. I couldn't do it, and he absolutely turned off on me and walked away."

Ralph chooses every image that reflects himself and his company. Look at one of Ralph's favorite ads: a photograph of a green, battered knit polo shirt. In the early 1980s the demand for polo shirts weakened and sales slumped. Ralph noticed that the kids were wearing stonewashed jeans, and in a staff design meeting, he said, "Stonewashing is what's going on. Let's take our knit shirt and weather it." The copy read: "The Polo knit shirt. Like all things of lasting quality, it endures." This was the first new style in knit shirts in years, and it worked because implicit in the ad was a guarantee that anybody whose shirt didn't wear well with age would get the amount paid for it back from Polo. That was how Ralph addressed the issue of poor quality control, which was one of the reasons his knit shirt sales had slumped in the first place. The next season, other knit shirt makers added stonewashed shirts to their lines.

One reason Ralph Lauren is so particular about his advertising is that he communicates best with images. This is how he explains creating the tens of thousands of products that bear the Polo label each year. "The line is designed with a story in mind, a story we discuss. We talk about clothes and how they are worn and where they are worn and why you wear it . . . If I'm working with a fabric I like I will say, okay, put this in all the accessories, put it into wallpaper, put it into this or that. I know where I want to see it. There's an overall picture. Do this, this, this. That's how I work."

The themes he uses — family, romance, elegant living — haven't changed in more than a decade. Neither have the basic images. Look at his earliest advertising, a mail-order catalog for his spring 1977 collection, which retailers sent their customers. Instead of posing models in studios or in exotic settings, he had the photographs taken on location in East Hampton and Santa Barbara. Ralph had been influenced by *The Thomas Crown Affair,* a thriller starring Faye Dunaway and Steve McQueen, and he wanted to recreate an atmosphere that was both adventurous and stylish.

"We both loved that movie, and some of the pictures in the catalog were inspired by it," says Les Goldberg, the photographer who both shot and produced the catalog. "There was a scene where Steve McQueen roars through the dunes in his red dune buggy. Ralph Lauren didn't have a dune buggy, he had a Jeep, but it represented his life-style and so we included a Jeep shot. There was also a montage in the movie in which Faye Dunaway watches McQueen playing polo. There's lots of cutting back and forth from McQueen to Dunaway, who was sitting on a Ferrari with a big hat and movie camera watching him. The polo player montage we have in this catalog came from those moments."

The opening introduces Ralph sitting in sand dunes, casually dressed in white painter pants and a dark blue sweater. The opposite page is a montage: Ralph in khaki shorts peddling a bicycle, Ralph playing tennis in his whites, Ralph and

Ricky and two of their kids driving in their white Jeep along the surf, and a second family shot of them walking by the water's edge. Together, they look like the all-American family, healthy, exuberant, successful. The concept was to show how Ralph's life-style influenced his work.

"Advertising is not supposed to be about buying," says Ralph. "When I started, people thought they had to stand there with a suit and say, 'Here's my suit.' That's how the industry worked. I said, 'No, the clothes have to be there but it's the mood that's important. Why do you become enamored with something? It's the image and mood of these people, who they are, what they feel like, you like them, and then you like what they wear."

Here are two pages of sweating tennis players, photographed at courts belonging to costume designer Edith Head. Then, a man dressed in khaki pleated gabardine pants with a 1930s-inspired camp shirt playing croquet on a manicured green lawn. Behind him, two elegant women watch in mock admiration. Then, on another spread, four men dressed in Polo suits walking away from a helicopter. "It was really a new way to show clothes," says Les Goldberg. "People thought, wow, this is conceptual advertising. These pictures made you ask who these people were, where they were going. One of these guys could be the head of a corporation or the head of the CIA. All you really know is he has style."

The photograph that caused the most talk showed a man wearing a white dinner jacket being chauffeured in a black, mud-covered Jeep. "You associate a man in a tuxedo with a woman in an evening dress and a limousine, and at first that's what we shot," says Goldberg. "But it didn't work. It wasn't interesting. Ralph liked Jeeps, so he said, 'Why don't you put him in a Jeep and see what happens.' So we shot it on a muddy road in California."

That catalog was quickly followed by a second, which promoted Ralph's fall 1977 collections. On the cover is a man riding a black horse across a snow-covered field, wearing a full-length coyote coat, Ralph's own battered cowboy hat, and riding chaps. A pair of old snowshoes hangs on the saddle.

"It was a stylish Marlboro Man ad," says Goldberg. "We

told the model to imagine he had just left his home and was riding to have dinner with his friends at their cabin. We also did a second snow shot in this catalog. Here he is dressed in jeans and cowboy boots, and underneath his beaver-lined steamer coat he is wearing an evening shirt, a tuxedo jacket, and a black tie." The copy line under this picture reads: "Style, not fashion." This photograph has since appeared in numerous publications. In 1987 it was used as a Ralph Lauren Christmas ad in the *New York Times Magazine*.

"Everything I wear isn't Polo, just as the way I wear it isn't a formula either," wrote Ralph Lauren in that catalog. "You see me in this book in an old army shirt, a down vest, and now old jeans. I have great respect for functional, authentic clothes that are forthright, not necessarily fashionable. They are timeless. That's what I think clothes should be. I design clothes with that end in mind, to look better tomorrow than today, to be an expression of your own style. And that's what Polo is all about."

Prior to putting out these catalogs, Ralph Lauren didn't do his own advertising because he couldn't afford it. Later he began to buy his own advertising space, running many of the shots in his catalogs as stand-alone ads. As he recognized the importance of his licensees, he promoted his entire product line across large blocks of ad pages in such publications as the *New York Times Magazine, Vanity Fair,* and *W.* (Ralph bought a block of ads only once in *Vogue.* Too crowded with advertising, he concluded.) Such advertising is expensive. An eighteen-page spread that appeared in the *New York Times Magazine* on March 16, 1986, cost $450,000. The licensees help pay the bills, contributing 2 to 3 percent of total sales each year. Ralph Lauren's own men's wear company, however, is considerably larger than any of the licensees, and it contributes more than 70 percent of the parent company's corporate advertising budget.

"I'm not selling one product, I'm selling many products, many worlds," says Ralph. "When people go to a movie they come out wanting to wear what the movie star was wearing. 'I want that hat, I want that dress.' Why? Because they liked that person. They liked the character. They were romanced by the mood, not necessarily by what a person was actually wearing. They may not know how to wear something, where it should be worn, how it should be worn. But when they see it worn in the right environment, they understand it. If you are selling a flannel shirt, you say, 'Where do I wear flannel shirts? Around a campfire, a nice place for weekends, a nice setting in the country.' That's what gets the customer: you want to be there. What made me think of that? I'm that person, that customer. I always loved environments."

Today everybody from Guess? to Jordache to newcomers like Tommy Hilfiger have imitated Ralph Lauren's block page approach to advertising. Hilfiger, owned by Murjani International, has even done it with a bit of wit, as seen in a four-page spread in an August 1987 issue of *People*. Page one, printed in bright green, states "Brooks Brothers" and is illustrated with the trademarked Brooks Brothers sheep hanging from a ribbon. It reads . . . "First the original button-down shirt led the flock . . ." The second page, in magenta, states "Ralph Lauren" and reads, "Then everyone in America wanted the Ralph Lauren version. . . ." The third and fourth pages, which are in orange, are illustrated with a blue, white, and red "Tommy Hilfiger" flag and conclude "Today it's Tommy Hilfiger with the new American classics!" Adds the body copy: "Every decade someone with talent and a sense of the times takes a good look at the great classics and makes them better. That's what Tommy Hilfiger did when he redesigned the button-down shirt, the polo shirt, the sweater, the classic Chino, and everything else modern men and women wear. Style marches on." Compare that to Ralph Lauren's oft-stated credo, "Style, not fashion." Compare it also to the clothes most associated with Ralph Lauren: his polo shirts, his sweaters, his chino pants, his fine cotton shirts.

The Europeans have also been affected. In Paris a chic, preppy French retailer called Façonnable sells Ralph Lauren– like cotton shirts, khaki pants, and silk ties. More striking, though, is the *Façonnable* magazine. Interspersed among the light feature stories on jazz musician Wynton Marsalis and weekend vacations are ten black-and-white ads that match almost perfectly the style, feel, and mood of Ralph Lauren's advertising. Here are the family portraits, the handsome young men in their tennis whites, the polo shirts, the cotton sweaters. When a salesclerk in Paris was asked about the similarities, he grumped, "We did it first," and walked off. Façonnable is said to be a terrific retail success.

Not all of Ralph Lauren's ads are enticing. Consider the twenty-one-page black-and-white spread that appeared in *Vanity Fair* in September 1987. Photographed in England by Bruce Weber, this is a "story" of wealth and reckless self-indulgence. With the exception of one page devoted to three large-tongued dogs perched on the back seat of an expensive car, what viewers see are haughty, bloodless aristocrats. It is *High Society* without the sparkle or the humor, and it falls flat. There are serious expressions and glasses of champagne, but nobody seems to be having much fun. Everybody is dressed in black.

Ralph knew these ads were elitist. That was the point. He wanted to attract wealthier customers to his store.

"A lot of people aren't aware I make evening clothes," he says. "They don't know I make tuxedos. What they know is that I make tweed jackets, but not the gowns. So what I did was paint a world. And I made a movie out of it by repeating it. These ads attract the customers who want evening gowns, who buy them. I want those customers to know I make them, and that they don't have to go to Bill Blass and Oscar de la Renta."

In an industry that caters to sexual insecurities, Ralph has disdained sexually suggestive advertising. Unlike rival Calvin Klein, Ralph Lauren has never promoted his products with pictures of naked men and women. Or with coy teenage girls. This means Ralph's appeal fulfills other needs, primarily the need for status and the need to belong. Indeed, on the golf course or at the tennis courts, his clothes are seen everywhere.

"Calvin Klein is different," says Ralph. "We are many miles away from each other in terms of our point of view. There are so many lines, so many people, and a hundred ways of promoting them. This is a very personal company. It's very personal in that it is a family which has built a concept. When I say family I'm talking about a family of people who have grown here with a particular point of view. This is not a Seventh Avenue, bang-em kind of a business."

So there is no sex. There aren't many words, either. Ralph

thinks words get in the way of the pictures. If you tell people what to think, they can't interpret the images for themselves.

"He's not wordy," says Sandy Carlson. "He brought restraint to advertising, because he didn't want his advertising to look like advertising. He's not selling a dress; he's selling what that dress represents, the romance of that dress. He hated ad clichés and clever copy lines. So, often we would just put his logo on our ads. Usually advertising is words and pictures. Not here."

All of which brings us to two key questions. Who is the Ralph Lauren customer and what does he or she want?

• "The guy who buys my things is a jet-set guy, a society type who travels a lot and knows quality. He's pleased that he can afford to pay more than most people can afford. He's somewhat of a snob," Ralph told the *San Francisco Chronicle* in November 1969.

• "I was sure there were other people like me, quality guys who were willing to pay for what they wanted. People with money who couldn't find what they wanted in fashion. I would give it to them," Ralph told *Gentlemen's Quarterly* in February 1971.

• "My collection is for the ultra-sophisticated woman," Ralph told *WWD* in May 1972.

• "I'm talking about the kind of woman who could afford to go to Europe several times a year and whose family kept horses, and owned houses with lots of grounds around them. These people were always dressed casually, and clothes represented a mirror or reflection of how they lived. They never wore that which was absolutely the latest fashion but clothes that could last for years. They wore cashmeres, camel's hair, suede, and leather," Ralph told *WWD* in November 1972.

• "I felt that there are women who are looking for elegant clothes, much of which have disappeared from the market. These would fall into a category just below couture clothes and might be described as worn by the young suburban woman in the so-called horsey set," Ralph told the *New York Times* in July 1973.

• "I started out with a fashion concept, a taste level, aimed at the traditional man, the kind of clothes I like to wear myself," Ralph Lauren told *Daily News Record* in November 1973.

• "I was aiming at the unfashionable fashion girl, a girl with enough authority to carry off very tailored clothes in a feminine way. You either loved it or you hated it," Ralph told *WWD* in October 1974.

• "The man I dress has a strong sense of style, he doesn't need to have his clothes create it for him. He wants to project his individuality without being too fussy. Clothes serve as a backdrop," Ralph told *Avenue* in November 1976.

• "I would say the customers want quality, design, and product consistency. They want understatement but stylishness at the same time. They don't want to look fashionable. They've been around. And they buy it not because it's the hot brand but because they know it's got class in terms of its consistency. You don't build a business unless people keep coming back," Ralph said during a *Forbes* interview in March 1986.

• "The people who wear my clothes don't think of them as 'fashiony.' They like good clothes and they like to feel comfortable in them." Ralph Lauren, public relations handout, January 1987.

So much for the perception.

In 1985, Grey Advertising decided to investigate the increasing national consumption of luxury products. The people at Grey were puzzled. If only 3.3 percent of all U.S. households qualified as affluent, who were the folks munching those expensive Swiss chocolates, quaffing the French champagnes, and buying their new Ralph Lauren suits?

The answer: a group Grey researchers tagged "the UltraConsumers." These customers were twenty-one to fifty, earned at least $25,000 annually, and numbered 26.2 million, or 15.3 percent of all U.S. adults. They were also the main body of luxury consumers. Grey researchers, however, suspected that many Americans not yet earning $25,000 a year also had "UltraConsumer" tendencies. The total universe of both groups of shoppers amounted to a bit more than 42 million people, or nearly 25 percent of all U.S. adults. Add the likelihood of Ultra attitudes in people over fifty with discretionary income, as Grey did in a study in July 1987, and the universe that emerges consists of 105 million people, or 58.6 percent of U.S. adults.

Grey defined them this way: "Customers drawn to the best, the latest, the ultimate, and they are eager to take things to the limit and then see what comes next. . . . their ultimate ambition: the most stimulating, entertaining and personally gratifying life-style possible."

Their incomes may have been modest, but their spending habits were not. Grey found that they preferred to eat in the trendiest restaurants, where environment counted as much as the food, bought the latest in home electronics, and were bent on self-improvement, from exercise classes to learning how to give speeches. They also were ardent shoppers of designer labels. Why? "For many people, clothes are a form of psychic armor. Even traditional consumers seem to feel confident and capable when they're well-dressed, vulnerable and uncertain when they're not. But for Ultras, clothes serve additional emblematic purposes, signifying not only the wearers' ambitions and social standings, but their personalities and creative impulses, too."

How did these people afford such life-styles? By sacrificing marriage, kids, and buying a house.

They also were eager borrowers. Consumer debt excluding mortgages in 1987 topped $606 billion compared to $535 billion in 1985. Evan Steffins, a therapist in charge of the Shopper Stoppers self-help program at Miami Valley Hospital in Dayton, Ohio, says many have become compulsive, hard-core shoppers. "It's as addictive as alcoholism or drug abuse," she says. "I see these people every day. They have an average of twelve credit cards, and they spend without any thought of the consequences. They're addicts."

Not every Ralph Lauren customer is an addict. But in most cases, they are committed.

Arthur Barens is a top Los Angeles trial attorney, best known for representing Joe Hunt in 1987. Hunt was the leader of the Billionaire Boys Club, a cultlike group whose members believed they were entitled to anything they wanted. (Hunt was later convicted of murder.) Barens may well be the number-one buyer of Ralph Lauren clothes in California, having been known to spend as much as $10,000 on a single buying trip. One former Polo store owner in San Francisco so valued Barens's patronage that he put a limousine at his disposal. Other than his watch, everything Arthur Barens wears is made by Ralph Lauren.

"I'm one of the few guys you will meet with a background in a foster setting most of my life," says Barens. "I'm all about the fact that anything is possible in America if you are willing to work for it and make a lot of sacrifices. One of the rewards of hard work is you get to buy Ralph Lauren's clothes. Part of the realization of the dream is also that you get to be the person you wanted to be as a kid. The guys we read about as kids, if we were reading *Gatsby* or Faulkner or stories about the people who had made it in America, wore Ralph Lauren clothing in our mind's eye. In many ways he represents the American dream, and the product line itself is particularly American in its look."

Joane Fitzpatrick is in her fifties. Having raised her family, she now works as an administrative assistant for an architectural and engineering firm in New York. She lives in Bronxville, a comfortable New York City suburb, and has been a Ralph Lauren customer for more than fifteen years.

"His clothes never go out of style," she says. "I like knowing that clothes I paid a lot of money for two years ago are still being sold. He doesn't force us to buy different things. Even now, if you go into the shops you'll see some short looks but you will see good taste, beautiful material, never a synthetic. He's had a big influence on lower-priced clothes, too. He was one of the first people to use linen and cotton, and it filtered down to the next price levels. Today people don't mind wearing things which are wrinkled. I remember when you couldn't find linen anywhere; he brought it back.

"Also, every year he makes one or two things which make me feel wonderful. This year it's a sweater with a scene of a polo match on it, and it's so subtle that it's almost private. I get this feeling as though he knows all about me."

Millie Graves, Bloomingdale's buyer, grew up with Ralph Lauren in the Bronx. Very much the successful New York career woman, she has brown eyes, closely cropped dark hair, and is wearing a gray business suit. Not only has she watched Ralph evolve from a teenager into a fashion designer, but she bought his collection, together with that of Calvin Klein, for Bloomingdale's in the mid-1970s.

"I have a sixteen-year-old daughter who would die for a Ralph Lauren comforter," sighs Graves. "When both my daughters transferred to Riverdale School [a New York private school] a while back, the Polo insignia was the emblem. One daughter was going into the fifth grade, one into the ninth, and everybody wore Polo as though it were a uniform. I don't think there was a kid who didn't wear Ralph's oxford button-down or Ralph's polo shirts. I couldn't believe it. And it wasn't just Riverdale. I looked into the whole world of New York private schools, and that emblem was everywhere. All the kids were wearing it. The same psychology which influenced the adults affected the eight- and nine-year-olds.

"Why do people respond? When I started buying Ralph Lauren and Calvin Klein for the store, I was very cynical about labels. But I learned that the labels made the customers feel secure. Maybe it's different for a man who buys a Ralph Lauren suit. But the Ralph Lauren women customers never filled in their wardrobes with other designers. They just bought Ralph because they only felt comfortable with Ralph. I always kidded and said it was like a horse with blinders . . . they wouldn't stretch their eyesight to the left or right. When they were done they'd have a pile of clothes two feet high, and the salespeople would be ecstatic.

"It all comes down to psychology. How, with the women's collection, can you justify the retail price in terms of workmanship? But it was so important to these people to feel that what they were doing was establishment, that it was right. And really, that's how it evolved. The Calvin Klein customer wasn't as cult-minded. If she felt a Missoni sweater was wonderful, that was okay. But a Ralph Lauren customer only bought Ralph Lauren. They were obsessed. They wanted to be total Ralph Lauren women. It became more than the status. It became a way of life."

Susan Ennis, thirty, is an executive in the marketing de-

partment at Home Box Office. Dark-haired and slender, Ennis lives in New York City and has worn Ralph Lauren clothes
since attending high school.

"The first thing I bought was a slate gray riding jacket,
which I still have. I had my eye on it for months. It was two
hundred and fifty dollars, but every time I went to Bloomingdale's I tried it on. Finally it went on sale and I got it for about
one hundred and ten dollars. I didn't buy it because it was
Ralph Lauren, although he did have a nice little department.
Rather, it was a very tailored and beautiful object. I wore it
for years. I stopped only because the lapels are very wide, as
are the flaps on the pockets. What makes it special are the
details. The underside of the collar, for example, is lined with
plaid. Most women's clothes don't have inside pockets; his do.
It's the added touch. Even now you can appreciate the workmanship. I've been cleaning out my closets but I'm keeping it.

"It used to be you'd pay a lot more for Ralph Lauren and
it was worth a lot more. These days I don't think it is. I love
his store, but his clothes aren't a special experience any more.
But I keep everything I have, and when I try them on they
still look fresh and new. When I bought those clothes, I didn't
know him as a famous person; I bought them because I liked
them."

Finally, listen to Pamela Street, who was raised in Greenwich, Connecticut. Pamela Street is perhaps the ideal Ralph
Lauren woman. She is attractive, outgoing, a jogger, and travels frequently. She attended Miss Porter's School in Farming-
ton, Connecticut, the same school attended by Jacqueline
Kennedy, and today lives in rural Oregon. She owns one long
plaid Ralph Lauren skirt, and several tee shirts.

That's all.

Why? Although she lives comfortably, she thinks Ralph's
clothes are too expensive.

"His clothes are so classic looking you think you can find
a counterpart without the label that has the same feeling or
fabric. And when I buy his clothes, I try to find things which
don't have the horse on them. I don't want to wear somebody
else's initial. I love the store on Madison Avenue, but that's
too expensive as well.

"There was a girl in my apartment building in New York who also went to private schools and everything, and her two children go to private school in New York. She's into a very WASPy, conservative point of life, but you never know what labels she's wearing. She always looks dowdy. She wears the same classics over and over again, the kind of clothes people wore a long time ago. Her clothes aren't old, but the styling is old.

"Actually, there are a lot of people who live in Greenwich and don't spend money on clothing. They're into L. L. Bean and Land's End as opposed to Ralph Lauren. God, you look at people my parents' age at the country club, and see what they have on. None of them are wearing designer clothes. They just don't care about making a fashion statement or having the latest thing. I remember one year going to Barney's for a Christmas present and buying my mother a beautiful Italian blouse. She never wore it. What she wore were the same things over and over again. So now I wear the blouse.

"The men are even more like that. My brother Tony came out here recently, and when he went hiking, he wore khaki pants. I don't think he's ever worn a pair of blue jeans in his life. It's a whole different mind-set. Go to a Greenwich cocktail party, and see what people wear. They aren't crazed by fashion or thinking about being photographed. I went back a few years ago for my twentieth reunion at boarding school, and there wasn't anybody dressed in earth-shattering clothes. Certainly they could afford them. But they don't buy the cashmere sweaters and the big-ticket items. They don't need to."

This is not such terrible news for Ralph Lauren, however.

Only 60,000 people live in Greenwich, Connecticut. His store there appears to be doing well.

Ralph Lauren's office at 40 West 55th Street has changed very
little since he moved here in 1969. The same pair of blue-and-
white ginger jars sits on the fireplace mantel his father once
painted. Toward the back, near the windows, is the large pine
table decorator Tom O'Toole chose as Ralph's desk. The table
is a failure as a desk because Ralph refuses to sit behind it —
too uncomfortable, he says. It is there mostly because it is covered with stuff, including a fleet of miniature antique cars.
Ralph owns full-size versions of each, including a 1963 Ferrari
250 GTO valued at more than $1 million.

Ralph Lauren runs a business that will do about $2 billion
in sales at wholesale in the fiscal year ended March 31, 1989,
but he says it is a personal business and that this is a personal
room. There are framed pictures done by his three children,
a stuffed bear dressed in a red English riding outfit, photographs of friends. On the floor is a Navaho rug; he also col-
lects Indian pottery. There are no books. On the wall behind
his desk is a framed picture of Ralph and his wife, Ricky. They
are kneeling in the surf, their arms wrapped around each other,
kissing. "You know, the scene from *From Here to Eternity*," says
Ralph.

He smiles. Things are going his way. His collections get
good reviews, his business in Europe is growing (although that
growth may slow if the dollar remains weak), and he has
launched several retail prototypes he calls Polo Country Stores
to sell his sportswear collections. Corporate expenses are increasing, and the overhead at his Rhinelander Mansion is a
problem. But Ralph projects self-assurance. Not a week passes
in which his name and his work aren't mentioned or appraised
somewhere in the national media.

A typical day means getting up at 6:30 A.M. and jogging
through Central Park. Back to the duplex on Fifth Avenue, a

shower, and into the office by 9 A.M. Ralph Lauren prefers a simple diet, avoids junk food, and he doesn't drink. Staying fit is important to him. Although Ralph does not lift weights, until recently he exercised four days a week at a nearby gym, doing stretching exercises. "I'm very basic," he says. Among his favorite New York restaurants are The Four Seasons and La Cote Basque for lunch, and Gino's for dinner.

At the office, Ralph goes from meeting to meeting until 7 P.M., when he is picked up by his chauffeur-driven limousine. He usually works Monday through Friday. This routine changes only when he is preparing a major spring, fall, or holiday collection. Then he works weekends. Although Ralph Lauren started as a men's wear designer, he no longer holds men's fashion shows. "They're silly," he says.

Ten years ago, Ralph Lauren knew every employee personally; his door was open, and anybody with a problem talked to him about it. Today Ralph Lauren employs more than 1,500 people, and that is no longer possible. Ralph likes to say, "My vibes are good. I hear it. Believe me, I'm all over the place. It's not like I just sit here and do my designs." But it is hard to stay in touch with a staff so numerous that even the stairways are crowded with people too impatient for a slow elevator.

"What happens is you develop teams," he said. "You have layers of people under them and they are afraid to go to me without talking to their boss. You don't want to call someone because you're afraid somebody else is going to say, 'Why didn't you talk to me first?' It's politics. It's how companies work. But I don't like that. I don't feel that way. I like to talk to people. That's how I operate. It's very straight. I say what I feel." Ralph Lauren was once closely associated with former presidential candidate Gary Hart, but he is suspicious of all politics. It makes him uncomfortable to know people may be saying one thing and thinking something else because they have a multitude of purposes. What he enjoys is going to design meetings and fighting to defend his work. "If I have a bad idea they laugh," he says. "I have to battle for my ideas. I want to fight. I could say, 'That's it, we'll do it my way.' But I don't. I want everybody to walk out believing in what we're doing. Sometimes you're cold. Sometimes they have an idea and I say, 'Great, let's build on that.' That happens. Absolutely."

Today Ralph is wearing a dark suit and tie, and he looks every bit the serious business executive. This is not always the case. Sometimes he comes to work in what appear to be gym clothes. Or in his western look, which typically means an old pair of Levi's jeans, a denim shirt with a button missing, red cowboy boots, an Indian bead bracelet, and a large silver belt buckle with the word *Chaps* written on it. Sometimes Ralph wears these clothes to sophisticated New York restaurants or fancy parties. The response is often negative. "The other night at Gino's, Ralph, in faded jeans and jacket with elbow patches, leaned over to the missus, Ricky. Lauren's whole back and shoulder were torn," criticized one New York gossip columnist. On a January evening in 1987, when Ralph was being honored as retailer of the year by the Council of Fashion Designers of America at a black-tie dinner, he arrived in a black dinner jacket, jeans, and cowboy boots. Some guests were furious. When Ralph went to the podium to collect the award he sensed the audience of 1,500 top retailers and designers was decidedly frosty. Trying to ease the tension, Ralph joked, "My kids made me dress like this." Nobody laughed.

Still, if somebody in the office questions his clothes by giving him a strange look, Ralph breaks into a big smile. Because he is the boss he can wear any damn thing he pleases. "Ralph Lauren was the best bum," says designer Robert Stock, who worked for him in the early 1970s. "Nobody could look as crisp and sharp and as bad at the same time. Ralph used to put these fatigues on, army fatigues, and he'd look like a garbage man. When he dressed down, you'd walk by and want to give him a dollar. It was impressive."

Ralph is eager to discuss his work as a designer. He is less willing to talk about his family. "I'm not saying a thing," he says at one point. He is concerned about their security; some years back, Calvin Klein's daughter was kidnapped. Besides, his family is private, he says. There are only occasional asides. "Sometimes I used to think we were sacrificing so much, because we had them when we were young. Now I'm glad because I can enjoy my kids." He told another interviewer: "I come home like all daddies do. And all three of them are at me at once, talking about school, about problems. I yell at them. I'm nice to them. We have a very good relationship. I'm not distant. I love them. I am with them a lot. I take trips, but they're short. I'm not a far-away father, and Ricky is there all the time. We are very together. We have the same problems that most families have — hoping that the kids are growing up healthy and happy and are nurtured with enough love." Ricky Lauren is most often described as shy and a full-time mother by those who know her socially. Several times a year, she is photographed with her husband at a formal affair; usually Ricky Lauren prefers to be at home with her kids.

Ralph was not always so protective of his family. In late 1971, Mort Gordon, the former editor and assistant publisher of *Men's Wear* magazine, talked Ralph into appearing with Ricky on the cover of that magazine.

Gordon told Ralph he was going to devote an issue to what he called "contemporary classics." Who better represented "contemporary classics" than Ralph Lauren, Gordon urged. Besides, you and Ricky will look great on the cover, he added.

Since Ralph was running a small business, and was barely thirty-two years old, he agreed that it was an okay idea.

The picture was taken. Ricky was seated in the foreground in a very modern chrome and leather chair. She wore a black jacket with gold buttons, a white ascot, a sweater, a black-and-dark-green tartan skirt, and dozens of gold bangles on her arms.

Behind her, standing with his hands in his pockets and his legs crossed, was Ralph. His hair was still black (although the sides had started to gray), and he wore a gray blazer with horn buttons, a dark caramel checkered sweater vest, a pale beige tie, gray pants, and dark tasseled loafers.

Ralph looked cocky and a little chubby. Certainly his face was much fuller than it is today. His wife looked as if she had been in a terrible accident and was paralyzed as a result.

It was not what Ralph Lauren had in mind.

"What had happened was that our art director set up this shoot with Ralph standing very elegant and Ricky, with her ash blonde hair, sitting in a Barcelona chair," says Mort Gordon. "When the color separations came back, Ricky's hair was Daisy Mae yellow. I didn't like it, but the art director said it was fine. The deadline was coming, and we thought the color would come down.

"Then the magazine came out in January 1972. Ralph called up, and he was livid. Absolutely livid. He said, 'My wife looks like a cripple in a wheelchair. And that isn't the color of her hair. She's absolutely furious with me. How could you do this to me?'

"I said, 'I'm sorry, but look at the coverage you'll get out of this.'

"It took him months to calm down."

Friends say Ralph and Ricky Lauren have a close family life. There is the membership in the Park Avenue synagogue, the long weekends in the country, the frequent meals with other family members. They live this way because Ralph likes it like that. Typically, Ralph refers to his brother Jerry as "my best friend." Ralph is also close to his mother and father, both of whom are well over seventy.

Ralph refuses to allow his parents to be interviewed. That's private, he said. One afternoon, however, they stayed in his office longer than he expected. When he walked them out, he saw me across the hallway, standing by the company switchboard. His parents started to head toward the elevator. Indecision. Ralph knew I knew who they were.

The question was, would he introduce us?

He took a step back into his office and then bolted out. "Mom, Dad, there's somebody I want you to meet," he said graciously. He gestured toward me. "Meet my friend," he said, putting his arm around my shoulder. That didn't quite explain what I was doing there.

"I saw the mural you painted in the fur market," I said to Ralph's father.

He smiled, gripping my hand.

"It's still there?" asked his wife. "You know, they called him a few years ago to come back and touch it up."

I looked at them attentively. Both appeared well; his mother, friendly, dressed in a handsome gray suit; his father, in gray pin-stripes complete with vest, still a natty dresser, sported the thinnest line of a mustache. They were both short and smiled frequently. Although Ralph's father had a serious operation in 1986, he had a strong handshake from years of holding and working with a paintbrush. As we chatted I wondered what it was that they did to mold a son whose name and products would be recognized around the world.

Then I realized they were probably as surprised and astounded as anybody. Their other children, especially their daughter Thelma and son Jerry, were more artistically gifted as children. One would have thought that if anybody would have a career as a designer. . . . But Ralph? Somebody whose main interest in high school was playing basketball?

(Those who knew him in the Bronx are also amazed. "Ralph and I both worked the same sales territory in the early 1960s," says Richard Blum, an executive at Swank who grew up in the Mosholu Parkway neighborhood. "It was easy for me, because Swank had a good name. Ralphie was out there with neckwear and gloves and he was bemoaning the fact that his bosses didn't have taste and wouldn't listen to how he wanted to build the business. Then I got transferred into international sales and lost contact with the domestic market. A few years later a guy says he is going to Bloomingdale's for a new American designer promotion and asks me to come with him. I get to the entrance of the store, and I'm flabbergasted. Every window on Lexington Avenue has Ralphie's picture in it.")

The elevator arrived and Ralph's parents stepped inside. Then they were gone.

"They're nice people," said Ralph, sitting down in his office and looking pleased because he has a close family.

He paused for lunch.

Ralph often takes his lunch in his office. This afternoon he was eating a tuna fish sandwich with tomatoes, potato chips, and a chocolate egg cream (a drink made with seltzer, milk, and chocolate syrup). It was served on a tray covered with a blue-and-white checkered napkin. "Don't forget the vitamin," he said, reaching for a small pill. "The gym guy says I should take a multivitamin." Ralph smiled. He doesn't believe in vitamins.

Health is a subject that is on his mind every day. In the

fall of 1986 Ralph was shaken by his father's triple bypass operation. Then, later that year, his brother Jerry suffered a serious illness. For Ralph, those pressures were only intensified by the knowledge that he had a brain tumor — a cluster of cells growing uncontrollably into a lump — and would soon need an operation.

"I'll never forget showing my spring collection in November 1986 and going out on the runway for the applause, and thinking to myself, 'I wonder if I'll ever see this again,' " says Ralph. "I had tears in my eyes, but only the video cameraman noticed."

His brain tumor was his most private secret. Back in 1977 Ralph had complained frequently and bitterly of a ringing in his ears. Nerves, his friends said. You get nervous when you're about to have a show.

That was true. Ralph did get anxious when he was working on a new collection. But this was different, he insisted. This hurt.

He went to a general physician.

"A lot of people have ringing in their ears," said the doctor. "We don't know what it is. Don't worry. It's not dangerous."

Not satisfied, Ralph went to a second doctor, an ear, nose, and throat specialist. He listened as Ralph described his symptoms and suggested Ralph have a CAT scan. A CAT scan produces sophisticated X-ray pictures of the brain.

"He probably saved my life," says Ralph.

Soon after the scan was complete, the doctor gave him the bad news.

"We think we know why your ears are ringing. It's a brain aneurism," he said. (An aneurism is a bubble that has formed in the worn wall of a blood vessel.)

Ralph nodded. He didn't know what a brain aneurism was. It sounded bad, but maybe not so bad.

He decided to ask his personal physician.

"I called him and said, 'They found out what was wrong with my hearing, all the ringing,' and the doctor said, 'What?'

" 'A brain aneurism,' I said.

"When I heard the concern in his voice, I sat down on the

couch and I wept. That was the first time I ever felt my own mortality. For a while I didn't know what to do. It was a very specialized thing, they weren't sure where to send me. I was very frightened."

A brain aneurism is very dangerous. If it ruptures and bursts, it is often fatal. Even if it is discovered early, there is still the possibility that a major artery might be ruptured during surgery.

Ralph then consulted Dr. Frank Petito, a New York neurologist. As a neurologist, Dr. Petito does not perform surgery. Rather, he defines himself as a diagnostician and a co-ordinator.

Dr. Petito listened to Ralph's symptons.

He looked at the results of the CAT scan.

And he concluded that Ralph's problems sounded more typical of a brain tumor.

He then suggested Ralph have an arteriogram, a test which involves the use of a dye that outlines blood vessels and aneurisms when used in conjunction with X rays.

The results showed that Dr. Petito was correct; Ralph had developed a very small tumor at the very bottom of the brain, located directly beneath the right frontal lobe. Although there is still debate over which functions this lobe controls, some specialists believe it influences a person's concept of the future, parts of his personality, and his daily energy level.

The tumor, Dr. Petito said, was called a benign meningioma.

It was good news. A benign tumor is much less dangerous than a brain aneurism.

"A tumor this small does not require immediate surgery," says Dr. Petito. "It may later have to be removed if it grows significantly. On the other hand, it may stay at that size for the rest of a patient's life."

"For the first few months I was in shock, and then I let it drift away," says Ralph. "I knew I had it but I wasn't going to let it affect my life."

The years passed. He was in terrific physical shape, his business was growing, the tumor seemed like an old nightmare. Then, in early fall of 1986, he decided to increase his insurance coverage. His insurance company, in turn, insisted he have a series of tests. Just to be sure everything was fine, the company suggested.

Ralph thought it was a waste of time.

"I didn't even want those tests," Ralph says.

When the tests were completed, Dr. Petito called and said he wanted to schedule Ralph for an operation. The brain tumor, said Dr. Petito, had grown faster than anybody had expected.

"It was about the scariest moment in my life," says Ralph. "Nineteen eighty-six was a very tough year for me. I even fainted at one point. The day my father went into the hospital, I was working out at the gym. Suddenly the floor began to spin. I thought, 'This is it, something is really happening.'"

Ralph immediately went to New York Hospital. He thought his fainting spell was related to his brain tumor. Instead, it was a mild case of vertigo, most likely brought on by stress. Relax, said Dr. Petito, and the symptoms will disappear. Ralph didn't faint again.

"I knew I was going for an operation, my father was in the hospital, it was a whole new stage in my life," says Ralph. "You bury your feelings somewhere in your body, and I guess it comes out."

Despite assurances from his doctors that his tumor was benign, Ralph worried that they might have made a mistake. Who knew? Anything could happen. The tumor might be malignant. He might have a stroke during the operation. It was very easy to imagine something going wrong. Especially as he decided to wait eight months before having the operation.

"It was a very strange time," says Ralph. "What happens is you have moments of being alone. You can be in the most beautiful place, or distract yourself at times, and then there is that moment of aloneness. When I was on the cover of *Time,* and everybody thought I was riding high and the king, I knew I had to go in for the operation. I was living through my worst moments. No one has it all.

"But you know, my oldest brother said a very nice thing to me. This gets me very emotional. He said, 'Ralph, you are a very good person. Nothing is going to happen to you.' [Lenny

Lauren, who worked with Ralph at Polo in the early 1970s, is today a partner in the Alsten Company, a major New Jersey manufacturer of custom packaging and displays for jewelry retailers.]

"What it does is make you stop and look at life in a very different way from most people. Anybody who has been through a very tragic moment in their life sees another side of life. People have a tendency to forget about the good moments and what they have and what is so precious. It made me appreciate the things that are passing, that go too quickly, the moments where later you think, 'I could have done,' or 'I should have done.' That's how it affected me."

Why did he put off his operation?

Because Ralph wanted to work on his fall 1987 collection. What he wanted to do was have his show in April and then take a vacation. Ralph thought he could have his operation in early April and be back at work so quickly nobody would notice.

Dr. Petito agreed. Another seven or eight months wouldn't make much difference.

Ralph didn't tell his kids until two weeks before he went into the hospital.

"I was so nervous about telling them; it was one of the most frightening things," says Ralph. "All along I had to deal with them, knowing I had something inside me that I couldn't tell them about. The thought of seeing their faces . . . scary. But they were terrific.

"For myself, the biggest shock was the fact that I wasn't physically sick. If you can't move your right arm, or all of a sudden you have a problem and you are dragging your leg, then you go to the doctor and get it fixed. That's one issue. If you are lying in bed and say, 'I need help,' that's another issue. But when you are perfectly healthy and you're running and you're going to the gym and you're at your prime, and then somebody tells you that you have something wrong and they've got to open up your head . . . that's a little shocking. You start to think, 'What's going to happen to me?' "

Ralph had his operation at New York Hospital on April 13, 1987, five days after he showed his fall 1987 collection at the St. Regis Hotel to mixed reviews.

"After the last fall show I went into the hospital not knowing how I was doing," says Ralph. "I saw the reviews from the
Times and *WWD* and they didn't get it, they weren't accepting
me. And you know something? I've never had a better season.
The clothes came in and blew out. That's what happened. That's
always been my story for some strange reason. I would do
something, believe in what I was doing, and of course not
everything went perfectly, not everything sells, not everything
is right, but I would do it, some reviews would be nice, some
fair, never great, never astounding . . . and then I'd feel like
I didn't make it. I'd feel embarrassed for my staff.

"After a show what happens is you do the clothes and the
immediate response is to open the *Times*, the *New York Post*,
WWD, and see what they think. I thought the show was beau-
tiful, but then I began to think I might have missed some-
thing. It was such a weird time for a fashion show, but when
I did that show I walked down that runway and I loved it.
Anyway, when I left for the hospital I left upset. I thought,
'Why didn't we get the reviews?' "

The operation was performed by Dr. Richard Fraser at
New York Hospital.

This is how it was done. First Dr. Fraser made an incision
above Ralph's forehead. Then he made a "window" in the skull,
which was essentially a door in the bone. Dr. Fraser then turned
that door back toward him, as though it were on a hinge. From
that vantage point he could see the brain. Dr. Fraser then lifted
up the brain and cut out the tumor growing below.

The surgery lasted five-and-a-half hours.

"It was shocking," says Ralph. "Shocking. That is it. It's
not easy for anybody. It's your body, it's your soul. There is a
major thing happening . . . But here I am."

Six days after the operation, Ralph got dressed and walked
out of the hospital.

"I couldn't stand it," he says. "I told the doctor I was leaving. I left. They wheeled me down and I walked out. But from
that moment your whole life is changed, your whole body is
changed, everything is changed."

Four weeks later, almost all of the physical scars were
healed.

In the months that followed, rumors spread in the fashion industry that Ralph Lauren was dying from an AIDS-related illness. This despite the fact that those who knew Ralph Lauren knew he was heterosexual and not a drug user.

The rumors intensified in June after he failed to attend a major industry dinner honoring Marvin Traub, chairman of Bloomingdale's.

"I was chairman of the dinner, and everybody was going to be there," says Ralph. "But I couldn't make it. I couldn't do it, too many people, I didn't have the strength. Marvin asked me to go. He said, 'Ralph, you okay?' I said, 'I'm okay, but sometimes I'm not okay.'

"What happens is that after a major operation like that you have to reacquaint yourself with life, with people, with walking the streets, even with going into a restaurant. I can only tell you I've been through it, I've done it, I've lived through it. As bad as it was, and I don't wish it on anybody, the experience was positive."

Soon after his operation, Ralph went to his home in Montauk to recover. Later that summer, he flew to his ranch in Colorado. He didn't return to his offices until early August.

Ralph realized he had to prove to both the press and the stores that he had recovered. So he appeared at the showing of his resort collection in August, making sure to greet his guests personally.

This was a business.

But it was a personal business.

He did not want people to think he was dying.

"After three-and-a-half months away from Seventh Avenue, Ralph Lauren returned yesterday, looking tanned and fit, to deliver commentaries at a series of small showings of his resort collection," reported the *New York Times*. "Recovered from surgery for a brain tumor, he said he had organized the presentations so that people could ask him questions and see that he was well again. That certainly seems to be the case . . ."

Then Ralph began to make appearances at various parties around New York, including a black-tie tribute honoring Audrey Hepburn and a cocktail bash held by the Council of Fashion Designers of America. He also attended a White House luncheon, where he was seated next to Nancy Reagan.

"I wanted people to know I was back," says Ralph. "I had to show them."

Side effects?

Five months after his operation, Ralph still looked thin. Psychologically, he was still recovering.

"I'm still suffering," he said. "I'm still . . . worn-out. Not worn-out . . . but wounded in my soul."

This day in early November 1987 is a particularly fine day for Ralph Lauren. A week earlier he had shown his spring 1988 fashion collection, and the critics were uniformly enthusiastic. It was a small collection. "I don't like long shows," says Ralph. "I like them short and sweet with a beautiful story. Fast, not slow. I edit very tightly. Not skimpy. Not lacking. But I don't want anybody falling asleep."

The show, held at 550 Seventh Avenue at his women's wear showroom, included several Ralph Lauren touches. Most obvious was the pianist, who played old favorites. The collection included tailored jackets with chiffon skirts and cashmere sweaters and satin pants. At a time when other designers were showing clothes better suited for bimbos, Ralph's collection was stylish and respectful. These were clothes that would look fine in five years.

"Not everything the press said to me personally after the shows appeared in the reviews," Ralph says. "But the next day John Fairchild called me to tell me how much he liked it. I'm told he doesn't do that very often. . . . You were at the show. What did you hear people saying?" He is eager to know. Ralph Lauren sometimes feels cut off. Because of his success people no longer talk to him as candidly as they once did. "They feel intimidated," he says. "It's not my fault. I'm still the same."

Ralph Lauren says he thinks of himself as a writer who expresses his thoughts in clothes. The description is a conceit. Ralph Lauren is not comfortable with words; he masks this by frequently saying in conversation, "I'm always direct, I always say what's on my mind."

Ralph says, "What you see is what you get," because he is not given to introspection. He distrusts complications. At one point, angered because he thinks he is being asked questions for reasons he has not been told, he snaps, "Why don't you level with me? I'm very straight as a person. I tell you the right things. You're not as straight as I am. You're working."

Fashion designers make their living by creating clothes that won't be worn by the customers for another six months. The fall collection Ralph Lauren shows in April doesn't begin to sell in the stores until September. It's no wonder Ralph doesn't like words. Words are precise, and Ralph Lauren is not in a precise business. There are no rules. Listen to him describe how he decided which clothes to present in his spring 1988 fashion collection. "Some of the line was designed as outfits, but much was designed piece by piece. There are jackets, there are skirts, there are tops. Then they come together. All of a sudden you take a piece of charmeuse and put it with a chiffon sweater. . . . I didn't know it was going to be that way. I could have done that outfit a hundred ways. I can simplify it, I can make it more sophisticated, I can make it all in chiffon, I can make it pattern on pattern. I decide. I put those clothes together. I pick each outfit, and I pick which outfit each model wears. I'm excited, my adrenaline is going, I want it to be perfect."

Nobody always gets it right. But Ralph does pay attention.

At least he does when it concerns his work.

When Ralph Lauren talks about his personal life he is absent-minded, vague about dates, forgetful of names and places. When it comes to a color or a particular piece of fabric or a skirt he designed fifteen years ago, the recall is precise. Part-way through one interview I asked him how his wife, Ricky, spelled her surname — Lowbeer, as one word, the way it appears on her New York City birth records, or Low-beer, with a hyphen, as it has appeared in print.

Ralph isn't sure. He thinks it has a hyphen. But if it does, he's not clear whether the *b* should be capitalized.

Two minutes later, I mention an incident involving Bob Ruttenberg, the former Warner/Lauren fragrance executive. Ruttenberg had bought a Polo topcoat in the late 1970s and then had his tailor sew on bone buttons. Ralph had noticed the change and had been furious.

"It was a navy blue coat and brass buttons," Ralph says instantly. "Of course I remember it."

He looks at me as though he is surprised that I would think he'd forgotten. This from somebody unsure how to spell his wife's maiden name.

Then again, maybe the incident shows why Ralph Lauren owns a multibillion-dollar business. Paying attention to detail sounds like a cliché today because Detroit advertises nonstop that it has learned the lessons of doing the job right. The advertising has not stopped the poor workmanship, but it has called into suspicion anybody who makes such claims.

Ralph does. What he is proudest of is not his possessions, which he loves, but the sell-through of his clothes at retail. Ralph Lauren is judged every day on the quality of every product that bears his name. That means about 10 million products a year. None of the customers cares about his problems. If a shirt doesn't fit right, the customer blames Ralph Lauren. It doesn't matter if one of Ralph's licensees made the product. It has Ralph's name on it.

When Ralph Lauren fails, he is always surprised.

Once, in the late 1970s, he told a newspaper reporter that he wanted to have a film career. It seemed possible. His friend Steve Ross ran Warner Communications, which included the Warner studio division. Maybe Ross could find him a script. "I know I couldn't become an Al Pacino in three weeks," Ralph said at the time. "But those are the type of roles I'd like to play, action-packed."

Ralph even thought of giving up the design business for a movie career. "I'm looking for a new challenge," he said. "If the right opportunity came along, I'd grab it."

A movie career? Not surprising. He has dark blue eyes, he projects immense confidence, and he loves images.

Listen to him describe his business:

"When you go into a store, there's a brand you ask for, a brand identity with a point of view. The point of view I have is presenting quality, subtlety, and understatement. But sometimes understatement is very hard to present. Cary Grant never won an Academy Award because his performances were so understated you thought that was what he was like all the time. [Among Ralph's favorite movies are *To Catch a Thief*, starring

Gary Grant; *The Godfather I* and *II; The Philadelphia Story;* and *Chariots of Fire.*] Sometimes actors are so low-key you never think they are acting. In fashion, designers can emphasize an arm, a shoulder, and people will say, 'Wow, oh wow.' When you are presenting a tweed suit or a beautiful plain shirt or a rep tie, people will say, 'So what?' "

Or this:

"In a movie you get to know a character. John Wayne presented a role and you saw him time and time again and you began to know something about him. Clint Eastwood presents a role, however narrow. There is a point of view and he gets a fan, and the fan laughs at his jokes. They know what to expect a little. There is a story and a mood that is presented. That's what I do."

Or this:

"When I first started to build this business, I spoke to some financial people. They said, 'You'll do a very limited business selling your merchandise at your prices. How far can you go?' Manufacturers tend to underestimate the quality the American consumer and the world consumer now want. We tend to look down and not up. I believe they want better television, they want better movies."

Still, Ralph Lauren never acted in a film. There were rumors of a cowboy picture to be shot with Clint Eastwood, this, that. . . . It faded away.

In the early 1980s, when Ralph realized he might not ever star in somebody else's movie, he contemplated bankrolling his own.

He had an idea for a movie project he called *The Conglomerate.* It involved Wall Street arbitrageurs. Ralph Lauren was fascinated by Wall Street, by the takeover game, by the ability to make millions of dollars in a few hours. And, he says, by the power he saw there.

"You get vibes," says Ralph. "Art directors, writers, have theories they write out of the world around them. Movies are a part of our culture. Something's happening, you're inspired. It's in the air, it's in the wind. Wall Street gets hot and you have five scripts on Ivan Boesky. You read something, you hear something, and you're inspired."

He never made that movie. But Ralph enjoys his ties to

Hollywood. In casual conversation he offhandedly mentions Robert Redford, Diane Keaton, Candice Bergen. He does not do this to impress; Ralph is cool. Rather, those actors are part of his world, or at least were at one time, and those memories and the pleasure of seeing his clothes in such pictures as *The Great Gatsby* and *Annie Hall* still satisfy. (He did not design a specific wardrobe for Diane Keaton in *Annie Hall;* rather, the clothes she wore in that picture — the Ralph Lauren oversized men's shirts and jackets — were her own.) Woody Allen once rummaged through Ralph's closets — the two men wore the same size — took an armful of clothes, and wore them in his movie *Manhattan.*

Certainly Ralph could afford to become a Hollywood producer. Remember, Hollywood itself was founded by a group of former New York garment manufacturers.

People who succeed in the clothing industry must have a sense of mass appeal and popular taste and how to market their product after they've made it. So do the winners in Hollywood.

And he still gets the occasional nibble. Not too long ago, Alexandra Penney, the author of *How to Make Love to a Man,* called Ralph with a suggestion for a film.

"I said, 'Ralph, I have this idea.' He said tell me over the phone. I said 'No, I have to tell you in person.' So I went over to his office and told it to him, and he immediately said, 'I hate it.'

"What had happened was that *he'd* had a great idea for a movie, but it was a period piece and it would have cost a fortune to produce," says Penney. "I updated it for modern times. But he said no. Why? Because it didn't fit into his fantasy world. It was too raw. To put him into a contemporary reality doesn't work for him. That's not his fantasy. So I said, 'Fine, that's all I wanted to know,' and then I talked to him about the Duchess of Windsor."

Ralph is patient. He is waiting for Hollywood to call.

What does it mean to have acquired a personal fortune valued at about $400 million?

It means owning antique cars and luxurious homes and

the luxury of not having to worry about bills. Ralph doesn't pooh-pooh any of this. It's great being rich. Besides, he makes a product, and the customers decide whether they want to buy it or not. Ralph Lauren is a top-notch mass merchandiser. If the customers didn't think the clothes wore well, they'd buy something else. Nobody builds a repeat business over twenty years by fooling people.

One thing it also means is the privilege of dreaming big dreams.

Consider Ralph's current fantasy: cattle baron.

Already Ralph has spent millions of dollars renovating his Double RL ranch bordering on the San Juan mountain range in southern Colorado. The spread includes a log cabin renovated by interior designer Naomi Leff, the same decorator who helped create his Madison Avenue showcase. In addition Ralph built an Indian teepee, new calving sheds and corrals, and used miles of rail fencing to mark his property instead of the traditional, but ugly, barbed wire.

There's more.

"While he left the ranching to his men, he paid attention to the esthetics," reported Jim Carrier in the *Denver Post*. "Cabins were stained old. Old sheds were left old on the outside but framed and modernized inside. Lauren's new house, built of logs, was torn down and replaced because the logs were too uniform. The fireplace was rebuilt, too. The swimming pool was dynamited and redone with the 'right' rocks. . . . Take the cook house. Built two years ago (in 1985) of aged barn board, it looks as old as the 1890 cabin beside it. The porch roof is supported by four knotty posts, the fourth set to be tried before Lauren accepted the right look. Inside, there are old cupboards, old lanterns, banged-up floors, tables and chairs. Inside the cupboards are Ralph Lauren dishes, Ralph Lauren towels, and in the dark and weathered bathroom, Chaps aftershave."

Okay, pretty silly stuff.

Still, Ralph Lauren intends to make this ranch pay. And in doing so, he may change the way Americans buy their beef.

That's right. Ralph Lauren intends to introduce what can only be described as "designer beef."

He already owns roughly 1,000 brood cows and another 900 steers.

"I'd like to come out with really great beef," he says. "One thing I've noticed about the cattle business is that people are struggling for pennies. They are all starving. I said, 'Why aren't there any brands?' It was like the tie business. When I had to raise the price from $2.50 to $3 the other tie manufacturers went crazy. They were so insulated they didn't understand that if something was beautifully made people would buy it. It wasn't a matter of ripping the customers off. It was a matter of making your product, designing it, and coming out with it."

Remember, until Frank Perdue put his name on a chicken, chickens were unbranded commodities. Ultimately, Perdue changed the direction of the entire chicken industry.

Ralph thinks that with the right marketing, he can do the same for the cattle business.

"Most people don't go to butchers," he says. "They go to supermarkets and take a chance on the beef. They buy what they are given. But if you knew a brand was good beef, you'd ask for it.

"I want to do that. I want to develop a brand from the breeding, to develop cows so that they have fine-quality meat. I don't want to sell cattle which have been fed fake things to fatten them up. Today, the ranchers grow them, and sell them for what they can get. I'm trying to do something different. I want a completely vertical operation. And I've got a manager at the ranch who knows the business and wants to do it."

Money isolates the rich. They've got it, others want it. They get burned once or twice, and then they discover they've been transformed from a person into a target.

Ralph Lauren has learned. There was the childhood friend from the Bronx who called because he desperately needed money for his sick mother. Ralph gave him the money immediately. Later Ralph learned the woman was never ill.

Or there was the troubling case of Bob Phillips, self-described California entrepreneur. Phillips opened his first free-standing Ralph Lauren store at 1030 Wall Street in La Jolla, California, on February 6, 1976.

Phillips knew a good thing when he saw it. And he acted fast.

"I formed a corporation called Polostore, one word, and then I registered a mark that divided the two words," he says. "In the center was a polo player making a shot under the neck. That was my mark, and it differed from Ralph's mark because his guy is holding the mallet high."

To make matters even more galling for Ralph Lauren, Phillips then fell behind in paying his bills. At one point he owed Polo $750,000.

"I had an agreement with them to put stores in major metro areas initially throughout the United States," says Phillips. "At the time I got my fourth or fifth store, it was the one in Phoenix, I was asked to come back to New York. The purpose of the call was left open. I felt, well, if they want to talk to me about furthering the details of what has been a laissez-faire arrangement, fine.

"When I got there, I was confronted with seven guys around a table in Peter Strom's office. The accountant's opening remark was, 'When are you going to pay us the seven hundred fifty thousand you owe us?'

"I said, 'Gee, I thought this was going to be a different kind of a meeting.' Then, before anybody could say anything else, the lawyer pipes up and says, "And your mark. We want your mark signed over right away or we are going to institute a lawsuit. We're a big company and that infringes on our mark . . .'

"I said, 'Gentlemen, I don't respond well to those kind of threats. As far as I'm concerned, I didn't come back to talk about that. The interview is over.'

"So I got up and left.

"What they did then was do everything they could not to ship me. They cost me hundreds of thousands of dollars. They put the squeeze on me and blackmailed me into signing over the mark to them, which I eventually did in exchange for their forgiveness of five hundred thousand."

In other words, after letting Bob Phillips buy his inventory on credit, it cost Ralph $500,000 to get back what many believe amounted to his own corporate name and trademark.

No wonder a person becomes suspicious. It's complicated being a wealthy celebrity.

Something else happens as a company gets bigger. It demands more time. The hours get longer, the hours left to see friends are fewer. Then the friends get angry because calls aren't returned, and the friendships start to peel away.

Look at Michael Farina.

Farina was an illustrator at *Daily News Record* who played an important role in getting Ralph's ties and early designs into the newspaper at a time when Ralph couldn't afford any advertising.

The two became so close that Ralph served as best man at Farina's second wedding. Not only did Ralph host a bachelor party for Farina, but he insisted on designing Farina's wife's wedding outfit.

But let Farina tell it.

"We went away on our honeymoon, and when we came back, Ralph invited us out for the weekend to a house he was renting in the Hamptons," he says. "That night, Ralph and I went out on the porch and talked for two or three hours. It was close-friend kind of talk: our lives, where are we going, how do you feel about this. We spoke about a lot of things, and that was it.

"Then, one day I called Ralph up and he said, 'Well, I'm pretty busy right now.'

"I said, 'Ralph, so am I. But I'm taking five minutes because I've got something I've got to talk to you about.'

"He said, 'Well, I really can't talk right now. I'm too busy.'

"And I said to myself, 'Wait a minute. You are too busy? There's no such thing.'

"So I said, 'Fine, give me a call when you get some time.'

"I'm probably as stubborn as he is, so I never called him again. I figured if you don't have time to talk to your friends, fine. I haven't talked to him since. But it wasn't as if we fought over anything."

What happened?

Farina thinks he knows.

"Ralph was so involved in his designing and wanted it so badly that he couldn't allow anybody to get in the way," he says. "Ralph had to devote his entire being to being creative and winning. And if he got too close to somebody, maybe, and I'm only suggesting, that it would take a part of him away from his designing and his business. I don't think Ralph had room for everything.

"It's a hard thing to stay on top. I don't think anybody can understand or feel what the pressure is once you've made it, when the world is looking at you expecting miracles every time you create something. It's got to be a tremendous pressure on anybody. Once you do better, how do you hold on to it, what do you do better the next time? I don't think people like that have enough room for everybody and everything. There are going to be hundreds of people who want to be your best friend. Or hang around. I don't think they have groupies in the fashion business, but maybe they do. People who are just clingers. I think that's what happened with Ralph. He didn't have room for everybody. He would hide, he'd go into his little corner and disappear. He'd cut one person off and go to somebody else."

Still, Farina was hurt.

After all, before they stopped talking, they'd talked a lot.

Especially about their childhoods. One day Farina told Ralph how much he liked to fish and hunt.

Ralph interrupted him, saying, "I had a gun once."

Farina was surprised. "Really?"

Ralph nodded. "I saved my money, and went into the store and bought a Daisy BB pump gun."

Farina was impressed. The Daisy BB pump gun was the most powerful and expensive gun that the company made. Every kid who wanted a BB gun wanted a pump model.

Ralph was different from most because he saved until he had enough money to afford one.

Then, when he got it, he did what every kid with a BB gun did: he took it outside to shoot it. This was the Bronx, though, and as he was walking over a bridge a police car stopped him, picked him up, and took away the gun.

"It was a very important story for Ralph, because that gun really meant something to him," says Farina. "Even then he wanted the classiest things. Anyway, just before Ralph and I stopped talking, I found a Daisy BB pump gun. I refinished it and put it back together in its original shape. Daisy even sent me some old parts. I redid it as a gift for him for being my best man. I had nothing I could buy him that made sense, and that story about his gun was always in the back of my mind.

"P.S. I still have the gun in my closet. I never gave it to him. I've thought about sending it because he'd know what it meant. I still have it. I hope one day I'll give it to him." (In the fall of 1987, Farina called Ralph, the two met, and Farina gave Ralph the present.)

As the Farina anecdote indicates, once somebody makes a lot of money and becomes a celebrity, his friends get very sensitive. Friends even compete with friends. Deciphering those ambiguities with one of the richest people in the world is tough because it addresses fundamental questions about how and why people relate to each other.

"People look at you from afar and think you've changed," says Ralph. "They look at you and say, 'I'm not going to call you.' But that has nothing to do with you. It's their feelings about you; it has nothing to do with your feelings about them. The only thing that happens is you get so busy, so barraged, that it gets tough. It becomes time. Your priorities are family and work. I'm so barraged I can't tell you. People say, 'Oh he's changed, he's too big to call me. I see his picture in the paper. I'm not going to call him back; he'll call me.'

"It's their reaction, not yours."

For more than thirty years Morton Sills has made some of the finest custom-tailored suits in New York. His shop, Sartor & Company, is on the seventh floor of 18 East 53rd Street. The wing chairs are made of leather, and they are as comfortable as one would expect in an old English club. The art consists of a solitary black-and-white painting by Fernand Léger. Here, among fine woolens, handfinished silk ties, and expensive men's pants, shop the wealthy and the privileged. Only a very select few can afford the $1,500 or $2,000 or so Morton Sills charges for one of his suits, and even they usually buy only two or three a year.

When Ralph Lauren was in his early twenties, he thought

he would one day have a business like this. He would attract only the wealthiest customers, buy only the finest fabrics, and stress quality rather than trendy fashion. He was drawn to Morton Sills and the late Roland Meledandri, also a New York tailor, not only by what they sold but by the dignity with which they presented their clothes and the certainty of their opinions.

Sills grew up in New Haven, Connecticut, where Yale undergraduates dressed in brown tweed jackets and gray flannels. Sills also saw how the rich lived, once watching as a young Yale freshman left the New Haven railroad station trailed by fourteen polo ponies with handlers. "That gives you a picture of life that was completely different from going to temple every Friday night with your father," says Sills. "You watch, and you pick it up."

Later, Sills would work for ultrapreppy J. Press as a salesman. One morning young Marshall Field came in and ordered six pairs of white flannel trousers. Those pants cost $75 each, which meant each pair cost more than Sills was earning a week.

Impressed, Sills asked Field what he did with such pants.

Play tennis, responded Field.

This is how Sills learned about how the rich lived, the clothes they wore, the level of service they demanded. Those moments shaped his taste, and they introduced him to a monied world. Later, to a select group, the name Morton Sills on a suit would signify old-fashioned hand-tailoring. When the customers stopped and asked him how he had learned all this, Sills would shrug and say it had been his life. Ralph Lauren, though, was different. With Ralph Lauren, in the late 1960s, Morton Sills would sit and talk for hours about the history of the clothes he made, the customers who bought them, the country estates they owned. Sills would talk also about England, and what quality fabrics meant and why one mill was better than another. Or he would talk about shirt collars and the proper width of a man's tie. Ralph may have been influenced by Fred Astaire and Douglas Fairbanks and Cary Grant. But it was Sills, Meledandri, and Clifford Grodd at Paul Stuart who explained where the clothes they wore came from, why they were worn, and what they meant.

Just as Ralph Lauren studied Sills, Meledandri, and Grodd, they studied him. As they watched his career develop over the years, they would marvel at how far and how fast his talents were taking him. If they envied his success and wealth, they would not show it, for they too were successful, although on a much smaller scale. For Morton Sills, though, Ralph's success would be bittersweet. Sills would always be proud to have introduced Ralph to a certain style of living; he would be less comfortable with how captivated Ralph had become by it.

"Ralph isn't a complicated human being," says Sills. "He's very simple. He believes if you put on the clothes you become an aristocrat. The fact that his customer can't recognize a Van Gogh from a Léger doesn't matter. Ralph thinks everybody is going to have a polo mallet in his hand and put some of his perfume behind his ears. That becomes pretty cynical because that dream is not supported by fact. Ralph never developed philosophically, never developed politically, never developed in other ways, in terms of his perception of life, his values. Sure he loves his wife and kids. But what world does he live in? Is Fifth Avenue the world? That might be the way he sees it, but that's not the world."

Sills is touchy because occasionally one of his customers reminds him that he's from outside their class.

"A guy said to me yesterday in the fitting room, talking about Ivan Boesky, 'The trouble with you Jews is you get caught.'

"So I said, 'Well, when Whitney got caught fifty years ago, how do you figure Whitney got caught?' [Richard Whitney, a Groton and Harvard graduate, bought a New York Stock Exchange seat in 1912, lived on a 500-acre estate near Far Hills, New Jersey, served as president of the stock exchange during the early 1930s, and in 1938 was sentenced to five to ten years in Sing-Sing prison for securities fraud.]

"And he said, 'Every now and then we let one slip through.'

"There was a smile on his face," says Sills. "But there was anti-Semitism in the remark."

Sills, then, sees both sides of the world he both caters to and disdains. There is the personal style and grace young Marshall Field brought to the tennis courts in his white flannels, and there are the doors closed to those born in the wrong neighborhoods.

Ralph Lauren, Sills thinks, sees only one side.

"Ralph reflects our society today, a consumer society," he says. "If you believe we have a viable society, then this is one of the success stories, one of the proofs to counteract the unemployment figures, the health figures, or money spent on defense budgets. Because it's all related. The customers who buy his clothes support the whole structure. Twenty years ago he had more integrity in his concepts. He isn't a furniture designer or even a women's designer. Yet the country buys it. That reflects what advertising is about, what public relations is about, what image building can do.

"Here we're trying to make the best damn suit in the world. It's a small goal. I've got a little house in Cold Spring Harbor, a guy drives me to work in the morning, I worked fifty years for that. I mean that's okay. But that's not what life is about. That's what hurts me about Ralph. His life should be more. It's a small life. Why all the pictures of himself in the papers? Because some smart guy said that was how to sell Ralph Lauren. And Ralph believes it. It's the same way personalities are consumed in North Korea."

A bit heavy here, comparing the merchandising of Ralph Lauren to the selling of Kim Il Sung in Pyongyang. But Morton Sills is a serious person; when he talks about Ralph Lauren he no longer sees the same young kid carrying a case of Abe Rivetz ties.

Then again, Ralph Lauren hasn't changed much in twenty years. He has acquired all the belongings associated with great wealth, but somebody who dresses in jeans and tee shirts at the office isn't working on the same emotional batteries as Wall Street brokers or investment bankers. What drives Ralph Lauren is not the opportunity to make yet more money. Mention his annual income to him, and Ralph Lauren's face curls up in a grimace. But watch as he thumbs through an article in *Esquire*. "Look at that," he says, smiling and pointing at a sentence which starts, "Ever since Ralph Lauren first told you to wear your blue jeans with a tie . . . " That simple sentence makes his day because it shows that Ralph has affected how his customers live and see themselves.

Ralph wants to be recognized as a creative personality. That's his itch. No matter how he scratches it, it doesn't get better.

After a certain point, more money doesn't mean peace of mind.

"It all has to do with people who have started out with very little in life," says Clifford Grodd, president of Paul Stuart. "Arriving they think, 'I'm going to be here and be happy.' But happiness is not having a steak dinner. Rather, it's recognizing what makes you content with your life at that moment. When you get there, and you have five homes — and Ralph is probably getting more pleasure out of these things than he thought — it's still tough to think 'I've arrived,' because you can never arrive to the extent that your success has led you to believe. You can be the richest guy in the world, yet you still have the same emotions. You don't walk away from your emotions because you have thirty-three million instead of thirty-three dollars. People think when they arrive they will be a larger person. They will be enhanced by it. But you are enhanced in a superficial way. Whether you have one million or three hundred million, it's relatively insignificant in terms of how it impacts on your personality. If you're insecure, you're always insecure and money doesn't change it. Ralph Lauren is very insecure. That's part of the reason for his success."

Actually, this doesn't describe Ralph Lauren as much as it describes the results of Ralph Lauren's work. Look at the Christmas card his office sent out in December 1987. The card itself is bordered in red-and-black plaid. In the center is a photograph of Ralph taken in the winter at his ranch in Colorado. He is on horseback, wearing chaps, heavy gloves, and an old brown weatherbeaten jacket worn over a red-and-black plaid lumber jacket. The sky overhead is heavily clouded, although there is a patch of deep blue off to one corner. Ralph is grinning broadly. Getting here has been a long struggle; but now that he is here he looks as if it is even better than he'd imagined.

This is a terrific image, an almost mythlike image. Here is Ralph Lauren on the range, riding free, owner of every acre as far as the eye can see.

And everybody knows he's the good guy. Because in this picture, he's the one wearing the white hat.

In the 1920s and 1930s, American industrial design blossomed and developed a character of its own. Designers like Raymond Loewy, Norman Bel Geddes, Russell Wright, and Henry Dreyfuss streamlined vacuum cleaners, thermoses, and radios, giving them wit and elegance. The things of everyday life gleamed, shone, and inspired. The marriage between industry and technology was never stronger. This was "The Machine Age," and it meant skyscrapers and the building of the George Washington Bridge, massive projects like the Hoover Dam, and sleek cars like the Chrysler Airflow. It was an era marked by a cocky "anything you can do, I can do better" attitude, but it wasn't smart-alecky because it didn't pander only to the rich. Rather, designers were reaching out to the middle class, and they were doing it with products whose imaginative styling gave them cachet.

Central was the belief that good design was an important marketing point. These designers believed that the customers would value sleek styling as much as they did a well-performing engine. In turn, these products would give their owners status as well as a sense of accomplishment and belonging. This was the start of aspirational marketing. ("A car of today for the sophisticated tastes of today!" reads the copy for the Chrysler Imperial 80 sold in 1928. "Chrysler's New 112 h.p. Imperial '80' has enriched even the experience of those most accustomed to and appreciative of the finest in motor cars." The bold black-and-white illustration, a frenzied tableau which includes flappers in a private box at the theater, is equally dramatic. This is a car, the illustration makes clear, for the achievers, the movers and shakers, the customers who know what the good life is and intend to get it. Dullards need not apply.)

The advertising became more convincing because it developed images with which the customers could identify. These were images that reflected not only who the customers were, but who they wanted to become. The industrial designers weren't marketing products; they were selling the good life to a postwar generation experiencing new and unexpected levels of affluence.

This marketing asked the customers to spend more, to rethink their tastes, to change their lives. Raymond Loewy made even pencil sharpeners inspirational. The products he designed not only worked, they let the customers who bought them feel good about themselves. There had always been a certain status associated with the Tiffanys of the world, artisans producing one-of-a-kind works of beauty. Now the middle class could also feel pride in ownership. Raymond Loewy explained his creed this way: "Good design keeps the user happy, the manufacturer in the black and the aesthete unoffended."

Loewy translated this concept into electric clocks, ballpoint pens, bathroom scales, passenger trains, sewing machines, tricycles, and cookie shapes for Nabisco. He took the simple and he made it stylish.

The new, streamlined look these designers introduced in the late 1920s and 1930s influenced not only how the customers lived, but their expectations as well. It was no longer enough to have any car; the customers wanted cars like the Ford Zephyr, with its elongated hood and high front fenders. Instead of mundane corporate headquarters, corporations demanded something extraordinary, such as Rockefeller Center, the "City of Towers." Everyday furniture was passé; instead the customers bought "skyscraper" bookcases and carpets decorated with wild, nerve-shattering geometric designs. Even cocktail shakers had to look like chrome bowling pins. "My early colleagues and myself helped create the life-styles of Americans and, by osmosis, of the rest of the world," Loewy told the *New York Times* in 1979.

The excitement made manufacturers of even the most ordinary products rethink their marketing. Technology was making such fast advances that most makers could not long count on quantifiable differences to justify the purchase of their products. For many companies, this meant offering a discernable difference based on design. It also prompted the birth of market research. If the customers were willing to pay more for style, maybe it was worth finding out what else they wanted. That meant asking them. It was a new approach, because until the 1920s products were sold primarily on the basis of performance: this lawn mower will cut so many more blades of grass, these tires will last so many miles. Designers such as Loewy, Bel Geddes, Wright, and Dreyfuss changed this by emphasizing style. They proved that all things being equal, the customer preferred products as handsome as they were efficient.

Hence one of Loewy's first great successes, the Coldspot refrigerator he designed for Sears, Roebuck & Company in 1935. This refrigerator not only sold 275,000 units in 1936, but it won first prize at the Paris International Exposition in 1937. "What I had instinctively believed was proved by hard sales figures," Raymond Loewy told the *New York Times*. "You take two products with the same function, the same quality and the same price: the better-looking one will outsell the other."

Industrial designers were creating an image and an aura around their products. When the customers rode Henry Dreyfuss's 20th Century Limited, they felt an excitement greater than that promised by the simple purchase of a train ticket. The very look of that sleek train made riding it a heady, even romantic experience. When the customers streamed in by the thousands to marvel at Norman Bel Geddes's "Futurama" in the General Motors Pavilion at the 1939 New York World's Fair, the future they saw there was a future brighter, sleeker, and more extraordinary than they had imagined before. No wonder "Futurama" was the most popular exhibit at the fair.

So, too, would the clothes men and women wore say much about their aspirations. This was never clearer than in 1947, when Christian Dior introduced what he called "The New Look," full dresses cut from yards and yards of cloth. The underlying message? That wartime quotas were over and better times were ahead. Later, in the 1950s, the big chrome fenders on America's cars reflected the nation's prosperity as well as its belief that it had the world by the throat. The proof was the big chrome monster with the fins sitting in the driveway.

There is only so much a designer can do to a shirt.

He can deepen the collar, he can taper the body, he can add more expensive buttons.

But he is still selling a staple. Unless, that is, he transforms that shirt into a symbol of something else. Make that shirt synonymous with a world of old-fashioned craftsmanship, a world in which the customers expect to pay more because they get more, and that shirt becomes a personal statement.

Copywriter David Ogilvy did just that when he introduced the Hathaway Man in the *New Yorker* in 1951. (The first Hathaway Man to wear the famous eye patch was Baron George Wrangell, a trim, ever-so-elegant Russian immigrant.)

Look at the ad copy, a clever blend of the hard sell with an upscale image.

"American men are beginning to realize that it is ridiculous to buy good suits and then spoil the effect by wearing an ordinary, mass-produced shirt. Hence the growing popularity of Hathaway shirts, which are in a class by themselves.

"Hathaway shirts wear infinitely longer — a matter of years. They make you look younger and more distinguished, because of the subtle way Hathaway cuts collars. The whole shirt is tailored more generously, and is therefore more comfortable. The tails are longer, and stay in your trousers. The buttons are mother-of-pearl. Even the stitching has an antebellum elegance about it. Hathaway shirts are made by a small company of dedicated craftsmen in the little town of Waterville, Maine. They have been at it, man and boy, for one hundred and fifteen years."

This ad promised the customers more than the satisfaction of owning another white shirt. It promised "antebellum elegance," and a sense of caring which had been handed down man to boy. By positioning itself as the purveyor of old-world workmanship, Hathaway hoped some of that respect the customers associated with old-fashioned workmanship would rub off on its own reputation. Which it did.

In his book, *Confessions of an Advertising Man*, Ogilvy bragged that the campaign was so successful it "put Hathaway on the map after 116 years of relative obscurity. Seldom, if ever, has a national brand been created so fast or at such a low cost." Eventually, such celebrities as Woody Allen, Bill Cosby, and Jonathan Winters would appear in Hathaway Man ads.

Compare this advertisement to one of the first promoting Ralph Lauren knit polo shirts, an ad that appeared in the *New*

York Times in December 1974. Remember, the knit shirt business was then owned by Izod Lacoste and its grinning alligator.

Remember, also, that few people had ever heard of Ralph Lauren.

"Nobody needs to be told about the superior breeding of Ralph Lauren's Polo shirt — the husky, lock-knit, 100% cotton, the perfect cut, the generous tails, the built-in comfort factors," read the B. Altman & Co. copy. "But perhaps you're curious, as we were, about Mr. Lauren's personal cachet, the miniature polo player appliqué that appears on each of his designs.

"To find out about it, we went, as it were, to the horse's mouth. 'My polo player,' Mr. Lauren told us, 'personifies the feeling I try to give my designs — the look of the American squire, the man who's at home anywhere from the Hamptons to Pebble Beach. There is nothing contrived about the look,' he went on, 'simply that if it's done by Polo, you know it's done right.'

" 'Right,' we echoed admiringly. Polo shirts are right for all seasons, right in every man's wardrobe, right for Christmas giving."

The muscle-length sleeved shirt cost $18 that year.

Note the similarities between the Altman and the David Ogilvy ads. Like the Hathaway ad, Altman's promoted Polo's knit shirt heritage ("superior breeding"), it emphasized Polo's quality manufacture ("the husky, lock-knit, 100% cotton"), and it promised increased status for the wearer ("Mr. Lauren's personal cachet").

It did not do for Ralph Lauren what the eye patch did for Hathaway; Ralph Lauren's knit polo shirt would not become a best-seller until the late 1970s, after it had been given national prominence by Neiman-Marcus and Bloomingdale's.

But the seeds had been planted.

Listen to Ed Carlo, the former national sales manager of Polo who helped launch Ralph's knit shirts on a nationwide basis.

"It was really a well-made shirt," says Carlo. "But I told the people opening Polo stores across the country that the product itself didn't really matter. It was the image we were selling. We weren't selling body coverage, we were selling ego massage. There was a romance to that shirt, a romance to Polo because of that polo player. And there was no romance left to the alligator."

Adds Robert Vignola, a former Polo salesman, "The concept was for every American with taste and money to be able to afford a little slice of Ralph Lauren. It was like being able to afford a key chain, but not the entire set of Gucci luggage. It was a taste and introduction to the rest of what Ralph had to offer."

The customer was no longer buying a piece of cloth, he was buying a life-style. A life-style represented by a polo player. It meant old money, it meant good taste, it meant the appreciation of a well-made product.

"Why did people buy my knit shirt? Because the entire middle class wanted to look better, not just the strivers," says Ralph Lauren. "People aren't stopped by price points. They wanted something that was well made. My polo shirt gave it to them."

Those were the messages conveyed in the first national ad for Ralph Lauren's knit shirt, which Neiman-Marcus ran in the *New Yorker* in November 1978. Arranged in three rows of eight were Ralph's knit shirts in twenty-four different colors, including five different shades of blue.

"People never settle for just one," reads the copy. "Pick the four colors you want, $104.00. Can't settle for only four, eh? All 24 shirts for $624.00."

Talk about image advertising. First there are the props, a polo mallet, ball, and hat, which are used to remind customers that polo is a game played by the rich. Then there is the message that wearing one of these shirts will enable the owner to share the same emotions and experiences of those for whom the shirts were intended.

"Neiman-Marcus was extremely influential in having the polo player recognized as the rising symbol of status," says Greg deVaney, a former Neiman-Marcus buyer. "Izod then owned the knit shirt business, and Ralph Lauren was barely known for his sportswear. But the whole preppy movement was starting, and I thought we could take that polo player and make it the new symbol for people to wear.

"We were also trying to establish the mystique about Neiman's. In retailing there are a lot of things you spend money on to develop business. Even if we didn't sell enough shirts to pay for the ads, building the image for tomorrow made it worth it."

This, then, is what Ralph Lauren would have in common with the designers of the 1920s and 1930s: he would take the ordinary products of everyday life, and he would translate them into stylish clothes or home furnishings or accessories that gave their owners cachet and status. Although only the most affluent could afford his top-of-the-line men's suits or women's dresses, almost everybody could buy his knit polo shirts, his men's and women's fragrances, his Chaps line, and his Roughwear (sports clothes) collection, much as customers could afford the sleek vacuum cleaners and radios of the earlier time.

Ralph Lauren's designs would be less obvious. Few noticed the real horn buttons, or the double stitching, or the finer quality of wool. But those were the details that would distinguish Ralph Lauren as a designer. Once he had established a name and a business, he no longer needed to shock the customers and the big stores. What Ralph did best was make clothes available to his customers that didn't rip or shred or shrink or bleed when they were cleaned. In doing so, he raised the expectations of his customers in terms of quality and fit and influenced other designers as well.

"Manufacturers tend to underestimate the quality the American consumer and the world consumer wants today," says Ralph. "We tend to look down and not up. I have never believed that." In 1987, this would mean ads in the *New York Times Magazine* that offered crocodile belts with silver buckles ($265); a man's cashmere shawl-collar robe with crest ($800); men's and women's crocodile loafers with gold buckles ($760); men's cashmere cabled sweaters ($335), and silk beaded scarves ($240).

These prices sound ridiculous.

They are.

But in its first year in operation, the Ralph Lauren store on Madison Avenue did about $31 million in sales. So some people out there liked what they saw.

(Those sales did not mean that the store was profitable. In

fact, the Rhinelander Mansion lost more than $5 million in its first year. Sales the second year appeared behind plan through the end of December 1987. More worrisome, the store's overhead was growing steadily. "Keeping control of costs is a constant headache," said Peter Strom, president. Polo/Ralph Lauren's biggest challenge in the next five years will be managing the company's operating expenses. Too much optimistic expansion too quickly could destroy the business.)

It is possible the Rhinelander Mansion will never make a profit. This does not mean, however, the store is a failure.

Look what it has done for Ralph Lauren's image.

For the fiscal year ended March 31, 1986, a few weeks before the opening of the Rhinelander Mansion in April, Ralph's licensees generated about $400 million in volume. For the fiscal year ended March 31, 1988, those licensees did $600 million.

Some of the gains Ralph attributes to the image of his company, which the Rhinelander store reinforces. In fact, the Rhinelander Mansion is now a New York tourist attraction, a place where people come to gawk and marvel and, occasionally, to buy something.

Just as the industrial designers of the 1920s and 1930s designed products that affected every aspect of their customers' lives, so too has Ralph Lauren branched into new businesses, the most important of which has been his home furnishings line, called the Ralph Lauren Home Collection.

The 2,500-piece collection of sheets, towels, glassware, silverware, and comforters was introduced by two dozen top retailers in September 1983. The stores included Neiman-Marcus, Bloomingdale's, J. W. Robinson, Bullock's, Macy's San Francisco, Marshall Field, and I. Magnin.

It was a debacle.

Blame it on trying to do too much, too quickly. Rather than developing one or two lines the first season, making the mistakes, and then growing the business in the second year, Ralph insisted on launching all the products at once. This meant that his main licensee, J. P. Stevens, was forced to deal with eight sublicensees at the same time that it was creating its own Ralph Lauren line of sheets and towels. Many of those secondary makers were unable to meet their deadlines.

Indeed, J. P. Stevens itself remade its Ralph Lauren plush towels more than thirty times before Ralph was satisfied.

Ralph also insisted that each of the stores that bought his line had to build a special Ralph Lauren Home Collection department in which to sell the collection. Including inventory, some stores were said to have invested almost $1 million.

The prices Ralph Lauren asked were high. Cotton shower curtains cost $100; all-wool blankets were $225; a set of 200-count, all-cotton sheets for a twin bed cost $64; a simple terry cloth robe was $195. (Later, the prices would go higher. For Mother's Day, 1987, the company suggested appreciative children might buy their moms hand-embroidered throw pillows for $225; a Belgian hand-embroidered flat sheet for $850; cotton tablecloths for $300; four embroidered cotton napkins for $240, or a white goose down comforter, full or queen, for $510.)

If Ralph had delivered the goods on time, and the customers had paid the exorbitant prices, he could have justified making such demands. But his sublicensees didn't deliver, which meant many of the stores that had invested in the home furnishings collection were left with bare shelves. Nobody makes money with bare shelves.

There were other mistakes, too. Ralph decreed that there would be no white sales of Ralph Lauren sheets and towels. (The bulk of the sheets and towels sold in this country are sold at white sales, regardless of whose name is on the label.) That meant retailers were stuck with hundreds of thousands of dollars in slow-moving inventory.

"The interest was phenomenal, because nobody had ever put together a collection like the one Ralph put together," says Peter Strom, Ralph's partner. "But the marketing was disastrous, the merchandising needed a lot of help, and the production was terrible.

"Deciding that all his products would be sold strictly in a shop concept limited sell-through. The domestic end of home furnishings is the most promotional area in the department store. It is promoted continually, and a lot of it is sold in specific classification areas: towels with towels, sheets with sheets. That's how people buy it. For Ralph Lauren towels to only be in the shop and not in the towel department was a horrendous error."

The business so deteriorated that in July 1984 Ralph took control away from J. P. Stevens and reorganized it under the direction of one of Polo's top young executives, Cheryl Sterling. The Home Collection company, however, remained a wholly owned subsidiary of J. P. Stevens.

Gradually, Sterling and Peter Strom turned the company around by reorganizing the sublicensees and canceling some lines altogether. In August 1986 the home furnishings business quietly became a wholly owned subsidiary of Polo/Ralph Lauren. A year later it was doing nearly $50 million annually in sales at wholesale.

What is most interesting about the home furnishings, however, is not whether it made Ralph Lauren more money, but how the collection was introduced. Ralph didn't set out to peddle sheets and towels. The customers already had sheets and towels.

Instead of selling cottons and flannels and terry cloth, Ralph sold the fantasy of how enjoyable it would be to share the same high-quality sheets and towels used in the best American and English homes.

As the company's promotional brochures explained, Ralph expressed this by segmenting consumer fantasies into four different categories and then giving each group a name that conveyed the concept.

One group was called "New England." This collection reflected Ralph's commitment to American traditions; it meant cashmere throws, solid and striped oxford cloth comforters, oxford sheets, and pastel, hand-loomed cotton rugs, as well as button-down pillowcases. The second, called "Log Cabin," suggested the rugged outdoor life. This meant cotton flannel ticking-striped sheets, reindeer-patterned rugs on top of larger, cotton dhurrie plaid rugs. The third group, called "Jamaica," was a collection of white linen, cotton terry towels, tablecloths in bold stripes of pink and blue, and a bamboo four-poster bed made up with embroidered linen pastels. Finally, there was "Thoroughbred," which conveyed Polo's horsey, English heritage. This meant Scottish wool blankets, shetland tweeds, and wallcoverings in tartans, checks, tattersalls, and foulards.

It was not coincidence that Ralph owned homes in Jamaica, Colorado, and Montauk. Much as he had done when he introduced his first catalog in 1976, Ralph was telling his customers that they could live their lives more richly by living their lives as he did. Few of the customers knew what 200-thread cotton sheets meant. (The tighter the weave, the softer the sheet.) What they did know was that their polyester-blend sheets were itchy, and that Ralph's were probably going to be more comfortable.

Few Americans had slept on flannel sheets, either. Three years later, flannel sheet sales were rivaling those of the 200-thread cotton sheets as one of the hottest categories in bedding departments nationwide.

Not many of the customers had ever been in English country homes. Ralph showed what they looked like through his advertising, and the English country home look then became popular with dozens of interior decorators. Books were written, lectures given, articles such as "Decor in True English Manner" appeared in the daily newspapers. Retailers that specialized in nineteenth-century English home accessories such as R. Brooke, Ltd., on Lexington Avenue in New York, would do booming businesses.

It was an old look, but Ralph Lauren had made it new.

The home furnishings industry, including the big textile mills, were skeptical at first. Then all the manufacturers copied Ralph.

The trade publication *Furniture/Today* both reported on this trend and borrowed from it in a piece called "Thoroughbred Images Salute the Elegant," published in October 1987.

"Recognizing the consumers' increasing desire for a home fashions statement that says they've arrived, upholstery manufacturers are saluting the opulent and the elegant in a look that says 'thoroughbred.' As part of this movement, manufacturers are romanticizing the classic. There are no better examples than Ralph Lauren's romanticization of a wing-tip shoe, as shown in the wing chair here with wing-tip-like stitching . . . "

Accompanying the article were sketches of "thoroughbred" furniture manufactured by such companies as Hickory
Chair, Century, Frederick Edward, Hickory/KayLyn, and Drexel
Heritage. At the Southern Furniture Market in High Point,
North Carolina, in October 1987, Ralph Lauren's influence was
notable in the number of paisley and plaid upholstered furniture pieces that almost every manufacturer introduced, furniture which looked as though it came straight from the old
family house in Vermont or Virginia. "Many exhibitors also
propped their showrooms with enough riding crops, dog portraits, and silver decanters to outfit all the hunt clubs in the
state of North Carolina," noted a *Newsday* reporter.

Ralph Lauren was certainly not the first American fashion
designer to put his name on sheets and towels — Russell Wright
designed a collection in the 1930s — but he would certainly be
among the most influential.

Look what he did to the bed.

A bed once meant several pillows, sheets, a blanket, and a
quilted bedspread, which was draped to the floor. Maybe it
cost $200.

Today, a bed is dressed in two standard pillow shams, two
regular pillowcases, three decorative pillows, a cashmere throw,
comforter, a fitted sheet, and a bedskirt that hangs from the
frame to the floor.

Put it all together and it looks like an unmade bed.

To do it right, at the Ralph Lauren store on 72nd Street,
can cost more than $1,500. (The cashmere throw alone is $640;
a Nanking pillow embroidered with a double dragon is $375.
And many of the famous paisley throw pillows are $200 or
more.)

Ridiculous. Nobody would spend that much money on a
bed . . . But toward the end of 1986, *New York* magazine reported the unmade-bed look had spurred sales of sheets, shams,
pillowcases, and comforters for all manufacturers.

It was the biggest growth the domestic linens industry had
seen in decades. For the first time in years, companies like
Fieldcrest, Cannon, Wamsutta, and Springmaid increased their
advertising. The interest in home furnishings was so great that
in 1986 makers of sheets and towels doubled their advertising
expenditures to $10 million. "It represents a giant leap in an

industry that traditionally spends little on consumer advertising," observed *Adweek*.

"I always believed everything was connected," says Ralph. "I have a home. My eye is attuned to homes. I'd look at something and say, 'Gee, that would be a fabulous pillow. Or that would be a great blanket, why don't we do it?' I went looking for sheets once with my wife and the sheets we saw were horrible.

"All the businesses I have ever started had the same starts and fits in the beginning. I put everything together in a collection rather than making one item, and then I put that collection in the right environment. It was difficult to deliver all these things. You go through growing pains, just as I did, and all of a sudden it starts to click. I couldn't deliver on time, prices were high, those were the growing pains of trying to get people to understand. Now it's moving right."

He also makes a good towel.

The fashion business has always been international in scope. The famous European designers like Valentino, Giorgio Armani, Yves Saint Laurent, Pierre Cardin have built big businesses in this country, witness the string of boutiques that stretches from Madison Avenue to Rodeo Drive. In turn, American designers, at least up until the early 1970s, looked to Europe for both direction and inspiration. Twice a year, the top American fashion critics traipse to Europe to review the collections.

With few exceptions, however, American designers do very little business in Europe.

They complain about cumbersome import rules, the headaches of doing business by letter of credit, a market which is smaller and more splintered than that here in the United States.

Fact is, most American design companies don't want to bother. The size of the market here, they say, is more than sufficient.

Probably they are right.

But Ralph Lauren didn't think so. In the early 1980s he decided he wanted to launch Polo overseas.

Joan and Sidney Burstein, who owned Browns, London's chicest fashion store, would provide the right entrée. Browns consisted of five attached townhouses on South Molton Street, and it was there that the Bursteins had introduced dozens of top designers to the London scene, including Giorgio Armani and Missoni in the 1970s, and Calvin Klein in 1980. Browns was most similar in tone and spirit to New York's famed Henri Bendel specialty store. It was a business whose character was a reflection of the Bursteins, much as Henri Bendel reflected the merchandising know-how of its former president, Geraldine Stutz.

Browns was not only the most famous retailer in London in the early 1980s, it was one of few that could boast an international clientele.

So when Joan Burstein approached Ralph Lauren in May of 1981, after seeing his fall fashion show, and suggested they talk about opening a shop together, Ralph not only knew who she was, he was willing to listen.

The Ralph Lauren venture would be marvelous for both, she said. For Ralph Lauren, it would mean his first exposure in Europe. Equally important, he could be assured that the opening would be done with taste and with prominent exposure in the press. For Browns, it would mean adding a second prominent American sportswear designer, a merchandising step sure to enhance the store's already considerable cachet.

Better still, the Bursteins were convinced both sides would make good profits.

Ralph decided to go forward when the Bursteins later assured him that his clothes wouldn't be shown at Browns itself but rather at a separate location at 143 New Bond Street. This bow-fronted, red brick building had sheltered the royal chemists Savory & Moore for 184 years. (Savory & Moore closed the store after being asked for an elevenfold increase in rent. The closing marked the beginning of a new phase in this street's character, one that has attracted Escada, Daniel Hechter, Louis Feraud, Lanvin, YSL Rive Gauche, and Giorgio Armani.)

The 2,800-square-foot shop, completely gutted and redesigned with two gas fireplaces, opened on September 24, 1981, after an investment of roughly $360,000. (The Bursteins and

Ralph Lauren were equal partners and invested $180,000 each.) It was the first time Ralph's clothes had been sold in Europe. Business the first day amounted to $23,000, about half of what the Bursteins' Calvin Klein store had done on its first day.

Still, the Bursteins said they were satisfied.

So did Ralph Lauren, who made sure he was at the opening. He wore jeans, a sport jacket, and his cowboy boots.

"Sure, some of my clothes are a little bit inspired by an English image, but it's the 1930s England as opposed to now," he told reporter John Byrne. "I love clothes that look better with age and that has always been an English characteristic." The shop, designed by Trician and Robin Guild, had Georgian moldings, wooden hat boxes, and English oak storage units.

The clothes were a smart mixture of Ralph's handknit Fair Isle sweaters, denim shirts, ankle-length flounced skirts, and Navaho belts and bracelets, as well as his more traditional shetland cardigans, long coats in Donegal tweeds, his polo shirts, and his other English-inspired clothes.

The Brits seemed bemused, if not overwhelmed. Years later, one London department store clerk would sniff, "We don't make a big fuss about rugby shirts, because we play rugby in them."

The months passed, and there were problems. The English weren't able to afford Ralph's clothes. Why? The pound was too weak against the dollar.

The Bursteins make an interesting couple. Joan Burstein is friendly, gracious, low-key, and still works the sales floor. All of Browns' top customers know her personally, and it is her fashion sensibility that has shaped the store.

Sidney Burstein is Mr. No-Nonsense. This savvy, gruff-talking shopkeeper dislikes fancy people, fancy ways, fancy attitudes. He says he has no pretensions about himself, and he doesn't like pretensions in others. Typical: "We're all ordinary people. All of us." He says he has made some excellent real estate investments over the years. He is also canny enough to let his wife do her job without interference.

The two sometimes finish each other's sentences, but in many ways they are two very different people in outlook and expression. And when their Ralph Lauren business started to go bad, they typically had different responses.

Joan: "You Americans aren't geared to export. It sounds wonderful, but in the end it's too much trouble for you. We gave Ralph a beautiful store, and we went into it with every good will in the world. But just like with Calvin Klein, there was a lack of cooperation with the prices of things." (The Calvin Klein shop was closed in November 1982).

Sidney: "Prices, deliveries, no cooperation, absolutely none."

Joan: "They weren't used to retailing overseas. A lot of organization had to be created on their side to give service, and that was foreign to them. We gave enormous orders at first. But if something was sent from Hong Kong we wanted a lower price-point. We wanted to be almost comparable to retailing in the United States, or comparable to the sort of clothes being sold here. But nobody there was realistic. That was the problem."

Sidney: "What happened when we opened the shop was that the dollar got very strong and the pound very weak. Prices just shot up. I said, 'While it's like this, drop your prices and we'll drop our markup.' No. They wouldn't. Nothing. That's what people are like. Human beings. Egos."

Joan: "Who knows why they wouldn't . . ."

Sidney: "Humans are illogical. It's peculiar. We couldn't make progress. It was very expensive to open the store, and then there was $300,000 a year in rent and overhead. It was high then, cheap today."

Joan: "Bond Street has since come up."

Sidney: "It was difficult to make it pay. They wouldn't lower their prices, and we couldn't get any cooperation from them. No follow-through, nothing. No special lines such as Ralph Lauren for Browns, not the slightest bit of extra cooperation."

Joan: "We were too small to be considered. I was very disappointed. I spoke to Ralph because the business wasn't good enough and the overhead was enormous. My husband told me he had an offer for the shop and was going to sell it. I said no, you have to offer it to Ralph first. I was very emotionally involved with the store. I loved it. I loved the image."

Sidney: "I was going to sell the lease to a dress shop."

Joan: "We were so fed up with not having any communications with anybody. Peter Strom was never available to talk with. And Ralph wasn't available to really talk, either."

Sidney: "I've got letters to them spelling it all out to them. A whole pile upstairs. Offering alternatives. Nothing."

Joan: "We had a great location. For all I know, he might have wanted to do it all himself. That was the flagship. It did start the whole idea. I'm not so sure . . . I don't think it was intentional, but it might have whetted his appetite. Maybe he didn't like the way we were running it, I don't know."

Sidney: "We'd put in a lot of merchandise, well over five hundred thousand dollars during the first year. So we went to New York for a meeting there. There wasn't the slightest bit of compassion, or feeling, or understanding. It made me sick, quite frankly. It made me sick. I went with my accountant. There were six of them, and all they were talking about was the bottom line, the bottom line. God, it had nothing to do with, 'Can we help you, is there anything we can do?' Nothing. After that I didn't care. Money isn't my goal. It isn't her goal either. We're nice people. We have enough, thank God. We wanted to make life more interesting, deal with nice people. There was no relationship, nothing."

Joan: "We carried everything, including children's wear."

Sidney: "We couldn't afford to stick it out. We were losing too much money every week. We're a solid business and we want to remain that way."

Joan: "When I first met Ralph, and he knew we had the Calvin Klein shop, he was amazed, saying, 'Calvin is so wealthy. I never had that exposure. *Women's Wear* never put me on the front page; it's always Calvin. I'll never reach his status. I'll never be able to.' I think our shop helped him very much indeed by putting him on another level."

Sidney: "Finally we sold it to him lock, stock, and barrel. I made money. I did very well. On the total venture, yes, we made money. It covered all the trading losses. He made us whole at the end, although not on purpose. I pushed him higher and higher, I'll tell you that."

Joan: "I wanted Ralph to have it."

Sidney: "She's a very nice person. Too nice. She has taste and flair. I'd have really taken them to town but she wouldn't let me."

Joan: "Why do the British buy his clothes? Because he puts

them together beautifully. He creates an image for people, and he captivates them with that image. When you walk into a Ralph Lauren store, the woman or man tries to associate themselves with that life-style. They walk in and become like that. Like the ancestors on the wall. I think it affects people. They feel when they buy something they are part of the whole ambiance. It's so clever. The British like it because it is also the ambiance they would like to be part of. It's what they think the London society scene looks like, how those people dress and put their things together. It's all part of an image. Why hasn't Jaeger done it, or Liberty of London? They can't. They don't have the business sense, the mentality.

"What is original about Ralph is that he is an upmarket Laura Ashley. It's a package. People want packages. They like images. It might have something to do with TV. People like soap operas. They love families, looks, fantasies . . . This is what he is selling: a fantasy life-style. If somebody walks in there and buys a polo shirt, they imagine that they look like his ads. It's brilliant. His ads are brilliant, and he uses exactly the same advertising as in the United States. The ads make you want to go and buy those clothes, because they make you want to be part of that whole environment."

The relationship between the Bursteins and Ralph Lauren was not helped when the BBC reported in October 1982 that the British handknit sweaters that retailers sold for over $400 in the United States were made by women earning 6 to 16 pounds, or roughly $10 to $27. This story focused resentment on both Ralph Lauren and Browns, and the Bursteins were roundly criticized. (It was not fair, but it made for great copy. Ralph Lauren didn't hire the knitters. Rather, he created the designs and worked through a British knitting company, which farmed the work out.)

In February 1983, Ralph bought out the Bursteins. He had no intentions of lowering his prices; he was a designer and manufacturer, not a currency trader. Moreover, many retail accounts asked him for exclusive collections; to do so would detract from his major business. Ralph thought he had done everything he could to make the Bursteins happy short of managing the store himself. He believed in his product, and he was convinced that eventually it would attract the customers. For a short period he took a new partner, Peter Bertelsen, a Dane who says he made a fortune in the oil business. That relationship also ended quickly; Bertelsen says the dollar was too strong against the pound and that he didn't know enough then about the fashion business to be more patient.

Today Polo/Ralph Lauren owns the shop and makes a profit. Many of the customers are American. Said Bob Everlanka, a marketing executive from Houston, "That store is everything I wanted an English store to look like. But the only store in London I saw like it was Ralph's."

On a summer afternoon in 1987 it is also a busy store. Inside are all the familiar trappings. This means leather chairs, leather-bound books, sets of old Louis Vuitton luggage, stuffed animals, riding boots. It is a narrow shop, and Ralph has only one floor; the others are rented to other tenants. The prices are stiff, but at $1.60 to the English pound, not shocking: leather belts (30 £); women's silk blouses (160 £) with matching skirts (368 £); jean jackets with corduroy collars (71 £); cotton socks (12 £); the famous polo shirt (35 £); cotton sweaters (125 £); and of course his ties (28 £).

There are no home furnishings for sale.

The shop is not the only retailer that sells Ralph Lauren clothes in London today. The Harvey Nichols department store has a separate Ralph Lauren men's boutique, as well as a Ralph Lauren women's wear boutique.

England would be the start of Ralph's international expansion.

Later would come licensed Polo stores in Belgium, Germany, and St. Tropez. There is also a 4,000-square-foot, two-story, mahogany-paneled Polo shop in Paris at the intersection of the Rue Royale and the Place de la Madeleine. This is one of the chicest areas of the city, as well as one of the busiest in terms of pedestrian and street traffic. Nearby are the stores of Mario Valentino, Rodier Hommes, Cerutti 1881, Hanae Mori, Karl Lagerfeld, Pierre Cardin, Cartier, Charles Jourdan, and Laura Ashley. Customers who aren't familiar with Ralph's clothes are invited to sit and watch videotapes of his latest collection. One customer was spotted making himself even more familiar: when he thought nobody was looking, he whipped out a tiny automatic camera and frantically squeezed off several dozen shots of the interior.

Altogether, there are forty-one Polo/Ralph Lauren shops outside the United States, excluding the shop Ralph owns himself.

It is the Japanese, though, who are the most eager of all Ralph's customers to share in a world dominated by images of gracious country homes, respect for traditional values, and luxurious living. Already there are three freestanding Polo/ Ralph Lauren shops in Japan, and the clothes are carried in many top specialty stores as well as department stores.

Seibu Department Stores, Ltd., has held the Japanese license since the mid-1970s; its business today tops $200 million at retail. The clothes are all specially cut for Japanese sizes and manufactured under license in Japan and Singapore.

"Since the late 1960s, traditional clothing has been a very strong marketing trend," explains Izumi Kajimoto, a buyer in the New York office of Seibu. "There is great interest in American products, not only products with a U.S.A. label, but which have a publicized image as being authentically American. The major appeal of Polo, especially the men's wear, is that authentic American image."

The clothes are a little more expensive than in the United States, but this has not prevented young men between twenty and thirty-five from becoming the largest customer segment. One recent market survey showed that Ralph Lauren's brand awareness ranked about 90 percent with men in that age group. This despite the fact that Ralph's only visit occurred in 1984.

It is unlikely, however, that Ralph will be able to grow his home furnishings business in Japan as quickly as he has developed his men's and women's business. The culture is different.

"Foreign influences can go so far in terms of changing how a population lives," says Kajimoto. "The home collection is difficult to sell, because its image is one that ranges from traditional English drawing room to a very opulent Duchess of Windsor look. What sells best are towels and sheets and pillowcases which can be used in any room. They don't need the chintz and wallpaper and furniture necessary to complete the image. Also, 65 percent of the population still sleeps on futons. Those customers don't need a bedskirt. The real estate market isn't going to change either. There is a limited amount of living space in Japan. There isn't enough room for everything."

What does it mean that somebody from the Bronx who starts out selling fat ties can build a fashion empire that stretches from New York to Paris to Tokyo?

Or that in 1987 *Forbes* magazine estimated his wealth as greater than that of financier Irwin Jacobs, film director Steven Spielberg, and retailer Sy Syms? Or that every year an estimated 10 million pieces of clothing, luggage, and perfume bearing his name or logo are sold in this country?

It doesn't mean that Ralph Lauren is the happiest man in New York.

Or that he is the most respected.

Or that he is even best liked.

According to a 1987 poll conducted by the Roper Organization for the advertising firm Doyle, Graf, Mabley, only 8 percent of 600 families earning over $100,000 ranked his label in the "most luxurious" category. This compares to the over 30 percent rating given the name Rolls-Royce. Indeed, that study found that the truly affluent don't pay much attention to fashion designers. Maybe it is fortunate for Ralph Lauren that less than 2 percent of the American public earns more than $100,000 a year.

Some say Ralph Lauren's success proves insecurity has become a national neurosis. Others say this is a brand-conscious society trained to respond to images that make people feel warm and cozy inside. That may be true. Then again, maybe Freud was right when he said "sometimes a cigar is just a cigar." Ralph's clothes are cut from beautiful fabrics, and they wear well. At least the men's clothes look as if they can be worn for years. In 1987 some customers complained that the women's collection was not made as well as it was once.

Economist Thorstein Veblen once observed that people consider things beautiful in proportion to what they cost. Much of the status inherent in any expensive product, argued Veblen, was derived from its price.

Ralph understood that when he charged $7.50 for his ties at a time when most other ties cost $3.

That was how he started to build his image. It is the direction he will follow in the years ahead. Even if a major recession strikes, Ralph Lauren's prices are headed in only one direction: up.

One would think that after all the awards Ralph has won and the money he has earned, he would be satisfied. Ralph is not. He is anxious and sometimes insecure. He also complains frequently that critics don't understand him, fail to give his designs enough space, and play favorites. He does not consider himself a favorite.

At one point in conversation, Ralph cited a cranky letter he'd just received which complained that "the only difference between a parvenu in a sharkskin suit and a parvenu in a Lauren blazer is that the latter has pretensions. . . . Anyone who deludes himself into believing that when he puts on his Polo shirt he is displaying his own 'English country' casualness is living in a fool's paradise."

"All through my career I've gotten this kind of treatment," murmured Ralph, who had jumped out of his chair to get a copy.

The letter turned out to be an article in the *Washington Post* written by Jonathan Yardley.

Managing Polo is a business. But it's a personal business.

Asking what Ralph Lauren means is another way of asking what he wants.

The answer is not more money. If Ralph wanted to cash in fast he could triple his licensees overnight and boost his income without taking any financial risk. He has not done this. Also, it is doubtful whether Ralph could eat, sleep, or live any more comfortably than he does today.

Ralph hasn't expanded faster because growth still makes him uneasy. Some businessmen dream of building big, powerful businesses. Not Ralph. He wanted money, he wanted luxury, he wanted recognition. But he never aspired to manage or own a $1 billion–plus company. As meticulous and fastidious as he is about his work, Ralph has never spent hours plotting his next career move. Maybe he suspected he would sometimes feel uncomfortable in a big company. If so, he was probably right. Ralph has told associates that he sometimes feels "like an alien" at his own designer staff meetings. Most likely, Polo/Ralph Lauren is a business that will go on for years with or without him. That is a strength, not a weakness, but it is not the same company it was when Ralph started it.

Fame? Ralph Lauren is already a celebrity. Often he is approached by strangers for his autograph, and such diverse magazines as *Time, Vanity Fair, Esquire,* and *Cosmopolitan* have written flattering stories about him. When he does decide to attend a big society party — such as the once-a-year Diana Vreeland galas at the Metropolitan Museum — the photographers treat him as though he were a movie star. Even his own employees sometimes treat him that way, especially the ones who rarely see him. When Ralph went to Polo/Ralph Lauren's Christmas party in 1987, his own employees reacted as if Paul Newman had dropped by. "You've never seen so many flashbulbs going off," said one. If Ralph still needs an extra lift, he can always appear in one of his numerous ads. Yet ask him, and Ralph says with a straight face that he never receives credit for what he's done.

"The critics don't quite know what I do," he complains. "They are still asking what I really do, what's got me here. In *Time* magazine they wrote, 'He rips off this, he rips off that.' That will be my epitaph. It's a little like Cary Grant. I was a friend of Cary Grant. Or he was a friend of mine . . . I don't know if I was a friend of his. The day he died at eighty-two, they never gave it to him. He was Archie Leach. It was always, what's the mystery? What was he hiding, what was he really? They never let him be what he was.

"This success . . . I don't want to tell you it's lonely, but it isn't completely fulfilling. Maybe other people feel the same way. Maybe many do. I've had all the success. But never quite a unanimous success. They always write how much money I made. They never write what I did."

It isn't the need for more celebrity that pushes him forward. No matter how much attention Ralph Lauren receives, it will never be enough. And Ralph probably knows this.

What motivates Ralph Lauren is fear.

It's the same fear that pushes Sugar Ray Leonard back into the ring, the same fear that drives Frank Sinatra to give that one last good-bye concert.

Ralph Lauren dreads getting old and being pushed out of the way by fresher talents. Anybody who reads the sports pages knows what happens to stars when they get old. They're fired, or the club puts them on waivers. Eventually their lockers are owned by twenty-year-olds.

For nearly twenty years Ralph Lauren has been at center stage in his industry. He likes it there, and he has earned the four-star billing. He also intends to stay there.

So deep are these feelings that Ralph sometimes describes himself as "the king." Not king as in royalty, but king as in "king of the hill." Ralph has fought hard to get to the top. Remember, he did not inherit money. He did not graduate from college. The stature and wealth Ralph Lauren has accumulated he earned with the help of his partner, Peter Strom. In an industry noted for its glamour, famous customers, and infighting, Ralph Lauren's survival at the top has made him subject to a certain amount of envy, jealousy, and disdain.

He understands. He reads the trade papers. Better than anybody else, he knows not only how hard it is to achieve success, but even more demanding, how hard it is to maintain it.

Even Frank Sinatra, Ralph's childhood idol, doesn't sing like Frank Sinatra any more.

Two bad fall seasons back to back and Ralph Lauren becomes yesterday's news.

It happens.

"I'm not creative in the sense, the way the critics think of being creative," he says. "I don't do a shoulder. I do a world. I have another approach to design. Another approach to my feelings. On every level I know what it takes to deliver. Because the product has to be great. You don't get anywhere unless the product has been fabulous. You're talking about very sophisticated customers who travel the world and who look for clothes. And I have a lot of competition.

"I never had formal training. I can't tell you I studied for twenty years with Christian Dior. But my things come out, and they touch people. They love the design. They love the clothes and treasure them. And that's how I feel about it. My soul is in what I do. I give all my feelings, like a writer, everything, about what I love. . . . Life isn't one narrow thing. People are many things. I love many things. It doesn't matter if I'm reading a book or driving a racecar or riding a horse or sitting on the ranch, I'm the same person. I love to live life. And I'm doing it."

Slow down? Not likely. This is a business, but it's a personal business. It's Ralph Lauren's name on the door, on the ads, in the store. He intends to keep it there, where everybody sees it, and where people express their feelings about him every day with their wallets and pocketbooks.

Ralph still pays attention to the details. He likes it that way.

And if nobody ever gives him a crown, hell, he can always design his own.

▸▸▸ ACKNOWLEDGMENTS

This book was suggested by Luis Sanjurjo, an agent at ICM. It is sad that he is not here to share in its publication.

Ralph Lauren and his partner, Peter Strom, met with me more than a dozen times while I was researching this book. They did not have manuscript review or approval. I would like to thank them for their cooperation. I want also to thank the following people at Polo/Ralph Lauren for their help and courtesy: Susan Akin, Meg Austin, Buffy Birrittella, Joanne Cea, Maryann Eboli, Wendy Gerber, Dedi McNamara, Alexander Vreeland.

At *Forbes* magazine, Jerry Flint, Allan Dodds Frank, Lisa Gubernick, Steve Lawrence, Gary Slutsker, and Sheldon Zalaznick were all supportive. Thanks also to Lawrence Minard, who first suggested I do a piece about Ralph Lauren for *Forbes*.

At Little, Brown, I was very fortunate to have the counsel and assistance of Ray Roberts, my editor. Ray's faith in this project was crucial. Thanks also to Elizabeth Power for her thorough copy editing and Laura Nash for her careful review. I also appreciate the legal advice given to me by Molly Sherden at Palmer & Dodge in Boston and Tennyson Schad at

Norwick & Schad in New York. At ICM I am grateful for the encouragement of Suzanne Gluck.

Martha T. Griffith did a terrific job helping me research this book; her assistance was invaluable. She was also a fine copyreader, and proved an inventive tracker of documents. I would also like to thank my parents, Morton and Frances Trachtenberg, for their support, as well as Joan and Elliott Sanger for their encouragement. The editing suggestions, patience, and delicious cooking of my wife, Elizabeth Sanger, were vital.

Many people offered me good advice or assistance during this project, and I want to thank them also. These included Lisa Anderson, Ben Brantley, Liesel Friedrich, Betty Goodwin, Tom Griffith, and Lawrence Kaplan.

▸▸▸S O U R C E S A N D
C R E D I T S

I interviewed the following sources for this book:
Joe Aezen, June Ainsworth, Gordon Allen, Frank Arnold, Julian
AvRutick, Bruce Baker, Jeffrey Banks, Arthur Barens, Joe Barrato,
Ike Behar, Steve Bell, Ivan Benjamin, Peter Bertelsen, Buddy Blake,
Mike Blum, Richard Blum, Frank Bober, Jerry Bond, Frank Bonura,
Ed Brandau, Martin Braverman, Barry Bricken, Ned Brower, George
Bruder, Joan and Sidney Burstein, Joe Campo, Pierre Cardin, Ed
Carlo, Sandy Carlson, Sal Cesarani, Rabbi Zevulun Charlop, Joe
Checkon, Michael Cifarelli, Arnold Cohen, Dr. Oscar Cohen, Phineas
Connell, Rich Connell, Mel Creedman, Dick Crose, Ron Cummings,
Ted Decker, Greg deVaney, Anthony Edgeworth, Susan Ennis,
Michael Farina, Phil Feiner, Don Fisher, Joane Fitzpatrick, Neal J. Fox,
George Friedman, Martin Friedman, Marty Gant, Steve Ginsberg, Ken
Giordano, Raleigh Glassberg, Dave Goldberg, Les Goldberg, Mort
Gordon, Rick Gossett, Millie Graves, Robert L. Green, Henry Grethel,
Clifford Grodd, Clara Hancox, Ron Harvey, Harvey Hellman, Norman
Hilton, Marley Hodgson, David Horowitz, Joel Horowitz, John
Horvitz, Steve Krauss, Bill Josephs, Izumi Kajimoto, Marilyn
Kawakami, Stuart Kreisler, Eleanor Lambert, Ted Lederman, Naomi
Leff, Jim Lehrer, Gloria Leonard, Armand Lindenbaum, R. Blair

Lindle, Bill Loock, Leo Lozzi, Erin Magnin, Jerry Magnin, Garry Marshall, Bob Matura, Linda Maxwell, John Moore, Julie Moses, Peter Newman, Carol Nolan, Tom O'Toole, Jimmy Palazzo, Bert Paley, Wallace Palmer, Alexandra Penney, Dave Pensky, Bob Phillips, Don Polley, Louis Praino, Bernard Price, Kelli Questrom, Dick Randall, Oriel Raphael, Jill Resnick, Ronald Roberts, Alan Rosanes, Bob Ruttenberg, Steve Ross, George Saffo, Jay David Saks, Isidor Schachter, Jack Schultz, Berny Schwartz, Sam Schwartz, Liz Serman, Gary Shafer, Seymour Shelsky, Alton Siebuhr, Herb Sills, Morton Sills, Stanley Silverman, Franklin Simon, Ozzie Spenningsby, Jo-ann Stadtmauer, Martin Staff, Michael Steinberg, Bruce Stelzer, Robert Stock, Pamela Street, Neil Tardio, Dick Tarlow, Gil Truedsson, Melon Tytell, Robert Vignola, Paul Wasserman, John Weitz, Alan White, James K. Wilson, Alan Wright, Michael Wynn, Frank Young, Danny Zarem.

I have checked as much of the dialogue as possible. People, however, make mistakes, especially when reconstructing conversations held decades earlier.

My source material also included numerous legal documents relating to the Michael Bernstein/Ralph Lauren court case.

I also read most, if not all, of the articles about Ralph Lauren that appeared in *Daily News Record (DNR)*, *Women's Wear Daily (WWD)*, and the *New York Times*. The stories cited below, from those publications and others, were especially helpful to me.

Introduction

1. "Puttin' on the glitz," Grey Advertising study, July 1986.
2. Born, Pete. "Bloomingdale's remodeled Lauren shop is a big hit," *Women's Wear Daily*, August 28, 1987.
3. Harmetz, Aljean. " 'Fatal Attraction' director analyzes the success of his movie, and rejoices," *New York Times*, October 5, 1987.
4. Sloan, Pat, "Rich folk may not care which label they wear," *Advertising Age*, December 7, 1987.
5. "Back to the middle ages," *New York Post*, March 10, 1987.
6. Born, Pete. "Lauren store tops $30M in first year," *WWD*, July 14, 1987.

Chapter One

1. "Lauren launches flagship," *WWD*, April 21, 1986.
2. Slesin, Suzanne. "Ralph Lauren's store: part palazzo, part club," *New York Times*, April 22, 1986.
3. Morris, Bernadine. "Ralph Lauren and Oscar de la Renta: a good day for fashion," *New York Times*, May 8, 1986.

4. "Ralph Lauren," fashion review, *WWD*, May 8, 1986.
5. Kornbluth, Jesse. "Polo/Ralph Lauren, refashioning New York's Rhinelander Mansion," *Architectural Digest*, October 1986.
6. Hoelterhoff, Manuela. "The house that Gertrude Rhinelander Waldo built (and Ralph Lauren rebuilt)," *Avenue*, December–January 1987.
7. Tauranac, Jeff. *Elegant New York*. New York: Abbeville Press, 1985.

Chapter Two

1. Friedman, Marty. "The parkway all-stars," *New York*, October 26, 1981.
2. "R. Lauren joins A. Rivetz & Co.," *DNR*, January 23, 1964.
3. "The professional touch," *DNR*, May 21, 1964.
4. Obituary. "Abe Rivetz," *DNR*, December 22, 1964.
5. Bond, David. *20th Century Fashion*. London: Guinness Superlatives Limited, 1981.
6. Horn, Richard. *Fifties Style, Then and Now*. New York: Beech Tree Books, 1985.
7. Flusser, Alan. *Clothes and the Man*. New York: Villard Books, 1985.
8. Mariani, John. "The not-so-fabulous 50s," *Newsday*, January 18, 1987.

Chapter Three

1. "Blass to debut in men's field," *DNR*, February 15, 1967.
2. Baumgold, Julie. "Polo ties saddling up for new fashion goals," *DNR*, August 22, 1967.

Chapter Four

1. Platt, David. " 'Understand oldness,' Lauren says of fashion approach," *DNR*, March 12, 1968.
2. "Men's wear pros move in," *DNR*, October 24, 1968.
3. Ad, *New York Times*, December 14, 1968.
4. Birrittella, Buffy. "The Lauren look," *DNR*, February 26, 1969.
5. "In the Coty spotlight," *DNR*, September 25, 1970.
6. Program. "The 28th Annual Coty American Fashion Critics' Awards," September 24, 1970, Alice Tully Hall, Lincoln Center, New York.
7. Morris, Bernadine. "Store suggests men think mink, instead of blue denim," *New York Times*, November 2, 1970.
8. Gale, Bill. "The thirties are alive and well in Ralph Lauren," *GQ*, February 1971.
9. "Polo: tied to the moment," *Clothes*, April 15, 1973.

Chapter Five

1. Chatfield-Taylor, Joan. "For the luxury-loving individualist," *San Francisco Chronicle,* November 6, 1969.
2. Ad, *New York Times,* December 12, 1971.
3. Morris, Bernadine. "The result has been pleasing clothes," *New York Times,* May 31, 1972.
4. 1986 interview with Ralph Lauren cablecast on the "Attitudes" show.

Chapter Seven

1. Skurka, Norma. "Setting for a fashion designer," *New York Times,* April 23, 1972.
2. Cunningham, Bill. "Nostalgia with subtle updating," *Los Angeles Times,* April 27, 1972.
3. "Between the lines" items in *DNR,* April 4, September 12, September 22, 1972.

Chapter Eight

1. "Between the lines," *DNR,* March 12, 1973.
2. "The GG mystery," *WWD,* March 22, 1973.
3. "Gatsby fittings," *WWD,* April 16, 1973.
4. Schiro, Anne-Marie. "Men's styles recall Douglas Fairbanks," *New York Times,* April 17, 1973.
5. "Fit for a Gatsby," *DNR,* May 25, 1973.
6. Gale, Bill. "Getting 'Gatsby' garbed," *GQ,* March 1974.
7. "Everything you ever wanted to know about Gatsby and should be asking . . . " *Men's Wear,* June 15, 1973.
8. *The Great Gatsby* souvenir book. New York: Souvenir Book Publishers, 1974.
9. Bahrenburg, Bruce. *The True, Behind-the-Scenes Account of Filming the Great Gatsby.* New York: Berkley Publishing, 1974.

Chapter Nine

1. "Ralph Lauren's label going on Kreisler items," *WWD,* October 11, 1973.
2. "Kreisler Group in new SA spot," *WWD,* December 20, 1973.
3. "Confirm Greif to make Chaps line," *DNR,* February 1, 1974.
4. "Ralph Lauren," fashion review, *WWD,* May 10, 1974.
5. Brady, Kathleen. "Stuart Kreisler: the new Ben Shaw?," *WWD,* July 3, 1974.

6. Cunningham, Bill. "A revival of class distinction," *Los Angeles Times,* August 13, 1975.

Chapter Ten

1. Wyman, Margaret Woodney. *Perfume in Pictures.* New York: Sterling Publishing Co., 1969.
2. "Warner's bad vibes," *Forbes,* November 15, 1974.
3. Jessee, Jill. *Perfume Album.* Melbourne, Fla.: Robert E. Krieger Publishing, 1975.
4. Ginsberg, Steve. "Warner Fragrances formed to market Lauren scents," *WWD,* October 7, 1976.
5. Sloan, Pat. "Fragrances to carry Lauren name," *WWD,* October 7, 1976.
6. Sloan, Pat. "Polo's new game," *WWD,* October 8, 1976.
7. Ginsberg, Steve. "Curtain goes up on Warner/Lauren show," *WWD,* January 6, 1978.
8. Penney, Alexandra. "Fashion in fragrance," *New York Times,* February 12, 1978.
9. Ad, *New York Times,* March 12, 1978.
10. Taylor, Angela. "Scents with designer labels," *New York Times,* April 1, 1978.
11. Lord, Shirley. "Fragrance 1980: the new big adventure," *Vogue,* November 1980.

Chapter Eleven

1. Bernstein, Peter W. "Atari and the video-game explosion," *Fortune,* July 27, 1981.
2. Pillsbury, Anne B. "Warner's fall from grace," *Fortune,* January 10, 1983.
3. "Warner Communications may sell cosmetics unit," *Wall Street Journal,* January 13, 1984.
4. "Warner plans sale of cosmetics unit for $146 million," *Wall Street Journal,* January 16, 1984.
5. Meyers, William. "Cosmair makes a name for itself," *New York Times,* May 12, 1985.
6. "President leaves post at Warner cosmetics," *New York Times,* September 5, 1985.

Chapter Twelve

1. Morris, Bernadine. "Top Seventh Avenue collections create people jams," *New York Times,* April 29, 1977.

2. Sheppard, Eugenia. "The Lauren look," *New York Post,* May 3, 1977.
3. Morris, Bernadine. "Lots of new collections, but Lauren steals the show," *New York Times,* April 22, 1978.
4. "Lauren: American fantasies for fall," *WWD,* April 24, 1978.
5. Taylor, Angela. "Lauren furs go wild and woolly," *New York Times,* May 22, 1978.
6. Cunningham, Bill. "New York goes western, too," *New York Times,* June 20, 1978.
7. Drier, Melissa. "Lauren, Gap form western wear venture," *DNR,* June 22, 1978.
8. "Lauren to design line for The Gap," *WWD,* June 22, 1978.
9. "Bright ideas for resort," *WWD,* August 31, 1978.
10. Anderson, Lisa. "Ralph Lauren: restless and reaching," *WWD,* December 11, 1978.
11. "Lauren's high in the saddle," *Men's Wear,* February 23, 1979.
12. Schiro, Anne-Marie. "Ralph Lauren's western classics," *New York Times,* March 31, 1979.
13. Lord & Taylor ad, *New York Times,* April 1, 1979.
14. Bloomingdale's ad, *New Yorker,* April 9, 1979.
15. Morris, Bernadine. "Lauren's impeccable tailoring, softened by color," *New York Times,* April 28, 1979.
16. Levine, Bettijane. "Ralph Lauren: riding out his fantasies," *Los Angeles Times,* June 1, 1979.
17. McCord, Jacqueline. "Ralph Lauren brands his own breed of duds," *Daily News,* June 10, 1979.
18. Alai, Susan. "Gold mining on the Lauren trail," *WWD,* June 27, 1979.
19. Macy's full-page ad, *GQ,* August 1979.
20. Alai, Susan. "Gap talking sale of Lauren unit with Polo," *WWD,* January 15, 1980.
21. Alai, Susan. "Gap set to close its Lauren unit," *WWD,* February 22, 1980.
22. "Gap confirms end of licensing pact with Lauren western line," *WWD,* March 19, 1980.
23. "Lauren's prairie gypsy," *WWD,* March 31, 1981.
24. Tucker, Priscilla. "Ralph Lauren and the new west," *Daily News,* April 24, 1981.
25. Morris, Bernadine. "Eclectic approach by Ralph Lauren," *New York Times,* April 25, 1981.
26. Morris, Bernadine. "American designers: the mood is playful," *New York Times,* October 30, 1981.
27. ZCMI ad, *Vogue,* February 1982.
28. Morris, Bernadine. "Divergent moods for fall," *New York Times,* April 24, 1982.
29. Hyde, Nina. "The old makes news," *Washington Post,* April 24, 1982.

30. Belkin, Lisa. "Lauren look permeating city," *New York Times,* December 8, 1986.

Chapter Thirteen

1. Chatfield-Taylor, Joan. "For the luxury-loving individualist," *San Francisco Chronicle,* November 6, 1969.
2. Gale, Bill. "The thirties are alive and well in Ralph Lauren," *GQ,* February 1971.
3. Review of fall collections, *WWD,* May 25, 1972.
4. Hanenberg, Paul. "Polo goes feminine with a line of shirts," *WWD,* November 8, 1972.
5. Koshetz, Herbert. "Catching on in the apparel field," *New York Times,* July 29, 1973.
6. Brick, Bill. "Lauren: candid comments," *DNR,* November 29, 1973.
7. Morris, Bernadine. "Fashion is quiet now and some designers say that's just fine," *New York Times,* March 31, 1974.
8. Sustendal, Diane. "Lauren likes genuine look," *New Orleans Times-Picayune,* June 15, 1974.
9. Cartnal, Alan. "Designer who dresses down fashion industry," *Los Angeles Times,* September 30, 1974.
10. Collins, Nancy. "Ralph Lauren: filling in the gaps," *WWD,* October 16, 1974.
11. "Lauren sacks it," *WWD,* September 19, 1977.
12. Breul, David. "Style," *Avenue,* November 1976.
13. Lockwood, Lisa. "Lauren dungarees expanding jeans pool," *WWD,* September 10, 1985.
14. "Puttin' on the glitz," Grey Advertising study, July 1986.

Chapter Fourteen

1. Gellers, Stan. "Lauren's contemporary classics: to make a label a lifestyle," *Men's Wear,* January 14, 1972.
2. "Brain Tumors: The Resource Guide," Friends of Brain Tumor Research, 1986, 2169 Union Street, San Francisco, California 94123.
3. "Designers: richest of them all," *WWD,* September 26, 1986.
4. Buck, Genevieve. "Sharing the good life," *Chicago Tribune,* October 8, 1986.
5. Adams, Cindy. "Multizillionaire Ralph Lauren," *New York Post,* February 10, 1987.
6. "Brain tumor surgery for fashion designer," *New York Times,* April 16, 1987.
7. Lockwood, Lisa. "Ralph Lauren OK after surgery, seen back to work in May," *WWD,* April 16, 1987.

8. "Lauren recovering well after removal of tumor," *Chicago Tribune*, April 17, 1987.
9. Lockwood, Lisa. "Sportswear scoop," *WWD*, July 15, 1987.
10. "Lauren resort," *WWD*, August 11, 1987.
11. Jacobs, Patricia. "Lauren does the island fling," *New York Post*, August 12, 1987.
12. Lockwood, Lisa. "Sportswear scoop," *WWD*, August 12, 1987.
13. Morris, Bernadine. "Lauren's quiet way with sport clothes," *New York Times*, August 13, 1987.
14. Alexander, Ron. "A glittering tribute to Audrey Hepburn," *New York Times*, October 22, 1987.
15. "Fashion cocktails," *WWD*, November 4, 1987.
16. Alai, Susan. "Ralph Lauren back in the saddle," *W*, November 16–23, 1987.
17. "Secret passion," *Playboy*, December 1987.

Chapter Fifteen

1. Morgan, Janet F. "The Lauren launch: aiming high," *Home Furnishings Daily*, April 25, 1983.
2. "J. P. Stevens takes the designer route," *Business Week*, September 19, 1983.
3. Lifshey, Earl. "The Ralph Lauren gamble," *Home Furnishings Daily*, September 19, 1983.
4. Markoutsas, Elaine. "Ralph Lauren, seeking his next conquest, has decided there's no place like home," *Chicago Tribune*, October 2, 1983.
5. Justice, Diane. "Ralph Lauren enters home furnishings field," *Independent Press Service*, October 20, 1983.
6. Anderson, P. K. "Ralph Lauren home furnishings," *Visual Merchandising & Store Design*, December 1983.
7. Bershad, Lynne. "Learning some lessons," *Home Furnishings Daily*, August 20, 1984.
8. Kanner, Bernice. "Sheet dreams," *New York*, December 15, 1986.
9. "Create the Ralph Lauren look at one-quarter the cost!" *Family Circle*, April 14, 1987.
10. Kinter, Kim. "Brand awareness: bedding makers finally wake up," *Adweek*, March 30, 1987.
11. Sherman, Beth. "High Point," *Newsday*, October 22, 1987.
12. Krebs, Alvin. "Raymond Loewy, streamliner of cars, planes and pens, dies," *New York Times*, July 15, 1986.
13. Anderson, Susan Heller. "The pioneer of streamlining," *New York Times*, November 4, 1979.
14. Five-page ad spread, *New York Times Magazine*, December 6, 1987.

15. "Decor in true English manner," by Rosemary Kent, *New York Post*, June 1, 1987.
16. K. D. S. "Thoroughbred images salute the elegant," *Furniture/Today*, October 19, 1987.
17. Full-page ad, *New York*, November 20, 1978.
18. Full-page ad, *New York Times*, December 9, 1974.
19. Byrne, John. "Browns to open full-line Lauren shop in London," *WWD*, August 3, 1981.
20. Chubb, Ann. "Away out west in Bond Street," *Daily Telegraph*, September 24, 1981.
21. Byrne, John."Lauren in London," *DNR*, September 28, 1981.
22. "BBC gives Lauren the needle," *WWD*, October 26, 1982.
23. Sloan, Pat. "Rich folk may not care which label they wear," *Advertising Age*, December 7, 1987.
24. Yardley, Jonathan. "King Lauren, conferring nobility," *Washington Post*, December 15, 1986.
25. Donovan, Carrie. "The Americans who lead," *New York Times Magazine*, June 28, 1987.
26. Slutsker, Gary. "Ode to a locomotive," *Forbes*, April 6, 1987.

▸▸▸ BIBLIOGRAPHY

Bahrenburg, Bruce. *The True, Behind-the-Scenes Account of Filming the Great Gatsby*. New York: Berkley Publishing, 1974.

Bond, David. *20th Century Fashion*. London: Guiness Superlatives Limited, 1981.

Boorstin, Daniel J. *The Image: A Guide to Pseudo-Events in America*. New York: Atheneum, 1985.

Brady, Maxine. *Bloomingdale's*. New York: Harcourt Brace Jovanovich, 1980.

Brooks, John. *Once in Golconda*. New York: Harper & Row, 1969.

Fitzgerald, F. Scott. *The Great Gatsby*. New York: Charles Scribner's Sons, 1962.

Gordon, Lois, and Alan Gordon. *American Chronicle: Six Decades in American Life, 1920–1980*. New York: Atheneum, 1987.

Horn, Richard. *Fifties Style, Then and Now*. New York: Beech Tree Books, 1985.

Jessee, Jill. *Perfume Album*. Melbourne, Fla.: Robert E. Krieger Publishing Company, 1975.

Ogilvy, David. *Confessions of an Advertising Man*. New York: Atheneum, 1963.

O'Hara, Georgina. *The Encyclopedia of Fashion*. New York: Harry N. Abrams, 1986.

Picken, Mary Brooks. *The Fashion Dictionary*. New York: Funk & Wagnalls, 1957.

Rosenthal, Howard, S., and Myron H. Ackerman. *Sell More Ties*. New York: Men's Tie Foundation, 1970.

Rybczynski, Witold. *Home: A Short History of an Idea*. New York: Viking Penguin, 1986.

Silverman, Debra. *Selling Culture*. New York: Pantheon Books, 1986.

Tauranac, Jeff. *Elegant New York*. New York: Abbeville Press, 1985.

Veblen, Thorstein. *The Theory of the Leisure Class*. New York: Penguin, 1986.

Walz, Barbra, and Bernadine Morris. *The Fashion Makers*. New York: Random House, 1978.

Wilson, Richard Guy, Dianne H. Pilgrim and Dickran Tashjian. *The Machine Age in America 1918–1941*. New York: Harry N. Abrams, 1986.

Wyman, Margaret Woodney. *Perfume in Pictures*. New York: Sterling Publishing, 1969.

▸▸▸ INDEX